THE MORAL LIFE
OF CHILDREN

Books by ROBERT COLES

For Children

The
Moral Life
of
Children

Robert Coles

HOUGHTON MIFFLIN COMPANY · BOSTON

For information about permission to reproduce selections
from this book, write to Permissions, Atlantic Monthly Press,
420 Lexington Avenue, Suite 2304, New York, New York 10017.

Library of Congress Cataloging-in-Publication Data
Coles, Robert.
The moral life of children.
Reprint. Originally published: Boston:
Atlantic Monthly Press, 1986.
Includes bibliographical references and index.
1. Moral development   I. Title.
BF723.M54C65   1987   155.4′18   86-27683
ISBN 0-395-59921-0 (pbk.)

Printed in the United States of America

VB 14 13 12 11 10 9 8 7 6 5

Houghton Mifflin Company paperback 1987

Published by arrangement with Atlantic Monthly Press

Chapter I, "Psychoanalysis and Moral Development," appeared, in
a different form, in the *American Journal of Psychoanalysis*, Summer
1981. Parts of Chapter IV, "On Character," appeared, in a different
form, in *Daedalus*, Fall 1981. Parts of Chapter VII, "Children and
the Nuclear Bomb," appeared in the *New York Times Magazine*.

0 395 431530

To the memory of Anna Freud
To the memory of William Carlos Williams
To Jane, with continuing thanks

CONTENTS

Illustrations follow page 148

THE MORAL LIFE
OF CHILDREN

INTRODUCTION

I F my wife had had her way, back in 1960, when our work in the
South with black and white children was just starting, the subject
matter of this book would have been our major preoccupation all
along. She is a high school teacher (English and history), and she
has always been interested in the moral side of her students' lives:
their ideals and values; their sense of what is right and wrong, and
how they state their reasons; and not least, the moral statements
they make in response to what she teaches. In New Orleans, twenty-
five years ago, when we were talking with young black children
passing through segregationist mobs to enter school, and white children also harassed even for attending a school with a black child in
it, my wife was quick to hear those children ask the old existentialist
questions (Why? Why me? Why such behavior from fellow human
beings?). She was also ready and eager to respond to that inquiring
initiative on the part of particular boys and girls — to hear them
at, to answer the questions put to us, to share her own ideas,
thoughts, worries, and hopes.

I have to say that such was not my inclination. As I indicated in
the five volumes of *Children of Crisis,* wherein I tried to describe
the work I have done in various parts of this country, among various
kinds of children, my training in child psychiatry has not always
helped me comprehend the ways in which those children have
managed. When they have been fearful, anxious, frightened, sad,

"sick," in a tenacious despair, I have known rather promptly what to think, how to see what is happening and why. But when the children in question have simply been "well," living their lives, I have often been at a loss to figure out how their mental life is to be understood. How are experts in child psychoanalysis to view the everyday behavior of children who have no clear symptoms, despite the severe stresses life has put upon them? Anna Freud has made an especially heroic effort to distinguish between "normality" and "pathology," to understand what makes for both in boys, in girls — and has warned against categorical explanations.[1] The subject begs research, more and more of it.

When my wife and I worked with SNCC (the Student Nonviolent Coordinating Committee), and lived in Louisiana and Georgia, during the civil rights days of the 1960s, I began to figure out one way of doing my work. Even though I was not "treating" children, as I had done in Boston's Children's Hospital, and even though these southern children weren't complaining of nightmares or appetite loss or constraining phobias (three somewhat common psychiatric ills of children), the boys and girls were experiencing moments of "crisis," were confronting threats, outright violence, were trying to survive psychologically as well as physically. And so I tried to work toward a version of documentary child psychiatry: to record how a historical crisis (school integration) or a social and economic crisis (the trials of Appalachia's mountain families and of migrant farm families), or a long-standing racial impasse (the conditions of Indians in, say, the Southwest, or of Eskimos in coastal Alaska) bears upon the mental life of young people.

I tried to uncover a psychology of everyday life; a psychology of turmoil and response to turmoil; a psychology of hope against hope with plenty of interludes of doubt and fear. It turned out to be a psychology not characterized by an overwhelming weight of symptomatology. Yes, I have seen a number of children in the rural or urban South — or in our northern ghettos, our working-class suburbs or affluent ones — who might have been helped by visits to a doctor who specializes in child psychiatry. Yet I did not seek out such children. In any community a child who is in substantial psychiatric trouble is usually known to the parents and teachers and ministers or priests of that community. Whether any medical help may be forthcoming is, of course, quite another matter. In a number of instances I certainly did help a child find his or her way to a clinic or hospital. "We need explanations for the vicissitudes of normality in childhood," Anna Freud has suggested — though we need, even before that, a way of seeing: a "methodology" that allows us to observe ordinary children going through their day-to-day lives.[2]

Even making such an effort, though, will not guarantee us the freedom to pursue whatever leads are provided by the children themselves. The observing doctor's ideological assumptions are hard to shake, and they can encourage one line of inquiry, discourage another. I am astonished at how stubbornly I turned my attention away from some extremely important messages I was being given by children, in order to pursue other matters. For instance, a *white* New Orleans child of eight, back at school after a 1962 boycott by white parents had finally collapsed, told me that she worried what God would decide, when He took up the matter of that boycott. I casually asked what *she* thought. She told me she was sure He'd have some trouble deciding. I asked why — certain, I'm afraid, that her sense of God's "trouble" came straight from her own mixed feelings. She became shy, suddenly; in time she told me she felt presumptuous speaking for God Almighty. I backed off, was only glad for such a spell of hesitation: *now* she and I might more directly address her own explicit reasons for not wanting to go to school with black children; and we might discuss her return to school, after months of idleness.

As the girl expressed her reasons for being glad to be back in school, I took note of the psychological difficulties she had to endure, both at home and at school: a child's psychology become, by virtue of one historical moment, an element in a city's political conflict. Here is some of what the child told me: "We were afraid to go to that school. My mother was sure that if they took in one or two colored kids, a hundred or two hundred would be there a month later, unless the white people showed the world we can't be pushed around. That's what we did, too! We just said no, and we showed we meant it! Besides, the colored aren't good at school, and they can ruin it for everyone. I have some trouble reading, and my mother was sure it would get worse, if lots of the kids in my class were colored, and they don't care if they read or they don't read.

"My mother says I should really work hard and get better at school work. She tells us kids we'll become 'little niggers' if we don't watch out! The next minute she'll say she shouldn't talk like that! She's always getting angry at us, then she'll apologize. The other day she threw a box of corn flakes at my brother and me, and when she missed, she picked up the broom and started chasing us. She called us 'niggers.' Then she bumped into the refrigerator, and I think she hurt her arm. She dropped the broom, and she told us she was sorry. She said we should sit down, and she'd make us our favorite pancakes, and she did. She told us she was sure glad we're back in school, and it didn't make any difference if there are a few colored kids there, because they're going to need an education, just like us, and God put them here, just like He did us, and even if it's not the right thing, to mix people up, just because some federal judge says to do it, there's no reason we should all end up losing out on our schooling for the rest of our lives. My daddy doesn't agree with her, I know that. He's ready to go fight the federal judge; that's what he tells us every day. He and my mother fight, and he" hit her sometimes, and she says he treats her like a 'nigger' when he's had some beer. So, she's ready to leave him one day, but then he 'comes around,' she says. She got him to agree with her on us going to school, even if he doesn't like the idea 'one goddamn bit.' "

Remarks such as these ought give all of us pause even today — reminders that social and economic jeopardy becomes, in a family's life, another kind of jeopardy: children caught between the complex and often contradictory inclinations of their parents, not to mention relatives, neighbors, friends, politicians, ministers. It was important to show that the so-called white resistance (in, say, the New Orleans of 1960–1963) was for some boys and girls a strenuous psychological challenge, the reasons for which they did not easily understand. And no wonder — their parents were themselves torn. Yet, I never did pursue themes the white child quoted above kept stating in her part of our conversations, and my wife always felt it was a pity I didn't. Here were people, she kept reminding me, who weren't only using psychological "defense mechanisms" of the ego to accommodate themselves to the thrust of "socioeconomic variables" upon their lives. These people, she observed, weren't only (as for smug Yankees) "rednecks," "segregationists"; weren't only (as for social scientists) the embittered members of a "marginal population," a "white lower-middle-class group." These were people, she repeatedly insisted, with a moral life that was chronically buffeted by conflicting commitments: loyalty to an (all-white) neighborhood; memories of what public figures and newspapers had been saying for years and years (the segregationist rhetoric of the time); devotion to a (Methodist) church; awareness of what education can mean in this century's America; and a notion of what constitutes their country's professed civic virtues. Each element in the foregoing list was part of what could be called an overall moral rhetoric to which the child somehow had to accommodate herself.

I think I understood how such a child ends up regarding the black children she sees at school or on the streets (being heckled) near school; also how she uses psychological maneuvers (rationalization, denial, projection, and so forth) to uphold parental mandates, to keep going in a confused and confusing educational situation. But I never did take a hard, close look at the actual moral content of such a girl's life — its private and public form, as expressed in reveries, words, and actions. When she supplied me with evidence of moral conflict, as she most assuredly did in the statement quoted above, I failed to pursue it as vigorously as I might have. On this subject, here are some remarks my wife wrote in the margin of a yellow unlined sheet of paper on which had been typed a black child's comments, which in their essential moral nature resembled those of the above-mentioned white child: "I wish you wouldn't only concentrate on the rivalry and envy and 'defensive hate' of the white children as proof of their 'marginality.' I wish you wouldn't only see the black children as victims. They are fighting for certain ideals, but the white children are also waging a moral struggle. Children receive all kinds of moral signals, and they have to figure out which ones to consider important and which ones to ignore. Sometimes they can't ignore what they've decided they'd better try and ignore, and then they're in a jam. Shouldn't we look at this, too — their moral life as it's unfolding here in New Orleans?"

Yes, I agreed — but in my mind their "moral life" meant their psychological ways of dealing with perplexing and even dangerous circumstances. I was not ready to chronicle the moral ups and downs of these children's lives; I wanted to show (when I paid any attention at all to the moral side of things) what kind of psychological turmoil a child's conscience can incite, or indeed, constrain, dampen. The conscience — its social, cultural, and ideological sources — was for others to study. For me, back then, a child's conscience was a given: years and years of a certain kind of family life had meant, at last, this or that child's superego — internal "voices" judging him or her, prompting the boy or girl to prove the judgment correct through a prescribed pattern of behavior. Whence the "voices"? They came from mothers and fathers, of course — "introjects," they are called; and by school age, are quite solid presences in a child's life, a psychological "force" whose everyday influence on the young can be ascertained without too much difficulty, if enough time is spent watching and listening.[3]

Yet, what of the child as citizen? The child as churchgoer? The child as the law's instrument of legal redress, as history's fateful actor or actress? The child as a parent's *hope*, not only as object of obedience, manipulation, punishment? The child as a civilization's major preoccupation, a society's obsessional regard? The child as a focus of imaginative play? (If film directors or storytellers or artists get involved in that last category, so also do social scientists, for whom "children" can be a means of constructing images, or even myths.) The child as moviegoer perhaps prompts us to think of mere consumerism, but even the silliest film, or one chock-full of violence, can be for some children a moral occasion. (I say this *not*, Lord knows, to justify such films.)

Why not, too, think of the child as moral protagonist or antagonist — as in the South's racial conflict? Ruby, at ten, looked back at four years of somewhat unusual school attendance. A black child, she walked past hostile mobs at age six to enter a once all-white school in New Orleans, and she will appear from time to time in this book, as she did in Volume I of *Children of Crisis*. Her view of her experience? "I knew I was just Ruby," she told me once, in retrospect — "just Ruby trying to go to school, and worrying that I couldn't be helping my momma with the kids younger than me, like I did on the weekends and in the summer. But I guess I also knew I was the Ruby who had to do it — go into that school and stay there, no matter what those people said, standing outside. And besides, the minister reminded me that God chooses us to do His will, and so I had to be His Ruby, if that's what He wanted. And then that white lady wrote and told me she was going to stop shouting at me, because she'd decided *I* wasn't bad, even if *integration* was bad, then my momma said I'd become 'her Ruby,' that lady's, just as she said in her letter, and I was glad; and I was glad I got all the nice letters from people who said I was standing up for them, and I was walking for them, and they were thinking of me, and they were with me, and I was their Ruby, too, they said."

Through those memorable sentences, a child reveals herself to be a self-observer, as well as an observer of others. But let us be more ambitious for her. Was she not, utterly, and daily, a moral figure? A person able to find a measure of moral transcendence: comprehending, through language, the essence of what a human being can manage to be? Ruby, Tessie, Lawrence, and Martha, the children we were meeting during those beleaguered and affecting days, were, in my wife's phrase, "moralists, but with no pretense." They led an active moral life that was not only part of a family's "psychodynamics," but the life of a neighborhood, a city, a country, a world; the life, also, of a religion, a culture. Might we not take stock of such a life by the use of the eyes and ears, questions put and answered, deeds observed and recorded? And especially through the children's own words, uttered in their own homes, transcribed, edited, and inevitably extracted from many human exchanges in a manner that might do justice to them.[4]

I suppose this is the occasion to take up directly, and yet again, the question of authenticity. "Children don't speak the way they do in your books," I was told at a psychiatric meeting once, and I could not disagree. I have assembled remarks made by children in the course of years of acquaintance, and tried to fit them into the confines of a book. The risks are substantial: distortion of what the children have said or intended to say; the intrusion of the observer's, the writer's subjectivity, if not outright bias. Under such circumstances there is a requirement of tentativeness with respect to assertions — lest a necessarily limited number of children, whose statements have been made in relatively informal moments, be turned into the vigorous spokespersons of the observer's beliefs, if not dogmas. There is a decided value to so-called objective research, to well-constructed surveys and to tests uniformly administered. There is good reason, too, that a few of us stay around specific neighborhoods, try to figure out, no matter the hazards, just what we've heard that seems to matter for the speakers and for us who have tried to understand not only today's utterances, but many months of them, enough to enable a sense of things, a drift of things — mostly vague, but at moments as clear and resounding as a giant bell, tolling to an entire country-side, or so it seems when a boy's, a girl's *cri de coeur* is uttered. And there *is* eloquence, Lord knows — powerful declarations, urgently persuasive analytic statements, stirring or touching asides.

By the time we were living in New Mexico (1972–1974), I had

begun to take more care for the moral activity of children. In *The Old Ones of New Mexico*, I tried to set forth a particular, rural, Hispano-American morality as I had come to see it through the eyes of some grandparents, who in towns such as Truchas or Madrid say so much about how the young think about this life. Similarly, in Alaska I tried to indicate (in *The Last and First Eskimos*) what happens to a cultural morality as it is transmitted over the generations, and as it runs into forces from the outside, bringing new social norms to the edge of the Bering Sea, or up rivers such as the Kobuk or Kugaruk. Finally, in the fifth volume of *Children of Crisis* (*Privileged Ones*), I tried to show some of the moral dilemmas that children of affluent backgrounds sometimes try to reconcile with a lived life. "I'm not your friend Ruby," one such girl warned me. After I had nervously assured her that I didn't hold that fact against her or anyone else, she explained the reason for her comment — not intended as "defensive" or accusatory: "I'm just like Ruby, though — in ways: I can see someone sneer, even if it's in fun. I can see myself starting to sneer, and then I say stop, and I do stop. I'll be held to account by God, like my mother says, for the bad thoughts, but at least I can shut my mouth and straighten out my face." She was waging her own moral war — not Ruby's, unquestionably, but a moral war just the same.

I noticed similar parallels as I worked abroad — starting in 1974 when I first went to South Africa and Brazil.[5] I explain that work, dealing with the way in which children acquire their personal sense of nationality, in another book, *The Political Life of Children*, which with the present book represents a decade of research. Once I had been struck by the moral energy in a few South African and Brazilian children, I was able, ironically, to see in other countries what for too long I'd failed to notice in my native land. In Soweto, in Cape Town's university neighborhoods, in Rio de Janeiro's favelas, I met boys and girls, poor and well-to-do, black and white, who were all trying to find moral answers for themselves through the daily steps they took — a word here, a gesture there, a sympathy announced, another sympathy denounced. I pursued the study I was making of nationalism as an aspect of childhood, but I also tried to regard how closely these same children, and others I would meet elsewhere, forged a moral life — an outlook that often followed, rather than preceded, a series of events.

Back in this country I decided to review all my records, all the transcripts of conversations, all the drawings and paintings, all the notes — before depositing them once and for all in the University of North Carolina library — with the hope of learning yet again from the Rubys of my working life. But I also decided, once more prompted by my wife, that I had better go back to the various parts of America we had once called home, and talk with some new children, or even with the children of the children we had once known. In Belle Glade, Florida, I met yet again with migrant children (during 1979); in New Mexico I visited Albuquerque and went north to the communities I had known — Truchas and Madrid (during 1980); I also returned (repeatedly, during the early 1980s) to Atlanta and New Orleans, and to the neighborhoods in and around Boston where I had worked in the 1960s and early 1970s; and not least, I was asked by the editor of *Daedalus*, the Journal of the American Academy of Arts and Sciences, to visit three schools in different parts of this country. Such visits were made (1980) by three of us (Sara Lawrence Lightfoot and Philip Jackson each went alone, as did I) in the hope that we would be able to report back to our colleagues on a committee organized by *Daedalus* whatever observations we found to be significant. In the chapter "On Character" I describe the "method" of that inquiry. In the five volumes of *Children of Crisis* I have described in detail how I did my work, and do so here, again, at the back of this book.[6]

The chapter "On Character," followed by the one on "Young Idealism," tells what I tried to do — get to know students, teachers, administrators from the top down, and in each case with an interest in the question of "character": what makes someone, in his or her eyes and those of others, a person of "character"? I pursued this last matter at greater length than originally planned — trying again and again to learn how it comes about that some youths achieve a moral stature, whether publicly recognized or simply among friends. The teachers I met, the school principals, pressed me as hard as I tried to press them, and I often thought of comments they made while I was trudging up the slopes of several Brazilian favelas, where schools play no part at all in the lives of even twelve-year-old children, and where *childhood,* one begins to realize, has to be considered in a different light from ours. The lucky ones I met in those favelas who had survived to the second decade of life (and to early parenthood) did not strike me as "adolescents." I fear, at times, my naive, ignorant, and self-preoccupied ways may have struck them as — well, not "adolescent," for none of them knew that word, but as, alas, rather characteristic of the Yankees they had met in Copacabana or Ipanema!

The Brazilian aspect of this work entailed much frustration, I have to say. I had long been interested in comparing the "poverty" I had seen in America with that to be found in the so-called third world, but my wife persuaded me that if it was lives I wished to compare, not merely statistics and indices, then I had best find some focus for the attempt, especially in view of the language barrier. My Portuguese is rudimentary and entails stilted exchanges mediated by an interpreter. Thus, I abandoned the original purpose of "comparison," in favor of an attempt over many years to puzzle out how some spirited children in Brazil's favelas manage to make do ethically. What sources give them the moral purpose they develop in the life they live?[7]

As I moved back and forth, one hour in the Copacabana, the next in a favela, I began to notice a continual reference to "them" by people I knew in both locations. I myself began to think of "them" all too commonly — "them" down there along the ocean, whence I had come to this or that favela, strung along a hill, and "them" up there on that hill, which I could see as I stood on the sand and felt the ocean lapping or lashing my legs. One day in a favela I was asked this: "Do you know what I think of them?" I said no — and not out of evasive psychiatric canniness, I really do believe. I knew there was, no doubt, plenty of envy or anger in the child's mind, but the child, aged only nine, wanted to tell me something that would help me see things a bit clearer, and maybe cut down on my lengthy indirections and halting, confounding asides, meant to give me time to consider *what next* in this series of questions and answers.

In a few seconds I was spared further speculative rumination. Words poured from the mouth of the child Carlos, the man Carlos, the youth who every day left a favela for Copacabana's oceanside boulevard, there to wash cars in exchange for whatever generosity a smile and a please and a declaration of hunger can prompt: "I do not hold it against them; I know they did not arrange Rio to be the way it is before they were born here! I know I didn't arrange things either! It's the luck of the draw! My luck is bad; theirs is good — the kids I see coming out of the big hotels and apartment houses in Copacabana and Ipanema. I talked with one boy last week — he stared at me, and I stared back. He had a suit on: poor kid. It was a summer suit, but he looked hot. I guess he was upset that the air conditioning stopped when he left the lobby of the building. Even the rich have to sweat sometimes! He was very nice to me: he asked me how I was doing. He had been watching me from the window of his apartment before he came down, to wait for the driver to take him to his father's office. He said he thought I was very strong, the way I worked so fast on the cars. He said he'd tell his father to pay me to do their cars. I asked how many they have. He said three.

"Then one of them came, a Mercedes: rich! The doormen tell me in our country a Mercedes costs four times what it costs in other countries, because of taxes. But he said 'these people, they can afford anything, and it doesn't bother them to pay lots of money.' He said, 'if they buy something cheap, they don't believe it's any good!' I'd love to be in their shoes, but it's not my luck. They sure don't want to be in my shoes! But that kid, I think he was curious, and I was very glad to speak with him. I thanked him for the job suggestion, and he was very polite; he thanked me for offering to do the job! Thank you, thank you, we were saying to each other, over and over — just two kids, not 'us' up here in the favela and 'them' over there in Copacabana!"

But such dissolution of an otherwise pronounced social polarization lasts only so long, as Carlos knew. The more he talked, however, about that incident, the more he was inclined to characterize not just the rich boy, but the rich boy's world that he knew as a hard-laboring person does when he has to approach and solicit work from people. As I listened to these stories, I began to realize how pointedly moral they were — statements that told as much about the child's interior, spiritual life as they did about the social life to which he had been witness for many years. I owe the chapter on "moral attribution" to that unforgettable moment, when Carlos talked as he did about a nameless age-mate, a fellow Brazilian, but of course, someone who lived figuratively on another planet. His comments and those of other Brazilian children, some extremely poor, some extremely rich, remind us that boys and girls are constantly at work noticing what is just, what is unjust, rendering their judgments.

I have also included similar attributions offered me by American children over the past ten years during interviews. I hope that my mode of approach to the moral thinking of children, my way of regarding their daily life from a moral perspective they themselves uphold, gives a boost to the tradition of "direct observation" Anna Freud urged upon us clinicians who work with the young. "Let us try to learn from children all they have to tell us," she said, "and let us sort out only later, how their ideas fit in with our own." Then she added: "Sometimes the children we see will even help us with our own problems, those of theory, because there can be many clues for theory in what a child chooses to say to an adult listener."[8]

I must explain, too, the chapter, "Children and the Nuclear Bomb." The research that I describe took place between 1980 and 1983, especially in 1981 and 1982. This work, as the reader will see, connects with the work on moral attribution — the way in which we regard potential enemies, and the way in which we regard those at home who agree or disagree with our views on the nation's defense or foreign policy. I was struck, yet again, by the implicitly moral nature of the opinions I was hearing as I talked with some of the children. Even those who refused to feel as alarmed as some of their American age-mates would often insist that they had their moral reasons for such an attitude. The matter of a nuclear freeze has become for certain families an issue of commanding significance, and sometimes for the children of at least some of those families. On the other hand, there are, as Carlos told me in Rio de Janeiro, several worlds in every country, and his shrewd generalization would have to include the United States of America. The issue of "class," of how one's background affects, even strongly determines, one's moral preoccupation, is an issue not sufficiently explored among children. When I was taking my residency in psychiatry at the Massachusetts General Hospital in Boston, I audited a seminar Paul Tillich was giving (1956) in "systematic theology." I will never forget a remark he made: "Morality for ordinary people is not the result of reading books and writing papers, as we're doing. Morality is not a *subject;* it is a life put to the test in dozens of moments. Morality and social class — that is a subject for us, an important one. For ordinary people it's not a subject; it's life affecting the views of people every day."

The present book is, in a sense, a continuation of the work of that seminar. Tillich was always encouraging us to look not only at the books he assigned, but at the lives we were living. He was, I suppose it could be said, a Christian existentialist; certainly he was interested in psychoanalytic thinking, and how that thinking applied to the world's many problems.[9] But, like Anna Freud, he worried that concepts might be worshiped like idols and hence be slapped indiscriminately and hastily on events and individuals. He urged upon us students what he called a "phenomenological approach," to pursue knowledge through an inquiry into the world: "Put ideas aside for a while, look and see what you see; the ideas are always there, and they are not meant to stop you from looking on your own." Those words reminded me of others I knew well: "No ideas but in things," one of the guiding signals William Carlos Williams dispatches in his epic poem *Paterson*. And, at another page in *Paterson*: "To make a start, / out of particulars / and make them general, rolling / up the sum, by defective means — / Sniffing the trees, / just another dog / among a lot of dogs. What else is there? And to do? / The rest have run out — / after the rabbits. / Only the lame stands — on / three legs. Scratch front and back. / Deceive and eat. Dig / a musty bone."[10]

I thought of those lines as I talked with children in the favelas — the dogs all over, as hungry as the people, but also as wily and inventive and stubborn, roaming and hoping and sniffing and poking and barking, eyes always alert, ears cocked, tails wagging — until, one day, the tail would collapse between the legs, and the dog would find a shady place under a tree, and the eyes seemed oblivious to the rude excitement of the favela's daily life and the ears seemed suddenly indifferent and maybe a soft murmur greeted the child who saw the relative stillness as he approached, and said to the Yankee man beside him: The dog will die today — a casual estimate, followed by a continuation of the walk.

I have put down on paper many times (articles, and a book) my deep obligation to William Carlos Williams, my affectionate memory of him. I simply state it again here, as I conclude twenty-five years of work. "Catch an eyeful, catch an earful, and don't drop what you've caught," he'd tell me as he pushed himself from building to building, that doctor's black bag in his hand, and the feverish brain working at full speed, waiting for the evening to set down its catch in those lines of poetry, those astonishing doctor stories, or in a novel, perhaps, which also drew upon a doctor's working experiences. Those of us who rather obviously lack his talents can at least be glad for his sanction, his encouragement, his example.

Some other gladly acknowledged obligations: Peter Davison, for his exceedingly careful and thoughtful editing; the Ford Foundation, and especially Ed Meade, whose considerate advice has meant a lot; the Rockefeller Foundation, and especially John Knowles, alas now gone from this earth, and Joel Colton, and Rebecca Painter, all three of whom were kind and encouraging at a critical moment in the life of this research; and not least, the MacArthur Foundation, whose five-year fellowship enabled me to pursue this work, and the work described in *The Political Life of Children*. I describe, with some detail in that book's introduction, the special help this fellowship enabled — the help I could obtain abroad from a number of individuals. No question, there is some carryover between these two books: a moral and political life is part of one's response to others as an individual and as a citizen of a country. But I pursue quite different lines of inquiry — and with different children — in writing the studies described here and those described in *The Political Life of Children*, as I believe a comparative reading will make clear.

I wish to thank the Association for the Advancement of Psychoanalysis for their invitation to give the lecture "Psychoanalysis and Moral Development," which appeared in the *American Journal of Psychoanalysis* (1981). I also wish to thank many friends in New Mexico, among them the Los Alamos committee members who invited me to give the annual J. Robert Oppenheimer Lecture (1984) — a memorable occasion for me, to talk about "Children and the Nuclear Bomb" in that setting. My debt to the editor of *Daedalus*, Stephen Graubard, is obvious — help in pursuing a line of inquiry further, in reporting on findings made (*Daedalus*, 1981).

I also dedicate this book to my wife Jane. Her interest in this subject was the essential force in getting the work planned and then done. She has suggested and suggested, said yes and said no, brought me back to the boys and girls we've both met, the boys and girls who have been our constant teachers. With our own children, now fairly grown — Bob, Dan, Mike — we have moved across this country, traveled widely abroad, tried to understand how it is to live under a wide range of circumstances. Though it is I who have written these words, a family has done this work. And speaking of the work, I make grateful mention, also, of the help given by Shawn Maher and Tom Davey and Bonnie Harris — constant friends, attentive critics of a bad scrawl called "my handwriting." Finally Anna Freud's intellectual guidance and painstaking criticism, rendered in letters and frank personal talks, have meant a lot to me, as have my years with Erik H. Erikson — years of studying with him, teaching in his Harvard College course. Their pioneering work has enabled others to follow their own directions with great confidence, with a sense of encouragement from highly respected elders. Even some of us inveterate loners and wanderers need to feel spiritually connected to certain kin, and for me those two have very much been that — mentors in my work these past two decades.

I

PSYCHOANALYSIS AND MORAL DEVELOPMENT

As Erik H. Erikson has shown us in his studies of Luther and Gandhi,[1] and as any number of clinicians come to realize in their everyday professional lives, neither among the great nor among ordinary people do defense mechanisms quite account for the entirety of psychological life. We all have them, and of course, the tone of each life has to do significantly with what defenses we use, with what frequency or emphasis, and on what occasions. But the moral texture of a life is, one suspects, not fully explained by a mere analysis of how the ego negotiates with the id and the superego. Nor is the ego or the superego, important though they are to an understanding of moral development, quite all we need to know in the face of specific dilemmas — the ethical behavior seemingly "backward" people display, not to mention the mischievous, sometimes deceitful, and certainly callous actions that one can find in highly intelligent, well-educated individuals, even those who have had the advantage of receiving rather a lot of psychological knowledge, whether in courses or in treatment.

A well-developed conscience does not translate, necessarily, into a morally courageous life. Nor do well-developed powers of philosophical thinking and moral analysis necessarily translate into an everyday willingness to face down the various evils of this world.[2] I was once helped in the effort at clarification by a black woman whom I suppose I'd have to call illiterate. She pointed out that "there's a lot of people who talk about doing good, and a lot of people who argue about what's good and what's not good." Then she added that "there are a lot of people who always worry about whether they're doing right or doing wrong." Finally, there are some other folks: "They just put their lives on the line for what's right, and they may not be the ones who talk a lot or argue a lot or worry a lot; they just *do* a lot!"

Her daughter happened to be Ruby Bridges, one of the black children, who, at age six, initiated school desegregation in New Orleans against terrible, fearful odds. For days that turned into weeks and weeks that turned into months, this child had to brave murderously heckling mobs, there in the morning and there in the evening, hurling threats and slurs and hysterical denunciations and accusations. Federal marshals took her to school and brought her home. She attended school all by herself for a good part of a school year, owing to a total boycott by white families. Her parents, of sharecropper background, had just recently arrived in the great, cosmopolitan port city — yet another poor black family of rural background trying to find a slightly better deal in an urban setting. They were unemployed, and, like Ruby, in jeopardy; mobs threatened them, too.

Still, Ruby persisted, and so did her parents. Ruby's teachers began to wonder *how come* — about the continuing ability of such a child to bear such adversity, and with few apparent assets in her family background. I reassured those teachers, I regret to say, with the notion that all was not as it seemed. Ruby appeared strong, but she would, soon enough, show signs of psychological wear and tear. Perhaps she was "denying" her fears and anxieties; perhaps her strange calm in the face of such obvious danger represented a "reaction formation." Then there was this bit of information: "I was standing in the classroom, looking out the window, and I saw Ruby coming down the street, with the federal marshals on both sides of her. The crowd was there, shouting, as usual. A woman spat at Ruby but missed; Ruby smiled at her. A man shook his fist at her; Ruby smiled at him. Then she walked up the stairs, and she stopped and turned and smiled one more time! You know what she told one of the marshals? She told him she prays for those people, the ones in that mob, every night before she goes to sleep!"

The words of a white schoolteacher — incredulous and, by that time, quite perplexed. As for me, I'd been interested in knowing how Ruby slept at night (an indicator of her state of apprehension, a measure of how well she was handling things mentally), but I hadn't thought to inquire about what she said or even thought each night before falling off. What to make of such a concern being addressed by such a child? I asked Ruby, after a while, about her prayers — first telling her what I'd heard from the teacher. Ruby was cheerful and matter-of-fact, if terse, in her reply: "Yes, I do pray for them." I wondered why. She said only, "Because." I waited for more, but to no effect. I started over, told her I was curious about why she would want to pray for people who were being so unswervingly nasty to her. "I go to church," she told me, "every Sunday, and we're told to pray for everyone, even the bad people, and so I do." She had no more to say on that score.

When I finally began to take notice of Ruby's churchgoing activities, and those of her parents, I'm afraid I was not very responsive to what I heard and saw. I kept wanting to fit what I was learning into what I had already learned — use what was, after all, a somewhat new "reality" for me, if not "human actuality" (James Agee's phrase), in order to say yes once more to the psychological theory I'd acquired before going South. Ruby was picking up phrases, admonitions, statements ritually expressed, bits and pieces of sermons emotionally delivered, and using all that in a gesture of obedience. She was being psychologically imitative. Her parents told her to pray for her tormentors, even as those parents had been told to do likewise by their minister, and Ruby said yes, of course. She did what she was told, but did she truly understand what she was doing? Was she not, rather, showing herself to be a particular six-year-old child: scared, vulnerable, not able to read or write, limited cognitively, vulnerable emotionally — holding on for dear life with brave smiles and silence outside and inside school, and with prayers at home?

Was she not, in addition, a poor black child in an extremely hostile southern city neighborhood, grasping at whatever straws came her way — hence her brave avowals of prayerful concern for those who, after all, wanted to kill her and had no reluctance to say so again and again? When I did prod the child a bit, I got this evidence of what I then concluded to be fearful piety: "They keep coming and saying the bad words, but my momma says they'll get tired after a while and then they'll stop coming. They'll stay home. The minister came to our house and he said the same thing, and not to worry, and I don't. The minister said God is watching and He won't forget, because He never does. The minister says if I forgive the people, and smile at them and pray for them, God will keep a good eye on everything and He'll be our protection."

She stopped and seemed positive. I thought I felt some doubt, some uncertainty. I asked her if she believed the minister was on the right track. "Oh, yes," she said; and then came a kind explanation for the benighted, agnostic, Yankee visitor: "I'm sure God knows what's happening. He's got a lot to worry about; but there is bad trouble here, and He can't help but notice. He may not rush to do anything, not right away. But there will come a day, like you hear in church."

She wasn't sure exactly what would happen on that "day." Even the remarks above weren't delivered as a brief sermon, but constitute an assembled collection of terse explications, delivered over an hour or two on a warm, moist spring afternoon in 1961, a terrible time for that American child and, arguably, for her country as well. Was she, with those explanations, whistling in the dark? Was she repeating in rote submission the clichés a long-impoverished and persecuted people had learned to rely upon — the analgesic self-deceptions of those who, through no fault of their own, have never quite learned to think rationally, logically, or, as some of us would put it, "maturely"? How well did she really understand what was happening to her city, to her neighborhood, to herself and her family? Set aside her composure, her pietistic avowals, her quick smiles, and one would find a terror-struck black child just barely in control of herself — or so I thought; and perhaps the same held for her parents.

Meanwhile, as already mentioned, my wife's skepticism was directed not at Ruby Bridges and her family, but at the kind of inquiry I seemed determined to make. The more I tried to understand the emotional conflicts, the tensions and responses to tensions, the underlying motivations, and the projections and displacements; the more I emphasized the automatic or reflexive behavior of the children we knew, a consequence of their short lives, their lack of education, their limited cognitive development, their inability to handle all sorts of concepts and symbols; the more I read and commented on various developmental points of view, which emphasized stages and phases and periods — and, of course, consigned elementary school children such as Ruby Bridges to the lower rungs of this or that ladder — the more my wife kept pointing to the *acts* of these boys and girls, the *deeds* they managed.

We had come to know an extraordinary range of children and parents. We had come to know, in addition, a group of poor and poorly educated people who, nevertheless, acquitted themselves impressively in pursuit of significant ethical objectives. I think of Rosa Parks, a seamstress, whose decision to sit where she pleased on a Montgomery, Alabama, bus in the middle 1950s preceded the emergence of the so-called civil rights movement and of Dr. King and Ralph Abernathy as leaders of it. I think of the four college youths who, quietly and without publicity (at first), decided to challenge the segregationist laws of Greensboro, North Carolina, in early February 1960. I think of the many black children my wife and I came to know, in Arkansas and Louisiana and Georgia and Alabama and Mississippi — and of white children, too, who braved awful criticism to befriend them: young leaders of a changing South, young *moral* leaders. Whence that moral capacity, that moral spirit, that moral leadership? How are we to make sense of such moral behavior in psychodynamic terms? And how are we, at the same time, to make sense of the well-known involvement of such towering intellectual and moral figures as Heidegger or Jung with Nazism, not to mention the justification of Stalin's vicious, conniving, murderous dictatorship by so many self-styled members of one or another nation's intelligentsia? More broadly, what makes for a moral *life* — for moral *action* — as opposed to moral reflection and analysis and argument? What do we mean, moreover, when we talk about "moral development" and, with the help of psychoanalytic theory as well as the concepts given us by Piaget and Kohlberg, define and declare who is able to reach what "stage" of such "development"?[3]

I think it fair to say that a child such as Ruby was in 1961 (aged six, black, southern, of extremely poor background) would not be a likely candidate for the usual kind of moral accolades. She was not "mature." She was, no doubt, right smack in the middle of an oedipal conflict. She had, without question, the kinds of cognitive inadequacies we have all come to find important to remember — and connect to the general (academic and social) behavior of the young. She was hardly a candidate for the higher level of performance, with respect to moral analysis, that Lawrence Kohlberg requires if he is to call one in possession of "postconventional" or "autonomous" moral thought. Here, by the way, is what Kohlberg tells us about the subject we were and still are trying to understand: "Moral development is therefore a result of an increasing ability to perceive social reality or to organize and integrate social experience. One necessary — but not sufficient — condition for principled morality is the ability to reason logically (represented by stages of formal operations).

"The main experiential determinants of moral development seem to be amount and variety of social experience, the opportunity to take a number of roles and to encounter other perspectives. Thus middle-class and popular children progress further and faster than do lower-class children and social isolates. Similarly, development is slower in the semiliterate village cultures that have been studied."[4]

I suppose Ruby lived in a "village culture" of sorts. Surely she wasn't a member of the middle class. For Kohlberg, she was a "preconventional" or "premoral" lass. Her prayers, her smiles, were, I suppose, mere gestures, not the careful responses of a truly reflective person — a Cambridge theorist, for example. As for many other children we knew in the South, both black and white, I doubt they would fare much better in Kohlberg's scheme of things. I have in mind the first white youth to speak to a black in one of Atlanta's desegregated high schools. He was from a family all too easily labeled, by the likes of me, "redneck." He was a tough athlete, a poor student, not a well-read boy of fourteen. God save him, he'd never been presented with all those moral situations freighted with twists and turns, alternatives and possibilities! He'd never been asked to say what he'd do if . . .

Nevertheless, the young man found himself, inexplicably and suddenly, without forethought (he later had to acknowledge this condition repeatedly, when asked by me and others), impelled to help out "a nigger" (the words of the helper!). He described the incident (and himself) in this way: "I didn't want any part of them here. They belong with their own, and we belong with our own — that's what we all said. Then those two kids came here, and they had a tough time. They were all by themselves. The school had to get police protection for them. We didn't want them, and they knew it. But we told them so, in case they were slow to get the message. I didn't hold back, no more than anyone else. I said, 'Go, nigger, go,' with all the others. I meant it. But after a few weeks, I began to see a kid, not a nigger — a guy who knew how to smile when it was rough going, and who walked straight and tall, and was polite. I told my parents, 'It's a real shame that someone like him has to pay for the trouble caused by all those federal judges.'

"Then it happened. I saw a few people cuss at him. 'The dirty nigger,' they kept on calling him, and soon they were pushing him in a corner, and it looked like trouble, bad trouble. I went over and broke it up. I said, 'Hey, cut it out.' They all looked at me as if I was crazy, my white buddies and the nigger, too. But my buddies stopped, and the nigger left. Before he left, though, I spoke to him. I didn't mean to, actually! It just came out of my mouth. I was surprised to hear the words myself: 'I'm sorry.' As soon as he was gone, my friend gave it to me: 'What do you mean, "I'm sorry"!' I didn't know what to say. I was as silent as the nigger they stopped. After a few minutes, we went to basketball practice. That was the strangest moment of my life."

His life had, in fact, changed. In no time, it seemed, he was beginning to talk more consciously (more self-consciously, actually) to the black youth. Soon, he was championing him personally, while still decrying "integration." Finally, he would become a friend of the black youth's and advocate "an end to the whole lousy business of segregation." Meanwhile, it was for me to explain that shift — in an ordinary, fourteen-year-old boy just starting high school; a boy who, by the way, had to endure lots of scorn himself from the many others who were not as swift as he to show a change in racial attitudes. Press and press that youth, and what does one find? He told me: "I'd be as I was, I guess, but for being there in school that year and seeing that kid — seeing him behave himself, no matter what we called him, and seeing him being insulted so bad, so real bad. Something in me just drew the line, and something in me began to change, I think."

That youth's tentativeness, his willingness to suggest the complexity of things, contrasts, alas, with the categorical assurance of some theorists who have moral development all figured out, as if life were a matter of neatly arranged academic hurdles, with grades given along the way. Here was a young person with a story George Eliot would have comprehended (as in *Middlemarch*): the *circumstances* that make for such a difference in our lives, the accidents, the incidents that come along out of nowhere, it seems. *Fate* is the word other generations used, and *destiny* — but, of course, to accept what such words imply about this life takes matters out of the hands of those of us who want control, who want to be able to predict all, explain all.[5]

Moral life is not to be confused with tests meant to measure certain kinds of abstract (moral) thinking, or with tests that give people a chance to offer hypothetical responses to made-up scenarios. We never quite know what will happen in this life; nor do we know how an event will connect with ourselves. It is no secret that we all contend with mental inconsistencies, contradictions — the disparate elements that each of us tries, day in and day out, to forge into a particular life. Meanwhile, there is the world around us, with various social and political and economic issues, the sweep of history even, which together offer us possibilities or, sadly, take them away, deny them. I have seen children such as Ruby, from the most unpromising of backgrounds, emerge brave, thoughtful, compassionate. I have seen youths such as the one quoted immediately above turn away from what seemed to be their quite definite moral selves — assume a new moral life, it can be said, it *has* been said, by them, by their teachers. Novelists know such developments, and so also do ordinary men and women the world over. Why not some of us self-styled psychological "experts," for whom words or phrases such as "will," "honor," "moral stamina," and "ethical choice" seem quaint relics of another age?

Ruby had a will and used it to make an ethical choice; she demonstrated moral stamina; she possessed honor, courage. The white youth I mentioned might have turned into yet another "redneck." His family had all the socioeconomic credentials. Instead, a series of events — in a nation's life, a city's, a school system's, a neighborhood's — enabled him to show other aspects of himself and his heritage: a mother's hospitable, warm side, a father's personal courtliness, even to a relentlessly poking, New England-descended doctor. When Walker Percy warned us, in *The Second Coming*, that it is possible to "get all A's, and flunk life," he had in mind the instructive discrepancy that occasionally develops between the mind's intellectual life and that larger life we all live. By the same token, there are those who never even have a chance to get respectable grades at a good school — yet they may acquit themselves impressively in their time spent on this earth.

Nevertheless, we need not abandon all efforts to figure out the mind's moral development theoretically. As I look back at two decades of work spent in that so-called field — ordinary human beings trying to get from day to day, with no pretense to an interpretation of how they do it, and with no claim to great competence, never mind success — I find some psychoanalytic concepts truly helpful in explaining what I have seen over and over again. Freud's paper "On Narcissism" (1914) is especially helpful.[6] Even before the "object-relations" theorists (especially Winnicott) and before the intensification of interest in narcissism that Heinz Kohut and Otto Kernberg have prompted, Freud had essentially sketched the essential particulars of the child's earliest moral life — the way he or she comes to (judgmental) terms with himself or herself. Mention is made of "the lost narcissism of his [the child's] childhood, in which he was his own ideal." Once there was that "garden," that innocence, that self-satisfaction, in the nonpejorative sense. Once there was life uncomplicated by language, by wordy speculation and frustration, by "knowledge." Needs were fulfilled. Attention was paid. Death was nowhere to be seen or heard. I suppose our human, developmental analogue to Eden lasts until the child begins to realize that those attentive, nourishing faces (and bottles and breasts), those smiles of eager, persistent approval, have to give way to another kind of concern. The baby starts noticing that the eyes aren't so widely affirming, the voice has an edge to it. Yes gives way to Oh! Oh! Then No arrives; then No! No! Soon it is not only the parents who are offering only qualified love; the child has begun to turn on himself, herself, with the gradually increasing vigor of a ready learner. Language appears — the precise particulars of its (neurophysiological, psychological) appearance still a mystery, for all the explanations. The body's functions become the subject of a struggle. The child who used to lie down and be the subject of grateful, enthusiastic demonstrations of approval is now up and about, caught in a series of negotiations — give and take; and "knows" about all that, to a significant degree, through the exchange of words, messages.

I am hardly breaking new ground here! But I think it important to emphasize the "ego ideal" Freud mentioned in his paper cited above. The ego ideal represents an effort on the part of the child to regain the kind of self-love once enjoyed so freely, relatively speaking. One thinks of a child looking upward, seeing eyes liquid-warm with adoration. One thinks of the child looking upward, hearing the cooing reassurance of all eternity, it must seem — the infinity, almost, of parental space. With the fall comes "development," "progress" — and yearning. The ego ideal is born out of the infant's inevitable entrance into the world of what Paul Tillich kept calling "finitude." Put differently, the ego ideal represents memory as well as desire — a recollection of everyday satisfaction (no matter the gas pains, the unease that culminates in diaper changes), which makes the new vicissitudes of growth seem a bad judgment of sorts.

Of course, we are idealizing, somewhat, that period when the ego ideal is born; no parent is perfect, and so every parent will add a quota of frustrations to those just mentioned, which are imposed by nature. The issue is a relative one: the joys of acquiescent, preverbal support, repeatedly offered, as against the hurdles that confront the child who speaks and understands speech, the child who must lose the breast and worry about cleanliness — indeed, worry about more and more matters, a world without end, it seems. The superego, we know, grows slowly — months and months, years and years, of lessons learned, disappointments severely felt, difficulties endured and not forgotten. It is not only a matter of "right" as against "wrong," of "conscience" in the vernacular sense. The superego has to contend with the disenchantment of self-love, with the child's increasingly critical eye, which responds to the vision of parents, teachers, friends; and with, not least, the self-judgment that naturally follows the experience of change — in Biblical terms the trek east of Eden. The ego ideal represents our effort to recover the past; we look upward, hoping to see what we once enjoyed so very much, a spell of uninterrupted sunshine. The clouds of a later life prompt us to look, to keep looking with hope and anticipation (if with, too, an edge of anxious doubt) for that lost radiance.

Meanwhile, we have to accommodate ourselves to the norms and values of the world we belong to. Not only must we measure up to the hopes generated by an early but increasingly challenged narcissism, to the dreams and values of the best side of our parents, to the grand and noble pieties of a more social nature — national imperatives, ethnic or racial slogans — we must also deal with the hundreds of no's, many intimidating indeed, which gradually make us run for various covers or learn to take (adroitly or truculently) a stand. There is wear and tear in this life, and our sense of our worth reflects that inevitable moral strain we feel. Entire modes of existence turn out to be, on close inspection, a response of a "personality" to various internalized psychological injuries: the superego registering its perceptions, and those perceptions calling for a day-to-day (protective) response.

I am, yet again, coming up with nothing very startling. But let me move from this brief, simply stated reference to some of the "variables" that touch upon our sense of ourselves, our judgment of what we'd like, what we miss, how we ought to behave, to an approach that is less explicitly psychological. In doing work with young black and white people in the South, I heard many a statement of willfulness, determination; many a statement of apprehension, fear, foreboding. Sometimes I heard both kinds of statements worked into one. I heard plenty of ideals defined, plenty of goals espoused, plenty of wrongs denounced and rights upheld. I heard a lot of people talk about themselves, their "rock-bottom self," their "deep-down self." I heard parents and teachers wonder about children or youth. What did they believe in? Why were they behaving as they were?

Here is a thirteen-year-old girl talking, in September 1964: "I'm glad we're finally standing up for ourselves. It's been such a long time! We can't be down and out forever! You have to keep your eyes on the goal. Otherwise, you'll get low. Even when those whites say the worst things in the world to you, even when they tell you that your days are numbered and they'll 'get' you, even then you have to smile to yourself, whether you smile to them or not, and you have to say to yourself what Dr. King says, and our minister says: 'We're headed for the Promised Land, and there's no stopping us now!' There will be days when I close my eyes, and I think of the Promised Land — lots of nice people, and all the food you want, and no one against you, and everyone trying to be of help, and everything where it should be, and no mobs, and lots of candy, especially chocolate bars! But then I remember that first we have to win the battles here, and only later, when we pass on, will we have a long rest. If we can turn around the white folks, the devil will be an easy one to take on! So I try to be good, to do what's right, and I know He's watching, the Good Lord, and in the end He'll call us to Him, and then there will be the bad folks, standing off somewhere, the people who wanted to kill us, and the Klan, and they'll be told by the Lord to wear their robes, whether they want to or not, and they'll be judged and they'll be put where they belong, and if we mind our manners and keep ourselves on the right side, we'll find our place, and it'll be a good rest, and we'll look back and say, *'We did it*, yes, *we did it,'* no matter the sheriff and all his buddies and their guns, and the Mississippi Highway Patrol and their guns."

Although from a poor family, she had somehow managed to obtain: strength to integrate a southern school; strength to be a young activist in the face of extreme hostility and plenty of danger; strength to believe not only in a social and political effort but also in herself as someone able and worthy to take part in it; and strength to maintain her high hopes, to keep her spirits up, no matter the serious obstacles in her way. Whence such strength — in a child whose parents were illiterate, unemployed, with few prospects? For years I have seen such children; they have lots of burdens to overcome, including, often enough, serious educational ones. But over and over I have witnessed their courage and tried to comprehend it — with little luck, as far as psychiatric characterization goes. If I had to offer an explanation, though, I think it would start with the religious tradition of black people, which is of far greater significance than many white observers, and possibly a few black critics, have tended to allow.

In home after home I have seen Christ's teachings, Christ's life, connected to the lives of black children by their parents. Even as Eden was the first Promised Land, and Christ (a second Adam) promised another Eden ("a new heaven and a new earth"), so too young children have been taught to regard themselves (and have been regarded) as anointed ones, of sorts: those who will lead their people to a better fate. Such a religious tradition connects with the child's sense of what is important, what matters — the ego ideal. And with the parents' sense, too — as anyone knows who has been in a black church and heard the statements and the hard praying, and seen the look of pain give way to the look of hope in countless faces. At the same time, of course, there is the superego we all mention so often — the scrupulosity of churches, the breast-beating, and the self-lacerating judgments one also hears in many black churches, where an emotional, passionate religion is in no way shunned. Blacks know that the way to heaven is long and difficult; that if one is to gain that final nod of affirmation (the sanction of the ego ideal), one has to pass many tests set up by a demanding world (whence the superego).

Such connections are not new to this century. Even as the child quoted above made the obvious leap from her race's struggle to her personal life and showed through her imagery the hopes she holds for herself, the worries she has about her goodness, her correct conduct, St. John of the Cross,[7] in the sixteenth century, eloquently analyzed the difficulties in the path of, say, a novice monk, a convert to a religious life: "It must be known, then, that the soul, after it has been definitely converted to the service of God, is, as a rule, spiritually nurtured and caressed by God, even as is the tender child by its loving mother, who warms it with the heat of her bosom and nurtures it with sweet milk and soft and pleasant food, and carries it and caresses it in her arms; but, as the child grows bigger, the mother gradually ceases caressing it, and, hiding her tender love, puts bitter aloes upon her sweet breast, sets down the child from her arms and makes it walk upon its feet, so that it may lose the habits of a child and betake itself to more important and substantial occupations."

The point is that a wise mystic knew how to draw upon human experience when considering the moral struggles of his own kind — and of our kind, too. It is in our nature, St. John of the Cross knew, and so too did the black child just quoted, to hope against hope, and in doing so, to be reminded of the first such episode — those strongly felt days, weeks, months, when hope seemed (in retrospect) so simple, so forthcoming, so free of impediments, obstacles, impasses, commands, threats, criticism, not to mention self-criticism. Still, it is our fate to lose those precious days, to hearken back to them in thought and fantasy and desire, to merge such a psychological inclination to look back with the imperatives that push us on. I believe that the active idealism we see in some of our young takes place — as I will try to show in a later chapter — when a beckoning history offers, uncannily, a blend of memory and desire; a chance to struggle for a new situation that holds a large promise, while earning along the way the approval of one's parents, neighbors, friends, and, not least, oneself.

In psychoanalytic language, we might speak of an ego ideal given a new lease on life and reality, and now in extraordinary harmony with the often skeptical if not overbearing judgment of the superego. In the everyday language of our lives, the moral life gets a wonderful charge of energy: an old dream has become newly sanctioned by a fateful turn of history. No wonder little Ruby, when she was nine, looked back and said, "We inched a little closer to God, and because we did we became a little better ourselves!" One childhood's "lost narcissism" had become, by the grace of a social struggle, an element in a *nation's* moral development. It is for others to speak of what, if anything, happens to us after we die. I know only that I don't expect, this side of the grave, to see anything more "transcendent" than the above-stated child's description of a particular kind of moral experience.

But there are other kinds of moral experience — and some of them, actually, make one hard put to use the designation "moral," even if one is encouraged to do so by knowledge of psychoanalysis and of a region's social history. I reported years ago my effort to understand the segregationist fervor of the 1950s and 1960s.[8] I pursued with mixed fear and revulsion men and women who loudly proclaimed their racist hate, and I eventually got to know their children, too. Such encounters provided few surprises. I heard the frustrations and resentments of white people who themselves felt almost competitively vulnerable with blacks. I heard men and women — members of what some call a "marginal socioeconomic class" — talk about the disappointments of their obviously aggrieved lives.

I tried to stay in touch with some of the black and white children I had met during those tumultuous days of the civil rights struggle. The issue, of course, was that of proper follow-up. I had been urged along that line of thought and research not only by my own clinical training but an increasingly helpful acquaintance with Anna Freud. In one of her letters she cautioned me hard — maybe admonished me — in this way: "I would be very careful to see how those children are doing a few years from now. I appreciated your kind words about my book [*Normality and Pathology in Childhood*], but if a book has any point, it is that the message in it be remembered by the sympathetic reader!"[9]

I also kept attentive to some of the families, black and white, I had met in New Orleans and Atlanta — the particular nature, I suppose I should put it, of those families. One does not easily forget Hank, one of the white children who eventually returned to the boycotted New Orleans schools during the winter of 1963. In fact, I found myself for a while not so much forgetting Hank as putting aside my observations of his personality in favor of the attention I was paying over the years to his father, who was a militant segregationist, a constant heckler of Ruby, and not least, a member of the Ku Klux Klan. The more I heard the father berate Ruby, the more I wondered about his own self-regard: street heckling as moral attribution, as an anxiety-relieving ascription of a sense of jeopardy and worthlessness to another human being. But for young Hank, all during the 1960s, such a dubious psychological accomplishment had not yet taken place. He had enough to do, during those years, simply contending with the difficulties, dangers, and demands of his family's emotional life.

The boy Hank, at seven, had told me that he thought Ruby was "crazy" for continuing her mob-threatened education. I wondered why. The boy was hard put to answer directly. He told me what I already knew about his father: a hard-drinking carpenter and house painter, he was the family bigot, so to speak. Hank's mother said "nothing bad about the colored," Hank knew enough, at seven, to mention — and the boy even had some speculations as to why: "My mum has five of us to watch over, and the baby is always crying, so she doesn't pay any mind at all, she says, to the nigger kid trying to go to Frantz [the elementary school]. My older sister [aged nine, then] told mum she felt sorry for the nigger kid, and mum said she'd better not talk like that or there'd be trouble to pay for all of us. My dad loses his temper when he's drunk: then we all have to hide, or he'll get you. He makes my mother cry."

This was a home with obvious psychiatric burdens to bear, and with no apparent interest in getting medical assistance — quite the contrary. Hank's father distrusted doctors, never mind psychiatrists; he had been poorly treated as a youth at the New Orleans Charity Hospital, and had never forgotten the consequences — nor stopped reciting them to his wife and children. The more I got to know Hank, and understand his moral outlook, the more significant I felt the boy's account of his father's hospital experience to be. I heard it in 1964, when Hank was ten years old: "My daddy was a teenager. I think he'd left school and he was learning his trade. He got a bad stomachache one day, and he kept throwing up, and he couldn't stop, but he wouldn't go to the hospital. He tried to stay on the job. He'd throw up, and then he'd do his work, painting a house, and then he'd throw up some more. He told the guy he was working with that he'd had too much to drink the night before. But the guy was smart; he saw that my daddy was sick, and besides, he knew he wasn't a heavy drinker. (Back then, he only took a few beers!)

"I guess he passed out. That's how he got to the hospital. He says when he woke up they were taking him to the operating room, and he told them to stop, and the next thing he knew they were standing over him, the doctors, and they told him they'd taken out his appendix, and he was lucky it wasn't worse. He was 'madder than hell,' he always tells us, because that was only the beginning. He got fevers, and he had terrible pain, and they did lots of tests, and then they had to do another operation, and they told him he'd been infected. It was a nurse who said she thought they might have left a piece of gauze, or something, inside him the first time they'd operated.

"My daddy says he was 'treated like dirt there,' and he swore on his mum's Bible that he'd never in his life go back to that hospital, or any other one, and he says he'd rather die, right on the spot, when God wants him to die, rather than go 'expose' himself [upon questioning the boy said the verb was the one used by the father again and again] to any doctors. If he gets sick, he tries to keep going. My mum says that's why he drinks a lot, so he won't feel the pains he gets. His head is always hurting. He takes lots of aspirin, and lots of beer, and sometimes some rum and Coca Cola, his favorite thing to drink. When he gets drunk, bad drunk, he shouts at us. Sometimes he opens the window and he shouts, and we hear the neighbors closing their windows, but he doesn't pay them any mind, he just goes on hollering. It gets bad when *he* closes the window, because then he starts pounding on the [kitchen] table, and he'll say the doctors treated him like dirt, like shit, and if he was a man with money, they'd have been nice to him, and careful, and not make mistakes, and if he'd been colored, they'd have patted him on the head, and adopted him, like a dog who's your mascot, and he obeys your every wish, no matter what you say.

"Sometimes you can tell he's going to explode. My mother knows. When he starts talking about the niggers, we're in trouble. He goes and gets the flyswatter; he starts with that — hitting the table and the refrigerator. If we're near, we'll get hit. We hide. If he's real bad, he'll come after us, but he's wobbly, and mostly he doesn't catch us. I mean, I get away. One of my sisters [two years his junior] gets caught a lot. He hits her with the swatter. A few times he used his hand. I think he tried his belt, and she screamed so hard my mother came back to the kitchen and she got a knife, and when my father saw it, he ran toward her, but she didn't move, so he went and sat down, and he stopped talking and he stopped drinking that night. He slept in the yard, and he had bites all over his face the next morning. My mum tells us she doesn't know how he can manage, but he never misses a day of work. He's always up and out of the house by six, even if he's been drinking and drinking halfway through the night."

When I have talked with Hank, or with his mother or his older sister, I have never heard this line of presentation alter much. Always there is the husband or father as a younger man, trying to get on, with the odds stacked against him because he is poor and has not had a chance to finish school; then he falls sick, ends up "mutilated" (his wife's word, and apparently his, too) by doctors, and becomes thereafter a heavy drinker; and now his family has to endure his occasional assaults, even attempted beatings, not to mention his tough, unyielding thrusts, directed at black people, Jews, members of rich New Orleans families, who live in "fancy homes," college professors and their gullible, "ass-kissing" students — the list can get longer and quite obscenely stated. Neither Hank nor his mother nor his sister ever showed any more taste than I for a full presentation of that list, but they knew its precipitants rather well — liquor, news of New Orleans' racial struggle, and especially, any reference to an indignity experienced by any black person, living anywhere. That last "factor" worked in this way, according to Hank: "If daddy hears of any colored kid in trouble, or a grownup, he says they all bring their troubles on themselves, and then he says they should be sent back to Africa. It gets him going, real bad, if he hears about any of the colored in trouble. My mum says: trouble for the colored means trouble for us!"

Over the years I began to understand themes central to this family's life — psychological experiences all its members had shared, and which all of them regarded as highly charged. The linkages were rather apparent: poverty, occupational insecurity, limited possibilities for personal and economic advancement, the vulnerability that goes with illness, including exploitation of the body — all these becoming connected to a sense that others, also vulnerable, like blacks, are getting out of hand, getting ahead, hence they present yet another danger in a world already fearful, threatening, even rapacious.[10] Moreover, the costs of a life such as that of Hank's father have been substantial: heavy drinking, bitterness, the constant effort (at work) of a cover-up, and at home, a never-ending, showy self-pity that can turn, all of a sudden, into combative truculence, culminating occasionally in family violence, a child chased and hit, a wife and mother chased and hit.

Not that others aren't targeted for violence, at least ruminatively, as Hank at eleven was quite able to declare: "My mum tells us that she thinks daddy would be a lot worse, if it wasn't for the rallies he goes to. They're ready to go find a nigger and beat him up, but they don't. Daddy thinks the FBI has someone spying for them but it's hard to know who the fella is, because they're all friends. There are two guys who are new, and they might be the ones. Sometimes they hold meetings without those two guys. Mum says when there's a long meeting, and they march, daddy comes home and he's quiet and he eats a lot and goes to bed, and he has nothing to drink."

The father's morality was hedged close by envy, resentment, and a despairing, powerless egoism. He railed at blacks when he meant to mourn his own lost hopes, which he feared they, fellow sufferers, might just possibly redeem for themselves, of course, rather than for him. He had never seen a lynching; he knew such an event was unlikely; but he dreamed of the violent past, and when drunk conjured up that dream with loud, vulgar, obnoxious depictions of what would take place — a bad beating, with death the "solution" to "one problem," though of course any listener was immediately reminded that there were, still, "millions of them left." This link in memory, between a family's spoken and listening life, between blacks and beatings of blacks and drinking and the experience of terror, gradually became part of a boy's moral awareness — so that, at ten, Hank could be a strange mixture to his fourth-grade teacher: "He's a very quiet boy most of the time. But he can suddenly erupt, and then he's almost a problem child. But he never does that, gets wild, here in class; it's always outside, during recess, or just before or after school, or during the lunch hour, that we hear Hank has gone and got himself into some real trouble. He's not a big boy, and he should learn to be more careful when he starts roughing with the others. Every time, it seems, he ends up taking as much as he gives. He gets into a fight, and there they are, those bigger boys: they knock Hank around. But he doesn't seem as upset as I am, or the vice-principal!"

This was surely not the first American boy to get himself into trouble for a rather long spell during elementary school. But Hank's manner of approach, as I heard of it in those school confrontations, told a good deal about a form of moral development certainly different from the kind I had been observing in, say, Ruby Bridges, who lived only a mile or so away in the same city of New Orleans. Hank had a habit, I learned from his teachers and fellow students, of teasing others, making snide remarks about them — only to infuriate them, of course. The result: he became, time and again, a victim. When he'd been so treated by others, he quickly turned into a complainer. Why had others treated him so? Why did the teachers let such episodes happen? What is wrong with his friend, Jim — who never rushes to Hank's aid when "they" go after him? When will Hank be old enough, at last, to leave this school, go to high school? And, more ominously, why had "all this desegregation" taken place? Surely *it* was responsible for much of the trouble in school, as Hank's father had often said!

One day, when Hank was twelve, and just home from a basketball practice workout, we talked about his hopes for himself as an athlete, a student, a fast-growing youth. He'd been shorter than average until a year or so earlier, and had suddenly gone through a surprising growth spurt. He wondered why that had happened: "My father isn't tall, and my mother is short. My mum says my dad's father was short, but he scared everyone near him, even so. I think he whipped my father a lot when he was a boy. Daddy never talks about his father. He died two years after I was born. My father didn't want to go to the funeral, but my mother said they should go, and they did. When I started growing and growing this last year, my dad said I'm lucky, I'll be able to defend myself. But there are always people taller than you are! I won't be *that* tall!

"I'd be a better basketball player if I could just reach up to that net and slip the ball down! No luck! There's one kid who's a giant; he can almost stuff the ball into the hole. I've had a few fights with him. He's a tough guy. I figure, if I can handle him, when he loses his temper, I can handle anyone in high school! I think I know how to do it — talk him out of going after me!

"I still wish they hadn't brought the colored kids here, but it's all right. I'm leaving. I used to feel sorry for them, but they're pretty tough, and they don't pay any attention to you, and they don't want you paying any attention to them. They're 'uppity,' my mum says. My dad swears at them, but he says you can learn from them: they know how to take care of themselves. No one's going to beat them up! I should go study how they do it, he says — then I'd spare myself a few bad times. But I'm still in one piece, like my sister says. If I could be something, I'd be the manager of a supermarket. I've done some errands for the guy who runs the market where my mother shops, and he's promised me a job when I get older, filling the bags, and that'll be real great. He walks around the store as if he's the richest man in the world, and the mayor of New Orleans, my mum says. He's on a salary, but you'd think he owns the store! He must know how to talk right with his boss! If he catches someone trying to steal, he'll murder him. He'll go right after him himself. He's tough. His brother is a cop, I hear. I wouldn't mind being a cop myself! I'd keep everyone in line! No one would dare mess with me, then! Even those big, tough guys you see downtown stop and think before they take on the police."

This child would soon, before leaving high school, be working in a supermarket and aspiring to a job not as a city of New Orleans policeman, but rather as a "private cop." He had heard many times when he was eleven and twelve that a number of businesses rely upon their own sophisticated kind of protection. As a teenager he became drawn to the prospect of having a gun, using it to defend property. He also became increasingly interested in wide belts, with big buckles — no rare preoccupation at the time among his friends, but worthy of this comment from his own mother: "Hank is trying to be a cowboy, and I guess it's a stage boys of his age [thirteen] go through. The only thing I worry about is that he doesn't seem to pay attention to his schoolwork, and he's nervous — so worried about how he looks. All teenagers are, I know — but that boy can't move without checking himself out in the mirror. He doesn't look at his face, though; he looks at his waist — his belt. Then, we catch him taking the belt out and polishing it and looking at it, and then putting it back on, and adjusting it — I mean, he'll think about which hole in the belt to use the way I think about what I'll be cooking for supper!"

I suppose all this can be dismissed as a not especially remarkable chronicle of youthful psychological change, if not turmoil — the boy Hank going through his emotional paces as an American of a specific social and regional and familial and racial background. Still, if Ruby could keep her moral position, through the years of her childhood, could remain the child who prayed that God forgive her street tormentors, it's worthy of mention that Hank's moral values, as indicated by both his words and deeds, underwent notable, even dramatic shifts. Moral development in children can be characterized not only by periods of moral stoicism, even Christian humility and charity, as in Ruby's demeanor, but also by extended stretches of moral stinginess, amoral self-absorption, even a persistent immorality that takes the form of spitefulness, rudeness, assaultiveness. Not that there isn't a sadly twisted moral message of sorts, often enough implicitly rendered, in these forms of behavior. Young Hank made it quite clear, when he, like Ruby, was six, that he was as sensitive to parental and cultural commands, injunctions, urgings as Ruby was. Just as she called upon Jesus, he called upon (more and more, I noticed) a common social ethic stated most pointedly and passionately by his father: "This is a tough world we live in, and I tell my children that it's sink or swim, once they're a certain age! It's an eye for an eye, and a tooth for a tooth, a hand for a hand and a foot for a foot, my dad told me. He'd always say that when we tried to get him to be easy on us. The trouble was, it never was like he said, 'burning for burning and wound for wound.' I think he went to church more as a kid than he let us go. *He* was our minister — but there was no appeal to God, because he was our God, too; and if we did the smallest thing wrong, we got the biggest beating from him, and I recall thinking it just wasn't fair, because a small wound got back a large wound, and a small burning got back a large burning, and my poor old ma just echoed what he said, because she was scared. Of course, now I realize that all a father can do is instill some fear, some respect in his kids. The mother hugs and kisses them, and the father has to tell them what a lousy, rotten world this place can be a lot of the time."

Such comments remind the listener, yet again, that a willful mind can find a justification for its expressions in any scrap of a culture's heritage. The Book of Exodus in the Old Testament offered humanity a powerful moral testimony — an effort to restrict the punitive rights of all sorts of individuals in accordance with an urgently stated Biblical faith. It is something of an irony that a man who hates black people, and wants them deported or subjected to the old constraints of servility, draws justification for his personal morality, and for the one he wishes to impose upon his children, through resort to the twenty-first chapter of Exodus.[11] That Biblical statement, after all, in the tradition of the Code of Hammurabi, had among its intentions the imposition of severe and rational limits on the discretion of slave owners with respect to their slaves. A standard of civilized behavior was to hold for everyone.

The *lex talionis* cited by Hank's father is worth a moment's reflection. He was not alone in offering this version of morality back in the 1960s South, nor does one fail today to hear a similar recitation in homes and pulpits all over America. Revenge was once an aspect of unqualified brute power — wielded as any man wished. The adoption of *lex talionis*, historically, meant that a significant curb was to be put on such power: tit for tat, but no more than that. When Hank's father and others tell their children that they will be rewarded (if that is the word) in kind for their missteps, they often also proclaim themselves as much ignored, even harassed citizens, whose country has fallen upon evil ways — a terrible softness, a moral (and political) corruption. Yet, *lex talionis* itself was met with substantial resistance when it was proclaimed, as indeed have many efforts to restrain the violently vengeful side of human beings. Biblical critics remind us that badness and its punishment obsessed the ancient world (and maybe obsess ours as well), whereas a concern for goodness and its rewards came into prominence only later. Of course badness was regarded in Biblical times as a deviation from goodness. What obtains normally, goodness, requires no special mention — though visionary prophets such as Jeremiah and Isaiah and Amos knew quite well how tilted their world was in favor of the bad. *Lex talionis* is stated repeatedly in the Old Testament, in Leviticus, in Deuteronomy, for example, and one can feel the Jews trying to be more precise (anatomically so), more rational, more procedural in their manner of condemnation and correction or (corporal) castigation, while dreaming of some better time to come.

The itinerant rabbi, Jesus, advocated yet another kind of justice, and without question directly challenged the Mosaic law. "Ye have heard that it hath been said an eye for an eye and a tooth for a tooth," Matthew has Jesus declaring atop the Mount of the Beatitudes, and He continues, "But I say unto you, that ye resist not evil; but whosoever shall smite thee on they right cheek, turn to him the other also." Those were words from the New Sinai, so to speak, and to this day they challenge, dismay, confuse, and confound us — all the more because they were not simply uttered, but worked into the everyday habits of a life, that of the Christ, Who submitted Himself to the Cross.

This reinterpretation, this enlargement, of an old law, this new way of regarding what is right and good for us to do with respect to each other (what the nature of morality is) has prompted awe and incredulity in many of us, including (understandably) any number of us who work with the very people Christ addressed in his demanding sermons, the poor and the much tormented, or as He put it, "the rebuked and the scorned." To them, and to those who would hurt them in any fashion (even when able to justify so doing through an elaborate recital of rules, laws, precedents), Jesus addressed his insistence that once and for all vengeance be abandoned, the other cheek be turned, and forgiveness be embraced — forgiveness of the evildoer as a measure of one's own faith, one's own worth to God.

Jesus regarded vindictiveness as a poison; revenge for Him was not sweet. Ill will feeds on itself; betrayals incite to new betrayals, some of them sanctioned by a legalistic self-righteousness. Vengeance is reserved for God alone: "Vengeance is mine; I will repay, saith the Lord" — and surely none of us can take it for granted that such a belief is in any way workable. As Hank's father told Hank, and as he often told me, "this is a dog-eat-dog world, and if you don't learn to bark, you'll just be muzzled, and locked up, and that's the end of you, and the next guy is laughing."

So much for the God of Love, for the ethic of personal forgiveness and charity! One hears Hank repeating those words, coming to believe them (even if a twinge of defiant humor enables him to wonder, once or twice, why anyone would need to muzzle a dog that hadn't learned to bark), and one realizes how much work it took him to become the moral agent of sorts he ended up being — a zealous law enforcer! Later, at fourteen, we heard him looking ahead, but also looking back: "I help the boss catch kids stealing. I go underground! I hang around, and when I spot them trying to hide candy or gum or some canned goods in their pockets or pocketbooks or raincoats, I follow them, and I have a signal that lets the manager know. Then we pounce!

"I wouldn't mind doing that all day — better than filling bags with groceries. I think my dad did a good job of teaching me to be a detective. When he was drunk, he'd always shout that people are lousy, and you have to take it as the basic rule: watch out for them! You have to keep your eyes wide open, then you jump, and you round them up! Out West they used rope, but we go right up to them and say we've got the goods on you! The other day this old lady told me I shouldn't be so mean with the kids, and she offered to buy them the candy they stole, and my boss blew up, and so did I! He just gave it to her, and she started crying, but she wouldn't admit she was wrong.

"I used to like people like her a lot; they seemed nice. But they can cause a lot of trouble. Now I see why my dad got so upset about those colored kids. Look at all the trouble we had to go through. Those colored kids must have wondered what they were doing! They got caught in the middle, that's what I think. They were pawns! The only way not to be a pawn is — like my dad says: bark! If someone's going to use you, then you be ready! If they keep on trying to use you, then you be ready to get even, or strike them down! I heard a kid say the other day that he'd always hit first, if he thought anyone was going to hit him eventually. I guess he's right; otherwise you're a sitting duck!"

This preemptive-strike mentality is not at all confined to seasoned military strategists, as many a schoolteacher in despair has had good cause to know, not to mention we who are parents! As I heard Hank speak about his future, heard talk and imagery that included mention of dogs and ducks, guns and belts, nightriders and store detectives, booze and bigotry, supermarket food and supermarket lust (for free food), black people and white people, rich people and poor people, Old Testament admonitions and New Testament pleas, I began to realize, yet again, that a child's mind is a window not only to a family's psychology and psychopathology, but to our world at large. Ruby's Christian moral spirit (which had her praying daily for men and women who wanted to kill her) seemed unyielding throughout her childhood, whereas Hank's moral instruction has had its own, no less tenacious, history. We in child psychiatry are right, I suppose, to say that elements of both Ruby's moral outlook and Hank's go to make up the stuff of everyone's conscience. But I really wonder whether such eclecticism does justice to the emotional reality we see every day, whether as clinicians or in our capacity as ordinary human beings. Did Ruby ever really have the slightest chance, given her background, of being other than the Christian moralist she was at six, and did Hank's developmental masochism and sadism both ever have the slightest chance of being in any way redeemed, sublimated?

The question is not whether moral behavior is determined, psychologically or sociologically. In Ruby's family, and in her community in New Orleans, one encounters plenty of calculating self-advancement, sly and open greed, mean and harsh assertions directed at children, and others. In the black church of Ruby's parents the long Sunday trial — the passionate statements, songs, readings, and responses to readings — offered evidence enough that the Christian message spoken almost two thousand years ago did not come easily to Ruby Bridges or to her parents, or to others they knew; even as, in the life of Hank and his family, one saw that message being held high, fervently espoused, and not least, ignored resolutely. Hank's mother, as I think I have indicated, was by no means his father; she could collapse in church or even occasionally at home in tearful, urgent prayer, and not only because she wanted her husband to stop drinking, stop acting abusive to her and her children. She spoke, one day, reflecting upon those elusive, para-doxical, utterly insistent and challenging Beatitudes, the basis of Ruby's spoken and lived moral life: "I don't understand those little colored girls. I don't understand how that one can go to the Frantz School, and those three can go to the McDonough School, and all the white folks screaming bloody murder at them, and they smile and look ahead and the next thing you know it's another day, and they've done it again! If it was me, I'd say to hell with it. If it was me I'd want to kill those people on the streets. If it was me I'd try with all my might to figure out a way to get even. But it's not me; it's them, and they must have someone rooting for them. In church last Sunday I wondered to myself if it was God! But you have those thoughts, and you lose them. You go on to the next thought!

"Maybe all of this is part of God's design! Who knows! My husband thinks it's the devil at work, but I'm not sure any of us can be completely sure how to figure out what's God's 'handiwork,' like our minister says, and what's the property of the devil. In church we hear that the devil has slippery shoes, and he could be wearing the mask of the law — like that federal judge ordering desegrega-tion! But we hear that Jesus was treated as though he was the devil, and that's enough to sober you up. I saw that colored girl the other day, leaving school with those federal police [marshals] protecting her, and I thought she could be going to some cross, to hang on it, one of these days, for all we know! I try to tell my kids to be careful and listen to the minister, and listen to what they hear in Sunday School, and try to be good Christians, but it's hard for anyone, and I'll bet those colored kids are finding it tough to go to school, just like we're finding it hard to boycott the schools: our kids are hanging around home, and they're not learning one damn thing, and they're bored stiff. Well, on second thought, they may be learning something, just seeing what some kids their age can do, when they have to do it, and that's that! I wonder what would have happened to those colored kids, if there hadn't been this desegregation trouble here. I wonder whether it's made any difference to them. My neighbor, the other day — she said those colored kids would be bored sick if they had to go back to being just *any* 'little nigger,' and here *we* are complaining about how bored our children are, not going to school. It's all too much for anyone to understand! Sometimes I remind myself that if it hadn't been for a fire, I'd not even be here: My dad was a fireman, and he met my mom putting out a fire in Baton Rouge! He helped save her life — rescue her. I tell my kids: Do the best you can, and leave the rest to God!"

She was struggling with all the vexing mysteries this life presents us. She never followed her husband morally and psychologically, and for a while I thought her son Hank would resemble her more than him in personality and character. As I think about Hank's moral development I am reminded of Freud's essay "A Child Is Being Beaten" (1919).[12] I never saw Hank or his parents in analysis; they were never "patients," nor (I judge) will they ever be. Psychiatry and psychoanalysis are realms they fear and distrust and shun. I came to them as a pediatrician, interested in stress, and though I told them I was a child psychiatrist, they never wanted to talk directly about that side of my working life — in contrast, say, to other children, other parents, black and white, who were endlessly intrigued about the meaning I found in their drawings and paintings. Hank treated me with silent, unquestioning obedience: what the doctor requested is done. Even so, the terms of Freud's discussion are not unrelated: a boy whose father was himself beaten badly, whose father is poorly educated, not always employed, of so-called "marginal socioeconomic background," an alcoholic, a sometime Klan member, someone who acknowledges candidly desiring to beat up certain kinds of black people ("uppity ones"), and a person of some violence himself, though his wife and children report it to be verbal and physically threatening more often than implemented in deed; a boy whose mother is relatively more gentle, introspective, considerate, kind-hearted, but who has herself at least once or twice been beaten, and (in clinical language) whose psychological 'masochism," with respect to her "character-structure," contrasts with her husband's "sadism" as a dominant "characterological trait."

As for Hank himself, he never told me that he was preoccupied with the fantasy that "a child is being beaten" — though he did see, every day, a black child taking a strenuous psychological beating. Ruby's vulnerability, her jeopardy prompted him to worry about her, wonder about his own ability to sustain what she, clearly, somehow, was managing to endure. I do not think, therefore, that I distort a long involvement with a boy when I say that he "identified" with Ruby, "projected" part of himself upon her, "used" her in the psychoanalytic sense as, yes, "a child being beaten," hence as a mental stand-in of sorts: one is being punished oneself, or one's envied or resented sibling is also getting punished, and even, as Freud suggested, one's long-suffering mother is taking it on the chin yet again. The living Ruby became, for the living Hank, a symbol, a mental condensation, an instance of that "multidetermined thinking" clinicians keep bringing up.

Yet, Hank's early moral and psychological resemblance to his mother yielded to the adolescent Hank — increasingly outspoken, tough, combative, and ready to "beat" others at one or another game, even "beat up" others literally if they should stray. One feels a bit battered to realize that a boy's developing success as his father's son implies a youth less and less sensitive to the pain and suffering of others (black people, poor people) and yes, less gentle, less empathetic, less responsive to the New Testament morality both he and Ruby heard espoused in different New Orleans churches. Freud's paper told us that a number of adults have long, maybe lifelong ruminations involving the beating of children, and that such obsessive ideas are connected to sibling rivalry, to one or another aspect of the Oedipal drama and its guilt. Freud's paper, too, examined a psychological disposition: "character" and its vicissitudes — sadism and masochism — as they get worked into the symbolic expression of a person's emotional and sexual life. Not least, Freud's paper takes up moral matters, albeit indirectly. After all, Freud writes that there is an element of reality that his patients have experienced in connection with (and as a prelude to) their later beating obsessions — the sight of children being hit by their teachers, or yes, the reading of books in which beatings figure prominently. He even mentions, in that regard, *Uncle Tom's Cabin* — Tom beaten badly by the infamous Simon Legree! I do not think Hank's father ever flogged a black person, though I rather suspect he many times has dreamed of doing so. If a paper titled "A Black Person Is Being Beaten" were to be written, I fear that, like Freud's paper, it would touch upon a psychological reality larger than that of one patient, or in this instance, one family. As Hank's father himself told Hank and his brother and sisters: "There are lots who sympathize with us [the Klan], even if they don't tell the world they do." That word "sympathize" has fairly widespread and deep psychoanalytic implications — a social statement with respect to "beating fantasies" that shows, yet again, how shrewdly prophetic Freud was.

The same holds for Freud's interest in Moses, his willingness to use the narrative form. (*Moses and Monotheism* was originally to be published as *The Man Moses, a Historical Novel!*)[13] Freud knew how intimately each person's life intersects with a social code, a cultural tradition. The "moral growth" more than implicit in the Moses story is the "moral growth" any child achieves, or fails to achieve for himself or herself, and by extension (for many people suffer the consequences of one wounded life) other members of the

communities that collectively make up this nation. As I think of
Ruby, of Hank, of others, I find myself struggling with exceedingly
vexing and perplexing matters. What makes some of us more honorable and decent than others, given the inevitable mixture of envy
and rivalry and possessiveness and fantasized meanness, of thoughtfulness and kindness and compassion? Ruby went one way. She took
her cue not only from her parents and her ardent church life but
got a big boost from fate, from history itself. Hank, I fear, went in
another way — though, as one got to know his family, one saw that
such a direction was not at all inevitable. Hank, too, was persuaded
not only by his family life, but by the "fate" that comes, finally, to
mean a given set of experiences in a region, a neighborhood, a
school, a workplace. We are left, perhaps, with the words of the
great English moralist, George Eliot: "Every limit is a beginning as
well as an ending. Who can quit young lives after being in long
company with them, and not desire to know what befell them in
their after-years? For the fragment of a life, however typical, is not
the sample of an even web: promises may not be kept, and an ardent
outset may be followed by declension; latent powers may find their
long-waited opportunity; a past error may urge a grand retrieval."[14]
One has sadly to say the obvious: that such may also not happen,
as in Hank's life and that of many others.

II

MOVIES AND MORAL ENERGY

WHEN my wife and I began our studies of southern children in 1960, we found that the television sets in the homes we visited got in our way. We wanted to capture the attention of the children, black and white, who were going through the trials of school desegregation. We wanted quiet, to make for good conversation and so that the children might sit at the table and draw pictures — portraying, thereby, what they saw and felt happening to them in school, on the streets, at home. Such emphasis on drawings and paintings as a means of getting on with children and understanding their concerns had given a great boost to my work in child psychiatry at Children's Hospital in Boston during the late 1950s.[1] I was now eager to pursue that mode of inquiry (which I would do first in Louisiana and Georgia and then in Alabama and Mississippi and Arkansas and Tennessee and North Carolina). I remember, when I was an intern, hearing Anna Freud tell a roomful of doctors how "visual" children can be — more interested, often, in seeing than in speaking. Certainly the southern children I met in the early stage of my research were not talkers. They were six and seven years old, and they were glad to draw pictures for me — but they were even happier when I left them alone, to watch the "pictures" others had done: cartoons, adventure films of various kinds, and movies, all on television.

Sometimes the children would pay little heed to the talks we were having, or the drawings and paintings they had agreed to try to make, because their parents had a habit of leaving the television set going so long as anyone was in the house, even though no one in the house, at any given moment, might be watching the set. Once, in a moment of annoyance and of what I thought to be helpfulness and now realize to have been ignorance and presumptuousness both, I marched out of a kitchen into a living room (also a bedroom) and switched off the television set. Quietly, tactfully, but immediately, the mother of the house went from the kitchen, where she and her six-year-old daughter and I had been — she cooking, the two of us "working" — and turned the set back on. I will never forget the little girl putting down a crayon and throwing me a quick glance — not so much in reproof as out of a compassionate regard for my haughtiness and provincialism. Much later, when I was a fairly familiar part of her family scene, the child told me: "Before she lost her job, my momma used to work in a home in the Garden District, and she watched her serials there, and the movies, and she said they kept her going. There was TV all over the house, and when she wasn't looking, she was listening."

The mother, I knew, also liked to go to the movies. At the height of the difficulties endured by the handful of black children who (accompanied by federal marshals) had to walk past mobs, this black child found weekend visits to the movies not only relaxing, but, it seemed, providential: "My momma says there's one thing we can do on Saturday, and that's go away from here. Sometimes the people who shout at me in front of the school, follow me home. The marshals have to stay here almost until suppertime. Then everyone goes home! But they've been keeping an eye on the house at night, too, I think. Momma says we're in prison! She lost her job because they put our name in the paper, and the missus in that big house uptown said 'nothing doing' to having her 'colored cleaning lady' being the mother of *me!* Momma got another job cleaning floors in a market at night, and she gave them another name, I believe. On Saturday, she just wants to go and sit and watch what's playing, and she doesn't care what the movie is, though she likes some better than others, I can tell.

"Mostly it's love, I think; she likes to see the woman get a nice man! That is when she leans over and tells me to be choosy, and don't just marry anyone. Every time I ask her if she was choosy with daddy, she says she was! There will be times, like now, when they both tell us they wonder why God gave all this trouble to the Negro people, and the white people have a better time. Then my mother will remember something she's seen in the movie, and she says you mustn't forget that the white people aren't all having such a good time, either. And she saw what was going on in the rich house where she worked: they were drinking all the time, the missus even in the morning, and it was like watching a movie, to see them and hear them talk to each other.

"When we come from the movies it's in the late afternoon, and my daddy has usually just come home himself. My momma tells him what we saw, and sometimes she has me tell some of the story. I remember the cartoons better than the long movies, though. I tell my daddy about Popeye, and he laughs. He says I should eat a can of spinach every morning before I go to school. Then, when we go by the mob, I could stop and hold my arm out, and the muscle would get bigger and bigger, and we wouldn't need the marshals, because the people there on the street would go away. But momma doesn't like spinach, so she doesn't make it. She said the marshals should eat the spinach, if they like it, because they're the ones who have to be strong. I told them what we decided, and they said they don't like spinach, either — but they'd be glad to stuff it down the throats of everyone out there shouting at us in the morning and in the afternoon. But my daddy said: watch out — then those people would be so strong, like Popeye!"

At the time, and for years afterward, I was rather impatient with this talk. True, I had often noticed, when I treated psychologically troubled children in Boston, that cartoons and television sitcoms and movies were used in various ways by children, not to mention their parents. In the comments above, which I've pulled together from a much longer stretch of exchanges, a New Orleans child, herself in jeopardy, loves to remember that an apparently innocuous, even vulnerable fellow such as Popeye (one no more attractive than she was to many foul-mouthed segregationists who threatened and cursed her) could, by some repeated trick (ingesting spinach) triumph over seemingly impossible odds.

I wanted to hear more about what was *actually* happening to this child. My training had taught that a cartoon or a movie essentially underlined or amplified an existing psychological reality — reactions to fear or doubt, powerlessness, insecurity, precariousness, not to mention danger. Similarly with my adult patients: when they would mention a movie that had especially touched them, a movie they couldn't get out of the mind, I always tried (of course) to figure out why, and asked them to help me. If the movie was about the vicissitudes of love, there was no small chance that the man or woman I was seeing had become a patient for just that reason — the vicissitudes of love for him or her had grown to be a burden, if not a disaster. If the movie was about someone who had gotten a raw deal, it wouldn't be hard for the patient and me to figure out what reasons prompted him or her to become so taken by such a film, so unable simply to forget it after an hour or two.

This clinical line of thinking dominated my mind. The movies offer us just about all the emotions, I kept telling myself, and so it is to be expected that any visit to a theater will put one or another emotion in the saddle. Still, my psychiatric duty was to direct attention to the life in question, rather than the film. If someone else's fantasy, rendered on celluloid, generates a responsive wave of feeling, then by all means the observer must take notice — but less of the film itself, or of what "going to the movies" means, than of the person's (inner) predicament: what does X reaction to Y movie tell us about Z — this man, woman, or child, whom I am now hearing, seeing?

Not that an analysis of the film itself will offer immunity from this psychological mode of explanatory categorization. The critic can do for himself of herself what a doctor like me is often inclined to do — generate interpretations of what has been happening emotionally in the movie, thereby telling something about the scriptwriter, of course. There is something static in all this — films as Rorschach tests, films as clues to the unconscious of somebody: the filmmakers (director, actor, actress), the ordinary moviegoers, not to mention those who make it their business to write about movies. Short stories or novels, of course, inspire a similar approach. There is an ample literature of psychologically insistent literary criticism. A somewhat more spacious, even mystical approach was told to my wife by Flannery O'Connor, when we were living not far from her in Georgia (1962): "When this story is finished, and published, the fun is just beginning! I've often wondered what happens to some of my stories. They have a life, and those who read them are touched by that life — and you never know the new life that will result!"[2]

An interesting way, indeed, of evoking the relationship between a writer's work and a reader's life — and one that has become helpful for my wife and me as we've tried to figure out what happens to people as a consequence of their seeing a movie. The children we knew in the early 1960s were, after all, not only watching at home contemporary shows — *The Little Rascals, Captain Kangaroo, Dr. Kildare, The Real McCoys, The Gertrude Berg Show, The Dick Powell Show*, or a police series like *New Breed;* they were watching old movies on the same home screen, meaning mainly those of the 1940s and 1950s, and they were also going to new movies. In 1961, the year New Orleans went through continued desegregation and Atlanta initiated its school integration plan, *A Raisin in the Sun* was issued, and a year later, 1962, *To Kill a Mockingbird* appeared on movie screens all over America. These are now classics of sorts — important social-interest films that, at the time, indicated that Hollywood was reading the newspapers. Almost all the southern black children we knew, and a few of the white children as well, got to see those two movies, and their responses were strong, voluble, and at times surprising.

Lorraine Hansberry personally adapted her stage play to film, and its themes were not hard for anyone to comprehend — the confinement of a formerly southern black family in a Chicago ghetto, the sometimes conflicting aspirations of members of that family, the continual tension between hope and despair in people who have had such a rough time and whose prospects are by no means cheerful. Black children had heard in church the Langston Hughes poem: "What happens to a dream deferred / Does it dry up / Like a raisin in the sun?" Theater and film audiences alike now hailed the question as an admonishing reminder that the time had come, at long last, in this seventh decade of the twentieth century, for an American whose young president talked of a "new frontier," to confront once and for all the twin tragedies of racial segregation and discrimination.

Ms. Hansberry created characters strong enough not only to sustain the story, but to be representative of a larger reality. The Younger family evokes an embittered and fearful but also proud and determined black people, still in great distress, but now at last able to plan, contrive, and launch initiatives. Lena Younger is the ruling grandmother whose clear religious convictions are at odds with the secular aspirations of her daughter Beneatha, a college student who aims to be a doctor. Beneatha's brother Walter Lee wants to find steady work, wants to own a liquor store, so that his wife and their son Travis may live with some dignity. Lena's two children aim to make a go of it in materialistic America — and though their elderly mother is no ascetic, she holds to moral principles that not only puzzle and anger her children, but take them back to the old-fashioned, intensely passionate religious practices of the black rural South.

For the secular-minded white liberal viewers of the time, it was not hard to be persuaded that the grandmother, for all her essential decency, was an anachronism of sorts — an aspect of black experience no longer useful for millions of people. The daughter, Bennie (as she is called), may sound a bit abrasive in asserting her black pride, her atheism, her denunciation of the white man's values, but her new attitudes make her a believable counterweight to the apathy and ingratiating fearfulness of the old tradition. Walter Lee evoked his own kind of sympathy, perhaps, from the more commercial side of our national life — someone determined to take chances, to win in competitive enterprise, the only game in town.

The grandmother worries about the immediate hurdles of her family. Although her children are of prophetic sensibility (what to do in the long run of things?) she is irreconcilably pastoral: what to do right now so that things may be made a bit better? She has been left $10,000 from an insurance policy of her late husband, and that money, inevitably, prompts disagreements, outright conflicts. The son wants to buy a *store*. The daughter will need *money* for her ambitious academic pursuits. But the grandmother wants to buy a *house*, to get her family out of the ghetto and into a "nice" (white) neighborhood. The movie ends with little resolution of those conflicts. The grandmother has heard her children affirm *their* hopes, thereby confronting her with the realization that in exercising control over them she is indeed a matriarch of sorts. The children exhibit their own truculent, bossy instincts. Having finally got a large share of the coveted money, Walter Lee promptly loses it in a bad investment. The daughter resists the move to an all-white suburb; she has had her fill of whites. She is, uncannily, a forerunner of what five or so years later would emerge as a movement toward "black power" in both our South and North. Walter Lee is tempted to undercut the move when a white member of the suburb to which the Younger family is headed offers to buy back the house at a good profit to the Youngers. But Walter Lee eventually has second thoughts, and we are left with the Youngers, for all their disagreements, disappointments and apprehensions, preparing to leave their present quarters and take up a new struggle, though on different, more bewildering, turf.

I give this précis[3] (and try to recapture some of the warm liberal glow that the movie prompted in white viewers such as myself) because the children with whom I was talking had other ways of responding. I fear, my own responses made me a poor (bored, antipathetic, irritated) listener to theirs. Ruby, for instance, she who braved terrible threats in order to go to school, found herself not liking either of Mrs. Younger's children. The most vividly significant scene in the movie, for Ruby, was the confrontation between Mrs. Younger and her daughter. The mother uses the phrase "God willing" as she talks (so too did Ruby's mother), and the avowedly atheistic daughter mocks such a way of putting things. The mother is enraged, exerts her authority, makes the daughter say: "In my mother's house there is still a God." Again and again Ruby hearkened back to that sentence, but with interesting comments: "The mother can make her say it, but the daughter might not believe what she says. The mother smacked her daughter on the face, and our minister says you don't hurt someone, even if someone tries to hurt you, not if you believe in God."

At another time, Ruby offered this interpretation: "The young lady obeyed, but she didn't like obeying, and she'll remember that she was forced to say what she said. The mother could have tried to be nice, and not push her daughter like she did. Then, they might be friends. But my mother said you can't be perfect, and I guess *they* both weren't perfect. My mother said the daughter can have her own opinion later on, and meanwhile you have to respect your parents. God doesn't want you to be fake with Him, though. If you're not really talking to Him in your prayers, He'll see through you every time; and it doesn't make any difference if you're old or just a kid, or if you're colored or one of the white folks, no sir, it doesn't."

Such remarks, I thought in those days, failed to address the essential thrust of the movie, not to mention the predicament against which Ruby and others were struggling. I fear that more than once I used the oracular word "defensive" to describe Ruby's concentration on questions of parental authority and religious faith, suggesting that the almost terrifying ordeal of integration was too much for her to contemplate at that time, and that her mind needed to banish ("deny") meditative activity in favor of sheer everyday survival. On occasion I characterized Ruby's movie preoccupation as "adaptive": if she focused on *this* aspect of *A Raisin in the Sun,* the obvious threats posed by the Younger family to Ruby's own situation would be mitigated. Ruby took no interest in the grave dangers that accompany blacks when they escape (go North), or when they start the traditional American socioeconomic rise (complicated by racial considerations), in the same way that she shunned looking too closely at her own perilous situation. In Rilke's words, "survival is all."

Yet, I heard a white girl of eight in New Orleans react quite differently to that same scene in the movie. Only then did I begin to remember that Ruby was, after all, a child whose mother was fairly religious (as was the mother of her white counterpart). The white girl, also attending an integrated school, had an interesting view of *A Raisin in the Sun* as a whole, and the "God willing" scene in particular: "The movie is supposed to make you feel sorry for the colored. My mother says the colored won't be helped by a lot of us people feeling sorry for them; then they'll feel sorry for themselves. When the mother slapped her daughter and told her to believe in God, she was being smart. If you walk away from God, you're walking toward a lot of trouble. Maybe the colored will get into more and more trouble, because everyone is telling them they're bad off, and they believe it, and then there's trouble, like now, in our schools. If those people in the movie only listened to the mother, they'd be better off. The trouble was, even the mother wanted to move. If she really believed in God, wouldn't she want to stay right where she was?"

These two girls had seen a movie and found in it not only what critics had discovered, a frank public airing of the black ghetto experience; the movie also resonated with their experience as children growing up in the South, always strong on the matters of family and faith. Obviously, it wouldn't do to forget race, or to concentrate singlemindedly on a region's particular values, or for that matter, to ignore the personal psychological difficulties of this or that child. Ruby had good reason — apart from being a black girl who resided in New Orleans, Louisiana — to take note of how a daughter deals with her mother, and how that mother responds. No doubt the white girl also had good reason — apart from her new daily experiences, of attending school with black age-mates — to look closely at a scene wherein a mother and a daughter test who has what rights with respect to the other. These two children may be regarded as having done precisely what Flannery O'Connor hoped readers would do with her stories. The white girl took a few seconds in a movie and made of what she saw the basis of a vigorous examination: the risks of self-pity, the utter demands of religious belief. A movie gave her moral energy a chance to exert itself in her life; and neither race nor sociology nor geography nor theology nor psychology, nor the aesthetics of a film, quite accounted for what happened. The same held for Ruby, for whom one fraction of a movie started some big thoughts, indeed: the relationship between avowed religious conviction and the everyday testing of its strengths, its vitality, its resistance to the various temptations this world constantly presents.

These children became, in their own fashion, moral witnesses. They watched a movie, selected a segment of it for ethical analysis, ended up having an idea or two on what was right and wrong — for themselves and others who were alive. Other children, by the way, black and white, and with religious and personal backgrounds not markedly different from those of Ruby and her white fellow student, were able to ignore the film entirely, or ignore the part of it just discussed. The child Tessie, who also desegregated a school, told us the movie proved just one point to her: don't leave the South! I asked her whether she meant that injunction to apply to her own people only, or to all people. Without hesitating a second, she said "all people," adding that "white people would sweat it out up there, and they would want to come back home." I tried like the devil (and with no success) to figure out whether a specific familial event or anticipated event (migration northward) accounted for the attention given *this* issue by *this* child. Tessie's mother was religious, and certainly not the meekest person in the world. Why did Tessie not pay heed to the "God willing" incident? One is left only with the mystery that takes place between each reader and each text, and each viewer and each film: the diversity of stimulation that emerges from several characters embedded in a complex plot, and the considerable latitude of awareness and moral concern in an audience.

All these children had in common not only a conscience that scrutinized carefully their family behavior, their reactions to parents, brothers, and sisters, and by extension, friends and classmates, but also (what else to call it?) a moral sensibility that, when provoked by artistic expression, responded with a personal statement. Such a statement itself is an artistic expression of sorts, an act of moral imagination. "I've been thinking," Ruby said to me — when I sensed she was actually "thinking" about the movie *A Raisin in the Sun*. When I heard nothing thereafter for a few seconds, I helped her along with the inevitable "You have?" and then waited for what I'd hear. She followed with this: "If all the [white] people on the street [who were heckling her mercilessly] saw that movie, they might stop coming out to bother us." I asked her why she thought that. She answered tersely at first: "Because." Then she amplified: "The people in the movies would work on them, and maybe they'd listen." Note: a child suggests that fictional characters have a collective voice that occasionally intrudes upon the other voices within us, and exerts an influence on how we behave. After Ruby saw *A Raisin in the Sun* she made a point of praying less casually for her parents before going to bed; she also added to her prayers (as if the list wasn't already long enough) "those people in the movie, who live in Chicago." She "knew," of course, that those people didn't exist; yet, they did after a fashion live in her head, in her thoughts. Characters in a movie had become aspects of a young mind's moral seriousness.

In the next year (1962) *To Kill a Mockingbird* appeared, and America by and large took the film to its heart, as it had, earlier, Harper Lee's novel. What a splendid time for such a film to be released — at the moment when the civil rights struggle was accelerating rapidly. Gregory Peck's Atticus Finch would become a national hero of sorts — the decent, pensive, kindly Alabama lawyer who defends a black man, Tom Robinson, against the charge of rape made by Mayella Ewell, a "poor white" stock character. Mr. Finch's role was welcomed by many white southerners, who felt themselves the easy scapegoats of all too many self-righteous Yankee accusers; in the North thousands of viewers were grateful to be reminded that honor and rectitude and gentleness of manner were also part of the beleaguered southern tradition. Yet, living in the midst of the civil rights South of the early 1960s, we heard from our student activist friends a certain incredulity about Atticus Finch: they'd yet to meet his kind of lawyer as they went about their controversial and dangerous work of attempted voter registration in the rural South, including Alabama. Some of the ordinary white people we knew, reluctantly involved in school desegregation or actively opposed to it, focused not so much on Atticus Finch as on "the girl" and "the nigra" — and regarded the whole thing as a kind of Hollywood "setup," some told us, to persuade everyone in the country that injustice is the ruling force all over Dixie.

I was surprised by remarks about the movie from some of the southern children I was then visiting. Three of them, Ruby included, concentrated their critical energies on a subplot, which, as I saw it, was meant to offer a bit of distracting drama, a bit of "local color": Boo Radley, played by young Robert Duvall, is the supposed loony who lives next door to Atticus Finch (a widower) and his six-year-old daughter Scout, and his ten-year-old son Jem. These children, along with their summer visitor Dill, are endlessly interested in what kind of person that neighbor may turn out to be. (He's been locked up in the home for years by his parents, and, of course, the children have heard dozens of rumors about his appearance, his manners, and not least, his odd behavior.)

For Ruby, and for a ten-year-old friend of hers, Boo Radley was an object of the greatest fascination, and ultimately, an intriguing hero. He *was* a hero, of course. After Atticus defends the black man, eloquently, yet in vain (an all-white jury condemns him), the white girl's father seeks revenge, and sets upon Scout and Jem as they walk through the woods. Boo Radley has been watching over them with benign concern, with affection, all summer (we have begun to realize), and now saves them by killing their attacker. The mysterious eccentric turns out to be a protective, loving person. (As the children had spied on him, earlier in the film, they had been frightened at his shadow, but also increasingly pulled into the orbit of his tenderness, and in time, gallantry: he leaves gifts for them, and when Jem, running in terror, discards his overalls, they are neatly folded and placed where they can be seen and repossessed.)

Ruby said of Boo Radley: "I was scared when the boy and the girl went near that house. I was afraid they'd get into a lot of trouble. I was afraid that man Boo was real crazy, that he'd harm the kids. For a few seconds I was wanting to leave and go outside. I stayed because my mother told me to stay, and she kept saying 'it's just a movie,' and I knew it was only a movie, but it didn't feel like that; it felt as if you were right there, and I was afraid."

I was surprised, indeed, to hear this young child repeatedly use the word "afraid" — in view of the fact that she'd abstained again and again from calling *herself* frightened, no matter what hectoring she received daily from a segregationist mob. If she "denied" her fear in that regard, then maybe it could be "expressed" in this way, or so I found myself reasoning! But Ruby took another tack: "I wasn't scared for the man, the Negro they all were wanting to kill. I knew they'd want to get him, and so did he! I was hoping they wouldn't be so mean. But I wasn't getting my hopes too high! Never get your hopes *too* high, my grandma tells us once a day, but then she says to get your hopes *high enough,* so you've got a good target for yourself!

"No, I was scared for the white kids, and I felt sorry for that man next door; he was in bad trouble, you could feel it. I was scared of him, too, like I said. You didn't know who he was, and he could be a real bad one. But he turned out good, real good. My grandma said it's people like him who get a bad name, but they're good people; and then it's the people standing out there in front of the school, and they're the ones who are the bad people, but no one's calling them crazy, because everyone's afraid to cross them, and they say they stand there for everybody in the city. That's what one man tells me in the morning: 'Hey, you little nigger,' he says, 'I'm here for the whole of New Orleans to tell you off!' I just walk on, and I think of all the people I know in New Orleans who aren't like him! That poor man in the movie who was in hiding, and he ended up saving the children — if he lived in New Orleans he'd sure not be out on the street screaming at us. I realized by the end of the movie that he was a shy man, and he liked kids, and he was kind: a good man, not a bad one!"

While the world, mostly, heeded this movie's explicit celebration of a lawyer's decency and rectitude (unavailing against a community's ingrained racism), Ruby was impressed by how a boy and girl roughly her age learn to distinguish between social appearance and moral reality. Interestingly, what caught Ruby's eye is now, more than twenty years later, the most arresting part of the movie for many viewers. Certainly the high school and college students I know who have seen the movie end up by discussing intently just the scenes Ruby and her age-mates, black and white, regarded as noteworthy in the early 1960s. Not that Atticus Finch, the brave, honorable, self-educated lawyer, doesn't also have his continuing appeal. Certain law school students of mine find the movie as instructive as novels by Dickens portraying nineteenth-century English law. In fact, Atticus Finch has been the subject of discussion in at least one law school journal — where his professional integrity underwent extended analysis and appreciation. The civil rights aspect of the movie has yielded in time to its truth of character portrayal, the ultimate consideration in the staying power of any story.

In 1962 another film of great influence caught the attention of the children we were observing: *The Man Who Shot Liberty Valance,* a John Ford western. This movie was especially exciting for the white boys we knew in Atlanta. Many of junior high school age went back several times, until I found myself knowing the plot long before I actually saw the movie. The plot was not terribly original, but of course Ford had a way of turning the conventional, even the banal, into the extraordinarily suggestive. Shinbone is the name of the movie's town, and we begin by seeing it in latter-day stability and affluence. The West now is quiet, attractive to the eyes of tourists who travel through it in peace. The movie opens with a train moving uneventfully through this calm countryside. James Stewart as a United States Senator and his wife (played by Vera Miles) are on that train, and it turns out they've come all the way home to attend the funeral of Tom Doniphon, the town derelict, whom everyone recognizes, of course, to be John Wayne. Why has the Senator returned for this occasion? Soon enough we see an earlier West, a West of decent and thoughtful people, yes, as was Senator Stoddard when a young lawyer; but also a West of wild, mean robbers, threatening violence anywhere and at any time. The young lawyer, traveling by stage-coach at night, becomes a victim of one of those outlaw bands. He is beaten savagely, left for dead. Liberty Valance (Lee Marvin) is the gang's leader. Tom Doniphon, a rancher, finds young Stoddard, brings him to Shinbone, asks the attractive and lively Hallie to care for the badly injured man.

The rest of this movie is not hard to predict. The chief outlaw, Liberty Valance, comes to Shinbone, struts about, makes a bid for power, and subdues a terrified town. But young Stoddard, healed, has his own aspirations for the town. He teaches children. He inspires all whom he meets with his idealism — the voice of our nation's better side. Soon enough he will confront the much feared Liberty Valance, and miraculously prevail (for all his ignorance of the West's gun-toting and shooting traditions). One shot and Valance is dead. Young Stoddard is now a hero, naturally, and on his way to national prominence. At the Territorial Convention he receives grateful applause, and is nominated to take the case for statehood to Washington. But he is uneasy with his popularity as the man who shot Liberty Valance. Now Tom sets to work to urge Stoddard to accept, to get on with the mission. No reason, anyway, for such scrupulosity: Tom had been the one, *really*, to kill Liberty Valance. Standing in an alley that day, knowing that Liberty easily would have prevailed over naive, defenseless Stoddard, Tom had pulled the trigger of his own rifle — and had not, thereafter, made the claim for the accomplished deed. Stoddard is free, now, to reap the harvest of his persistent goodwill, his untarnished innocence: win the attractive woman, Hallie (whom Tom had also liked very much), and, eventually, the high office of Senator.

Not unlike other westerns, this movie is filled with guns and booze and fearfulness and raw intimidation, and earnest, well-intentioned talk and cowardly onlookers and sociopaths on horseback. This movie is, however, especially well directed and acted; and the plot has a larger, historical scope: the nature of not only the outlying West, but of our country. Who has clean hands? Who protects us against whom — and who gets the credit? What truths go unrecognized, while legends grow? What was *lost* as a consequence of the taming of the West? Our weakness before the Liberty Valances of this world, no question. But Tom Doniphon/John Wayne had a direct decency and a bold, unpretentious honor that have also been lost to us — we who live amidst the hesitations and indirections, the pomposities and banalities that characterize bureaucratic life. Once there were the bad guys, true, but also the exceedingly good guys. Once our community was challenged constantly, but with utter and exhilarating candor, by a moral polarity. Now we have law and order, without question — but if Liberty Valance is gone, so too are Tom and his breed, for we no longer need them to challenge Liberty, a usurper of other people's liberty.

My wife and I went to this movie with a young man (aged fourteen) who came from a staunchly segregationist Georgia family — whose members did, though, also worry about "law and order," an expression quite often used in the South of a generation ago to signify, among whites, their grudging acceptance of the school desegregation then being required by one district federal court after the other. The youth was in the ninth grade, had stood up in class to announce that he wished "the people in Washington, D.C., would leave us alone," meaning Georgia's racially separated schoolchildren; but to announce, further, that he'd "be damned" if he'd let "some bureaucrat up there have the satisfaction" of seeing Atlanta's boys and girls, such as himself and his brother and two sisters, become violent or members of a mob or in any way lawbreakers. I had heard the statement (a speech, really) and had been startled by the eloquence of its shrewd exhortation to respect the law, by its evident acknowledgment of reluctance to conform, yet its canny assumption of a higher ground, so to speak — a move which adroitly disarmed segregationist criticism, and which left the speaker free to make his plea to the many listeners assembled before him in the all-school meeting.

While we sat watching the movie, I could see and feel this boy's intense involvement — as I could notice, occasionally, how caught up my wife and I were. Afterward silence reigned as our car moved through the city's streets — a sure sign, in my experience, that a movie has hit home. When we got to the boy's modest brick bungalow, built twenty years before but already deteriorating quite noticeably, we started talking a bit, and my wife and I were invited by our movie guest to come in: have a proverbial Atlanta Coca-Cola. We drank, we talked. The life and death of Liberty Valance and of Tom Doniphon became subjects of heated discussion, as did, we all began to realize, the rise and fall of the American frontier. In fact, none of us had realized until we began discussing the film just how much it had meant to us. We all were "with" Tom/John Wayne, were admirers of his stoic sacrifice: Stoddard/Stewart gets the woman, gets public recognition, gets high public office, whereas Tom/John Wayne gets — oblivion, the boozy decline of the town recluse. What kind of justice is that?

On another day, we had a second long conversation about the film with the young man for whom, apparently, Georgia was also a part of our West! "I keep thinking of that movie," he declared, and then, as we exchanged opinions (I herewith summarize his, spoken during a long afternoon's discussion), he let me know why: "I'm pretty sure the people who made the film wanted us to be on John Wayne's side! I'm always on his side! But they want you to be on the side of that Senator, and I'm *not* on his side. I mean, he was one of the good guys; he was *the* good guy. But who believes anyone like him is for real? He was Mr. Nice, and you can't go wrong with a Mr. Nice in a movie — but he'd have been the one shot if Wayne hadn't been there. We're all supposed to admire the nice lawyer who we know is going to be Senator, because he was so modest, and he didn't want to be a big success to people because he killed Liberty Valance. To me, the really modest guy is Wayne: *he* could have stepped up and told people that it was his doing. But he wasn't that kind of guy!

"What kind of guy was he? He was the really good man who gets a raw deal. Everyone thinks he's odd, or he's rough and tough. He hasn't got any polish on him, none of it. He doesn't think so much of himself that he goes telling other people how to behave. He's not even sure himself how *he* should be behaving! But he's tough, and he's not going to sit back and watch someone push everyone else around.

"What happens to him, though! He gets nowhere. The young goodie-guy gets everywhere! When Wayne dies, a Senator comes all the way from Washington, D.C., to his funeral. Big deal! I'm sure Wayne didn't ask him to come! If he could have gone to his own funeral, he wouldn't be so impressed that this guy came to wave goodbye. If you ask me, I think Liberty was the big crook, and the guy who became a Senator is Mr. Nice who picks up the chips all the time, and Wayne is the guy who's *too* good. You're supposed to think that future Senator is *too* good, because he doesn't know how to use a gun, and he's so worried about the education of the kids, and he's 'pure' — he won't just brag, because he has his principles, and to brag you've killed someone, even Liberty Valance, is not behavior 'high' enough for this guy with the big shot soul! But by the time Mr. Nice has left the town for Washington, Wayne has had it, and if you ask me, that means the *town* has had it!"

At such a moment one is intrigued, eager to hear a good deal more, and is not disappointed. Merely asking "why" elicits a Dixie eruption: "It's like here; by the time these lawyers from the Justice Department are through with us, and these federal judges, who have to order their own neighbors to do what they're told, or else — by that time this won't be the same city any more. My mother and father have been watching all this, and they say there was once a city here of people who would help each other, and even if the colored and the white weren't equal (and a lot of whites aren't the equal of other whites!), there was some spirit in the city, so that if someone was in trouble on a bus, or the street, or in a store, people would stop and try to help. It was like it still is where my grandparents live, in Moultrie, Georgia. In that part of the state the colored and the white are still segregated all right in schools and in the restaurants or the moviehouses, but I'll tell you, if someone gets into a jam, race won't stop people from trying to give some help, no sir. People stick together. People belong to the same place, the same town, the same county, and they know each other, and they know they've got to live with each other, so there's so far anyone can go, and then everyone will say, *stop!*

"The same in that town out West before the shoot-out. Sure, Liberty Valance was trying to take over. But you see, Wayne could have taken care of him in his own way, and that would have been that! But no, this outsider comes, and he's full of sermons, and he wants to tell the whole world how to behave. God, has he a bad case of the preaching bug! So he starts a school, and he gives his lectures; and he says he's going to clean everything up — he'll even challenge Liberty Valance, that's how brave he is, and that's supposed to show everyone that here's a guy who will risk his life, and he's not one of those fake, compromising types. So he does what he's said he'll do, and he shows the town that he's as good as the people who wrote the Constitution and fought the British in the Revolutionary War; he's a knight in shining armor, and if it wasn't for him this two-bit western town would be a sinkhole, and the people there would be (like our minister says) headed for hell faster than they knew.

"What happened was that the town was headed for the end of its independence! You could argue that, yes sir! You could say that once people like Wayne stopped being the strong people there, out West, and all those outside lawyers and teachers came in, then it was a different place. Maybe for the better, in ways, I'll admit; but maybe for the worse, too. There's probably a building in that town, like there is in all our Georgia cities and even our smaller places now — a building full of big bureaucrats, and they talk their mumbo-jumbo, and they get their court orders, and if you cross them, you're through, washed up, and no one calls them Liberty Valance people, just guys who work for the same government that Senator and his buddies run out of the Capitol, Washington, D.C. Try to talk with a senator, even one of your own, my daddy says, and see how far you'll get. Senators have time for big shots, not for the ordinary guy, whether he's colored or white, not for John Wayne types, unless it's the real John Wayne, and then every senator in Washington will come rushing to his side, so the photographers can catch a few pictures."

As with *A Raisin in the Sun* and *To Kill a Mockingbird*, the 1962 movie critics did not review *The Man Who Shot Liberty Valance* as some southern children were inclined to see it. Not that there was a chorus of agreement among all those children for the critical approach just presented. But this lad wasn't the only Georgia child or youth to observe a certain self-righteousness, albeit modulated, in the James Stewart character who went on to fame and national power. Nor were such young observers only white — or segregationist. A number of black children, girls as well as boys, found themselves drawn unmistakably to John Wayne, but also quite unfriendly to James Stewart, who is rarely cast as anything but good-natured and decent. Why?

John Wayne by 1962 was well on his way to becoming a personal legend, even as one of this movie's themes has to do with how a legend is made, and by the same token, how a legend may require the nourishment of half-truths, evasions of truth, even clear-cut falsehoods. As a legend, Wayne could not ultimately do wrong. He could stumble. He could scorn the conventions of society that most of us demand that others obey — except for those larger-than-life individuals whom we choose to honor, helping ourselves to a bit of disobedience by proxy. The challenge to Wayne, some children saw, was from the Jimmy Stewarts as well as the Liberty Valances of this world — and such a complexity of social analysis bespoke the presence of considerable moral energy in these viewers. They did not assert themselves, naturally, in a carefully reasoned and utterly coherent, consistent way. They equivocated, advanced ideas (or plain old family hand-me-downs of opinion, if not demagogic assertion), retreated to publicly sanctioned banalities (such as "I guess it's hard to police *any* society"), and so hemming and hawing, expressed their perplexity, their mixed feelings, their confusion — about, obviously, not only the frontier West but the contemporary South.

It is a mistake, however, to regard these children as mere moral puppets, driven by the workings of some contemporary sociodrama to hunt down cheap symbols in order to help express whatever psychological tensions were at work inside their heads. In the case of *To Kill a Mockingbird,* a number of boys and girls were inclined to emphasize childhood rather than race. The human mind in the first decade of life can conjure up the demonic even in the close-at-hand world of a small and familiar rural setting, and that same mind may be instructed in the error of its ways by life's events. In the case of *A Raisin in the Sun,* race could yield again (even in those children hard pressed by its consequences) to the quandaries of authority: Who has authority in a family, and who doesn't, and why? Moreover, how long will the status quo remain — not only the racial one, but the one that obtains in my home?

John Wayne could prompt a wide-ranging regard not only for himself, and not only his beloved West, and not only the (then) beleaguered South, but for our mid-twentieth-century nation, in the midst of winning big moral gains, but (the young critics observed) at the cost of bureaucratizing our ordinary lives. A boy here, a girl there, was reminding me that a legend, just partially true, had become enshrined, and that the dying man had taken with him a good deal of the town's former moral spontaneity. If the price of that perception — in, say, the youth whose words are offered above — was an outburst of callous, racist pieties (which I know that boy, grown up, an Atlanta physician, would quickly and sincerely disown!), then the listener might well have hearkened back to the movie itself, which hints at a similar predicament: the mixture of reason and unreason that attend so many of this life's moments, be they routine or dramatic.

Perhaps the word imagination is, again, the one required to do some justice to us moviegoers: moral imagination as it is lent energy by that inert celluloid going round and round for a hundred minutes or so. After those eyes have watched the hundreds and hundreds of frames that in their sum become a film — then the mind recovers the remembered words, the scenes that engage with a person's own scene, his or her life-situation. An impression is left, perhaps, of one or another character — an impression that may linger and stimulate a viewer's mind. It is not a matter of reflex reaction, a behavioral consequence of sociological and psychological stimuli finding their mark. Rather, those behavioral stimuli are, not infrequently, ignored, or absorbed in some broader moral vision of things that even small children seem unself-consciously able to construct for themselves.

As Flannery O'Connor spoke about readers, so too the young southern viewers quoted here managed to create a "new life": not, strictly speaking, either their own views, but not those of the film-makers, either. We all know how easily children are supposed to be swept off their feet, turned into the putty of one or another pied piper: the advertising executive who wants to make them buy a product; the teacher or minister who persuades them to believe such-and-such; the parent, of course, who molds them, for years on end; and nowadays the television or moviehouse screen exerting its seductive power over them — an immersion of their senses (the eyes and ears, at least) in what amounts to an irresistible spectacle. There may well be a moment and longer of surrender: the "passive" child (or adult) will be no match for the self-styled artists, the ma-nipulative magicians who are "doing" sound and lights, or coaching, cajoling, lording it over the actors and actresses.

The passive response is not the only one available. We have it within our power, young or old, to attend selectively, to summon a sense of proportion, to call upon humor and common sense, to assume a varying or even quite insistent critical distance from the subject under scrutiny in the film, and later, in a given mind's life. I think another child can be of help here, a youth of fourteen whom I got to know fairly well when living and working in Albuquerque in the early 1970s. This boy's father often remarked that he'd "up and educated" himself; he worked for the Interior Department. The son, however, wanted to revert to his father's earlier occupation: an Anglo rancher living amid a growing number of Spanish-speaking neighbors. He found the ninth grade boring, and the movies a delightful alternative: "I can go to see John Wayne over and over. Any western will do for me! Any western is better than sitting there in that class and listening to the teacher go on and on and on about prepositions and why algebra will make a difference in my life! I look at her, and she's so fussy about everything and she brings in a peppermint patty every day and — would you believe it? — cuts it into four parts, and eats a quarter before the first period and another piece before lunch, and another piece after lunch, and the last piece before we're dismissed. Lady, I say to myself, eat it all, and then take another one and eat it all; don't use that penknife on that little piece of candy! But that's what she's like! She rations everything in her life, I'm sure. She belongs on a ranch, preparing grub for the hands! No, God spare us, she doesn't!

"When I go see the cowboys and Indians fight, I forget all this city stuff — Taco Bell and Safeway and the TG and Y, and figuring out when a word is an adverb and that stuff. This country wasn't built up — not out West, anyway — by people who were worried about the semicolon! In a movie, you see people leveling with each other: the guys who are honest, and the crooks; the people who are going to grab what they can, and the people who won't let them, and who will stand up and die, if they have to, so the rest of the folks won't be in danger every minute of the day.

"You can't take a movie too seriously, though; I know. I forget a lot of the movie pretty fast! I know the Indians got a raw deal. But I don't think about that when I see the movie. Later it'll occur to me — maybe when I see them selling their stuff downtown or up in Santa Fe. I feel sorry for them. They got cheated. To me seeing a good western is like taking a vacation: you get into the swing of things, and you're right there while they slug it out. I don't try to remember my American History that she teaches us, Miss Peppermint Patty we call her, while I see the cowboys going after the Indians. But I don't forget my history, either. I try to tell my mother when she says we're seeing too many movies, and there's all the shooting in them: Ma, I won't forget a single fact, just because I go and see that movie; and you can stand on Fourth Street here in Albuquerque and watch those cars fighting it out with each other, and the drivers are as mean as any bad guy in the movies, and the drivers are out for blood, just like the bad guy in the movies is out for blood.

"Anyway, when I leave the movie I know what's ahead of me: a spelling test, maybe. And I don't believe everything I see, and I don't try to imitate everything I see. If I did, I'd have to stay away from Albuquerque as much as the movies! I saw two guys fighting in the supermarket about who was first, and they had to get the cops in, and each of them got his punches at the other, and the doctors had more business, as usual! People don't give you credit a lot of the time for having your head screwed on straight! They say kids are influenced by this bad thing and that bad thing, and it's always the movies: they're not as good as Mark Twain, that's what the teacher says. But I'll bet Mark Twain might like going to the movies, if he was around, and he wouldn't think *they* are the reason people act bad. He said people were pretty bad back when he was around, and there weren't movies then."

There is nothing in his words that deserves inclusion in a definitive anthology of film criticism. This Albuquerque boy (both his parents were born in Wyoming) was struggling, even at twelve, when I first met him, to figure out what kind of a life he would live. He was not headed for the University of New Mexico. He had no interest in the federal bureaucracy, where his father has found security. He had his own horse, loved riding. He knew the land well, and looked forward to spending his life in some intimacy with that land. Western movies quickened that resolve, put him in a happily anticipatory mood. The movies did not, however, sweep him away from his mooring in the 1970s, in a rapidly growing American city. He left the theater ready, as always, to deal with automobile traffic, with high school, with a job he had bagging in a local supermarket. He did not become excessively nostalgic or simpleminded as a result of the westerns he saw. They did not cause him to forget the real history his earnest and conscientious teacher had taught him, nor to embrace an updated version of "frontier justice." The sight of certain Indians made him feel sad, evoked confusion and pity rather than the anger and bitterness of a moviegoer who has seen many nice Anglo girls carried off, turned into the property of Indians who spend their time harassing courageous and high-minded Anglo travelers or settlers. This American youth even remembered a few stories his parents, both born to rancher families, kept telling their children: how much not only the Indians but the western land itself had suffered at the hands of those cross-continent Anglo adventurers.

A young moviegoer can thus repeatedly expose himself to the excesses of a Hollywood genre — sentimentality, violence, blatant misreading of history, racial prejudice, simplemindedness — and somehow emerge unscathed intellectually as well as morally. It can even be argued that he becomes stronger in both respects. True, film enables him to "escape," to experience vicariously the pleasure of shoot-outs, of a raw life replete with galloping horse-riding, or enormous breakfasts and shots of gulped whiskey, and of an untouched, pastoral mountain landscape that makes even a national park seem impossibly cluttered with cabins and road signs for the tourists. But each movie helps him learn to sort matters out, stop and think about what is true and what is not by any means true — in the past, in the present.

This youth becomes stirred morally — not simplistically to join some cowboy vigilante group, not to simplify America's nineteenth-century frontier complexity. He doesn't forget what he's learned in school, learned at home, from hearing people talk in his family and his neighborhood. But he does take westerns to convey a truth — the self-deceptions people so commonly contrive in order to justify their various purposes: "A lot of people came out West because they'd had trouble back East. They couldn't get work, or they'd done something that wasn't right. Then they hit the Plains and the Rockies, and they wanted to make a million fast, or they wanted to build up a little empire for themselves, and no one would ever take it easy. Meanwhile, those Indians were there, and when they weren't fighting to keep what they had, they were just standing and watching, or sitting on their horses and watching. That must have been murder for our people — all those eyes on them! I think it's too much, plain too much, when that Miss Peppermint Patty stares at me!"

Such moments of moral reflection ought not be turned into occasions for overwrought psychiatric comment, for banal connections between the western movies, say, and the collective American conscience, or woven into that boy's effort to settle his attitude toward schooling. (He *would* eventually attend and graduate from the University of New Mexico, where he took a "minor" in film studies, and go on to that university's law school! And he still enjoys a "good old western.") He was simply stating his own awareness that interludes in the dark are inevitably interrupted when the lights go on, are affected by such artifacts as popcorn machines and freezers full of ice cream sandwiches, by counters stocked with colorfully wrapped gums, chocolate bars, sucking candies, and racks full of soft drinks. He notices there are, even, a pile or two of peppermint patties. Outdoors there is the beaming sun of the semi-arid Southwest, and all those New Mexico license plates proclaiming "Land of Enchantment." There is a wallet that has five dollars less in it, hence needs replenishing. His horse has to be fed by emptying grain from a bag, not by being put out to pasture amid the uninterrupted grassy countryside that seems to stretch into infinity. Soon there will be the teacher, and her crisp historical asides and wonderfully cynical injunctions ("Don't bother memorizing the names of all the Presidents: most of them aren't worth the time and effort."). Even as historical men and women went West to face down the requirements of a given reality, this youth realizes upon leaving a movie that he has a particular world, staring and glaring at him, whose imperatives he must learn to fathom, a practical, demanding life all around him. That life, inevitably, has a moral side to it, as the Albuquerque boy constantly, keenly observes. If a child does not have such a life, one with perceived moral dilemmas, the movies will momentarily bestir, maybe, but will present little overall meaning. If a moral life has strength and coherence, the movies aren't likely (at their worst) to topple things. At their best they can prompt the kind of ethically charged reveries the children mentioned here have experienced.

I have thought of those boys and girls as I've listened to children from "working-class" backgrounds in New England's so-called factory towns (Lowell and Lawrence), or from upper-middle-class homes, pleasantly situated in the spacious suburbs to the west and north of Boston, and outside other northern cities, as well, such as Chicago. Without question these northern children, too, are as prepared for the movies as they are for schools, maybe more so for the movies. Many of them have been exposed to day-care centers and nursery schools before they are marched off to kindergarten. By then nearly all of them have had a sustained fling or two with a television adventure story, a weekly cartoon program. They have come to know, over the years, the antics of *Gilligan's Island,* the sudden power and authority of Hong Kong Fui in his Fuimobile. They have become familiar with a variety of odd-shaped creatures whose magical powers amaze millions of viewers.

We, who are older, worry, and ask: What *is* this all about? We forget, sometimes, our own childhood — the "funny books" with spacemen such as Flash Gordon (the initial inspiration to George Lucas for *Star Wars*). We forget *The Shadow* on the radio. We forget ancient myths, like that of Icarus, soaring in space (for a while), and Prometheus making men out of clay and stealing fire from Olympus — the endless supernatural intrigue and hanky-panky (sex, violence, revenge, murder) that characterize respectable Greek mythology. We older people forget, too, how today's fantasies become tomorrow's reality, the connections between any mind's imaginative constructions and the constructions of our singular inventors, or our technology. Centuries ago Leonardo da Vinci dreamed of initiating the conquest of space, of deep water; dreamed of flying and of penetrating the oceans in an underwater ship. Surely he had his many predecessors, many quite ordinary men and women, even as we today have our futurists — among them, children who delight in 2001: *A Space Odyssey*, not to mention the *Star Wars* series. Not that the time machine always pulls us *ahead* of ourselves. It is no great leap from Robinson Crusoe to Gilligan and his friends on their island. We want to imagine what it was like in the past as well as what it may well be like in the future. Entertainment is an expression of our nature — the creature who asks where and how and why and whither. Such curiosity is, of course, especially prominent in children, who know full well (and are reminded all the time) that they have a lot to learn. Nor is the knowledge they get going to be, as some scientific philosophers have put it, "value free." Anyone who has taught a baby of one or two where he or she might go, and must not go, and why, knows the linkage between exploration and morality established for all of us early: it is good to go here; it is bad to go there; it is good to try this; it is bad to try that. When I lived in the Southwest I saw the look of horror on the faces of Hopi parents and children both as they struggled to understand the moral meaning of sonic booms — a source of great pride to us Anglos out there. Those children had already acquired a notion of what is not allowable technologically.

The *Star Wars* trilogy George Lucas has given us is a brilliant addition to this continuing existential tradition — ours, not that of the Hopi! Who can see these Lucas films without getting drawn into their epic power, their almost apocalyptic moral confrontations, interrupted by marvelous moments of good cheer, easygoing everydayness, and touching good fun? These movies embrace all of the industrial world's history — from primitive man through the age of chivalry, down to the spaceship world of the third millennium. For years now I've heard children say as they parted, their eyes lighting up: "May the Force be with you!" A fad? A joke? Maybe something more, as one realizes how many times so many children have seen these movies, and with what excitement. The Rebel Alliance and the Imperial Troopers are now elements in America's moral iconography, as are, needless to say, Luke Skywalker, Obi-Won Kenobi, the Jedi Knights, Princess Leia (for all her stiffness, there's charm and beauty there!), and their antagonists, Darth Vadar and Grand Moff Tarkin. The two robots, C3Po and R2D2, have also become part of us — reassuring proof that machines will not escape the influence of our human instincts. (They remind my mother and father, among others, of Laurel and Hardy!)

Parents and teachers have not failed to notice the mental activity these movies stir up — perhaps in themselves as well as their children. I have found among rich children, poor children, black children, white children, American children, children of Ireland or England or Brazil or South Africa, that all are intrigued by the mixture of release from earth, and the persistence of our earthly capacities for decency and for malice, for good deeds and bad deeds. The combination is irresistible. I could fill hundreds of pages of print with transcriptions of what I've heard children say about these films. Yes, children share the well-known moments of great technological diversion and sport, and the memorable moments of almost sweaty, feverish concern for Luke and Solo and Princess Leia, and for the fate of their Millennium Falcon, and the moments of stark, gripping horror at the prosect that the Death Star and its rulers will win out. But I notice that one theme, again and again, captures the worried, compassionate moral attention of so many children: the sad fate of the planet Alderaan.

There are, to be sure, other planets that intrigue the viewer: Tatooine, where R2D2 and C3Po crash, where Luke Skywalker lives with his uncle, a moisture farmer, and where the dangerous Sand People also live, not to mention the old Hermit Ben Kenobi, alias Obi-Wan Kenobi; and Yavin, where the Rebel base is located, and to which the Falcon repairs with our heroes, who have in their own small way dared take on the giant Death Star. But Alderaan is the planet we never see. It is where Princess Leia's father lives. She has pleaded with Ben Kenobi to deliver the secret Death Star plans, stored in R2D2, to Alderaan, so that her father may be forewarned, forearmed. Solo and his Falcon were recruited to take Luke and

Ben Kenobi to Alderaan; it is on their way to Alderaan that the ship
gets caught in Death Star's tracking beam. We learn that Alderaan
has been summarily destroyed, because Princess Leia won't tell
where her Rebel friends are, and where the stolen Imperial plans
have been hidden. The movie is fast-moving, to say the least; and
yet, many children pause, fret — worry hard about Alderaan while
watching the movie burst onward.

Later, those children come back to Alderaan in their thoughts,
as did this ten-year-old black child who attended a ghetto school in
Boston. He had, one might suppose, other urgent matters on his
mind, such as the serious illness of his mother, who was on welfare:
"First there was Alderaan, and then it was gone. I don't remember
the names of the other planets, but I sure remember Alderaan. You
think it might be like this place, the Earth. There were people
there, and then all of a sudden something terrible happened. They
say it might happen to us one of these days — we'll sink into a 'hole,'
the man said on a science program the teacher showed us in school.
Then there won't be a planet left, and we'll all be gone — like
someone snapped his fingers, and that was it! The minister tells us
in church that we should live every single day like it's the last one,
and boy, it's hard to remember his sermons, but sometimes I do,
and when I heard that Alderaan was gone — while I was watching
the movie — I thought of what our minister says, that we're here
for a second, and gone before the good Lord can even wink His
eyes!

"That was the only time I was really sad, when Alderaan was
wiped out — just like that! You had the feeling they were good
people there, nice people; they were just minding their own business. Maybe they made a mistake when they took people who fled
from other places, I don't know. But you think to yourself: it can
happen right here, to you and your family! My uncle was coming
home one day, and he was just walking on our street, just walking,
and a car came down, hitting a hundred, people say, and the kids,
they were so high, they were on their way to "hyperspace" — out

of it, totally out of it. And then it just happened: they went up the sidewalk and ran down my uncle, and he was dead right away, right away they told us, and they hit this kid, he was five, and the same with him, he died before he even knew what happened, they say, and then this woman and her groceries, they went all over the place, the eggs and the cans of tomato paste, and the slices of bread, Roman Meal bread, I remember, and she had blood pouring and pouring, and the Pepsi mixed with it, and we'll never forget it. She died, too.

"You want to know something: those guys, all four of them, just walked away. The car stopped, and they got out and walked away. I saw them. If we didn't tell the police, they'd have gone and got more to snort, and what the hell! Who cares about Alderaan! Who cares about anyone — just so long as you can get high! That's those guys! I agree with my mum: there's a lot of people who are out for themselves and they could see someone out in the street, right before their eyes, in real bad trouble, and they'd say: man, that's not my worry, that's someone else's worry.

"You think about Alderaan. You think, it's coming to that, it's coming to that, there will be planets wiped out, presto! It might be with nuclear bombs, or maybe later, with something else they're developing. If I could get an education, and learn computers, something like that, I'd like to do it, and fight fire with fire: there would be power on the good side, and it could win over the bad side, like in *Star Wars*. It goes back and forth, you see — *The Empire Strikes Back*, but then there's *Return of the Jedi*. It's like playing on the seesaw in Franklin Park!"

Sometimes, watching that boy struggle with this world, I think of him as a candidate for *The Cool World*, a tough 1964 film about Harlem's low life. Other times I think of *Nothing But a Man*,[4] a film I use every year in my college course — an extraordinarily sensitive, low-budget ($200,000) effort to convey the complex texture of black experience in America, and a worthy companion, indeed, to Ralph Ellison's *Invisible Man* precisely because both narrative chronicles, film and novel, connect the trials of their people with the trials people of all classes and colors and creeds have as human beings, trying to make sense of (as the expression goes) the things of this world. The boy, however, stands only for himself, one Boston black child with a life that has its own determinants, limitations, possibilities — and without question, moral underpinnings. Those last center on survival, to be sure, but also upon the ancient antagonists: virtue and evil, God and the Devil, Luke Skywalker and Darth Vadar.

For this boy, as for many others in our ghettos, the problem *is* black and white, though there are more shadings, more nuances of color to that symbolic black-and-white polarity than Luke and Darth are allowed to suggest. How many of us who aim to be Luke Skywalkers end up skywalking like jugglers on a moral tightrope! How many Darth Vadars are unrecognizable — all too cozily part of a community's, a nation's establishment, what the Bible calls "principalities and powers!" When one hears a "slum kid," as boys like this one were once called, wistfully say that he wishes "you could spot the Darth Vadar types faster on the street," and also say he thinks Luke Skywalker (so blond and agile and strong) "had it made from the start," one is in the presence of, again, moral imagination at work. Not that Mr. Lucas's trilogy has been begrudged its due. Children also understand *realpolitik* — or, as the Boston child observes: "It's best when the enemies are right there and look completely different — then you can place your bet and you can see the one you've bet on. And I guess you have to bet on the side you think will win — if you want to win!"

Young people like him make up the majority of persistent moviegoers. They are the self-described fans. They follow the flicks. They latch on to movie heroes and heroines, to genres that become fads. They take to Faye Dunaway's powerful mixture of skeptical anger and edgy fearfulness; to Jane Fonda's cool sexiness; to Clint Eastwood's macho, solo drive; to the twisted, confused, obsessive moral preoccupations of Charles Bronson; to the strangely suave mannerisms Roger Moore uses to vent his anxieties; to Sylvester Stallone's subdued watchfulness or John Travolta's exciting, volatile egoism, and Dustin Hoffman's experienced, safely warm versatility and brilliance. They are, themselves, not without some of those qualities, these youthful ones — knowing, observant, frightened, self-centered, and, oh yes, sexually alert yet isolated, so they feel, even when surrounded by friends. And morally awake — or not yet ready to be morally inert.

On some days one wonders about the use of that word "moral" in connection with certain movies — say, those of Clint Eastwood and Charles Bronson. Who is this Eastwood, this Dirty Harry, this High Plains Drifter? What cruel, abrasive, arrogant, super-tough, woman-hating streak in us does he address? And how to comprehend Bronson — another loner, another vigilante, another fiercely desperate, trigger-happy executioner whose splendor is marred continually by cunning and even murderous mischief? And what of Mr. Moore, the exuberant misogynist and narcissist, the man of sad past and endlessly stressful present and of a future limited, say, to the next five minutes of jeopardy? Slim pickings for a moralist — other than as subjects for voluble expression of dismay!

Yet, I am always surprised when I hear young people talk about those individuals and the movies that feature them. A thirteen-year-old white *girl*, who lives in a splendid home in an old New England town, remarks that "Clint is tough, he's hard to figure out — but so are a lot of the troubles we have." She adds: "Sometimes the only answer is for a detective to fight fire with fire." As for Clint the cowboy: "He's a mystery man. He gets you wondering where he's going next, and what will happen to him — I mean, eventually, when he's older." She wonders about him, as she says; but in a minute or two, it's quite clear, she is worrying about herself, and not only in the selfish way we all do at moments. "I'd like to be fighting bad people when I'm his age," she observes — though she qualifies her desire quickly: "I won't be doing it on horseback out West, I know, or in a San Francisco police car!"

I suppose there are at least two ways to approach Clint Eastwood or Charles Bronson or Faye Dunaway or Jane Fonda, not to mention their movies, all movies; and each mode of analysis was described by Kierkegaard, who died in the middle of the nineteenth century, long before Hollywood was built. A cranky social observer, a God-haunted melancholy Dane, a major spokesman for modern existentialism, he had an artistic side to him, and knew the temptations of the critic. He distinguished (in *Either/Or*) the positions we take toward the world — one of aesthetic appreciation or one of moral seriousness. These are not meant to be exclusive or necessarily antagonistic. Some of us notice how the camera is used, how shots are sequenced, how a scene is framed, how black and white or color are called upon, while others pay relatively more heed to the nature of the case being made, the essential message put forth, the moral implications of a (literary, theatrical, artistic) performance.

For him these were "stages" — the aesthetic, the ethical. Walker Percy has done a glorious job of applying these "stages" of Kierkegaard's, and their quite subtle psychology, to our moments of moviegoing — the ways in which we evoke nostalgia, crave distractions: anything sensual or "aesthetic" to help us *not* dwell on the important moral questions this life poses. But Percy is always hinting (as Kierkegaard did) that we can be too clever by far with ourselves — those few who are moviemakers as well as millions of us moviegoers. We sit down to be diverted, amused, entranced. We are offered suspense, catharsis, exorcisms, erotic stimulation, an outlet for every mean or evil streak. We are also offered, commonly, an obvious and trivial afterthought, some moral justification for what we've allowed ourselves to experience: the good guys do win, the Force prevails, or the gang of villains gets done in, finally, by our desperate (and desperately hurt) midnight protector.

Binx Bolling, Walker Percy's moviegoer in *The Moviegoer*, turns quite serious about this celluloid life, though with no sacrifice of a pleasantly ironic manner that keeps him from being a big, self-righteous bore, and any number of other moviegoers seem to do likewise. Moviegoing is common to ghettos and favelas, to pleasant country homes and swank apartments — and on our high school and college campuses. I am always being told about the movies by the high school and college students I meet. But what I hear only prompts questions. Why does a group of young college men band into a Clint Eastwood Club — movies hired and played over and over, the posters of him displayed everywhere? Why does a group of young college women assemble to watch soaps, or declare Faye Dunaway their heroine? Why do junior high school boys, or for that matter, college students, even a few of the medical students I teach, go to see *Star Wars* or *Return of the Jedi* three or four times, and listen to John Williams's scores, and buy the posters and books?

A fad, a cult of the person, a diversion, a crush — the victimization our various "media" successfully implement? True, and these fantasies can form a foolish shield against looking at what we are all about. But the shield can be dropped, deliberately or unwittingly, with astonishing ease by young people often judged to be hopelessly misled, wayward, dopey. Suddenly the morally foundering, the lost or blind ones, start speaking, and we hear how a vision (the movie) is affecting their own vision. Unquestionably, some of this introspection can be fittingly dubbed "psychological," our favorite American way of "explaining" anyone, it seems, who does anything. No doubt those Eastwood fans huddle together out of male anxiety; those soap fans out of female withdrawal, out of a curbed romanticism furtively espoused. No doubt, also, *Star Wars* is one big indulgent emotional cop-out, and every western an all too convenient historical simplification of our contemporary requirements as individuals threatened constantly by hostile forces.

Still, we are not only that, lost in our marketplaces, our schools with their ladders we strive to climb, or abandon. We are also, in the tradition of existentialism, travelers, wayfarers, wanderers, alarmed castaways, or transients who find ourselves here on earth, and try to figure out the moral significance of that realization. Nor is such activity only the province of self-conscious intellectuals. Children display similar moments of introspection in their conversations with one another, in the statements they utter to parents or teachers, in the compositions they write. And so we go to the movies to take what we can get: we go to see them out of all the boredom and confusion of our lives. We expect pleasure, we expect some kind of helping hand, we expect, even, instruction, or an example or two: how to do A, what to do when B takes place. We sort them out in our minds — and every day one hears even elementary school-children doing so.

All the while our lives go on — the happy and welcome spells, and inevitably, the tough times, the moments and longer of weariness or melancholy. A movie can give us a psychological boost, or it can help us affirm our already high spirits. But psychology yields to moral and philosophical reflection even in emotionally preoccupied analysands — hence books with titles such as *The Moralist* or *Insight and Responsibility*, written by psychoanalysts such as Allen Wheelis and Erik H. Erikson.[5] No wonder *Five Easy Pieces* keeps pulling in my students. I take the lead, I use it in my college course. But the moral intensity of the responses to that movie written by the students reminds us, yet again, what a good narrative can do — in this instance, the story that comes out of director Bob Rafelson coaxing actor Jack Nicholson to be Robert Eroica Dupea: vain and self-lacerating, snotty and modest, obnoxious and charming, naive and wily, brusque and blind, disarmingly knowing and obliging. And Karen Black's Rayette Dipesto — hurt and confounded and clinging, yet willful and mocking and able to spot weakness and vacillation masked as pride and machismo and surly independence. The title of the movie itself prompts an often dramatically self-involved speculation and exegesis: the *Five Easy Pieces* piano students must master, and then put aside in favor of more demanding compositions — as in the lessons of life itself.

No wonder youngsters often can be heard telling their parents, their teachers, that a movie is "hard to forget." I've heard that phrase a million times, it seems, and a million times I reflexively have asked "why?" And a million times I hear, often with unaffected charm, a movie hailed for its memorable scenes, for its scary music, for the great aesthetic spectacle provided, the mind-boggling contrivance; or for the emotional truths explored or given concrete psychological form. Not least I hear a movie praised for a disturbing or encouraging or thought-provoking line of argument, or stretch of events: the moral element, introduced intelligently or omitted by wanton negligence.

Our best film critics have struggled with these different aspects of what it means to see a movie, even as their written efforts emphasize their own ways not only of seeing, but sorting — what they find "hard to forget." For Manny Farber[6] "space is the most dramatic stylistic entity," and all films can be considered in accordance with the way "film space" is (aesthetically) used — what fills the screen, how the actors and actresses handle their "psychological space." For James Agee[7] the matter, again and again, was ethical — the wrenching choices embedded in certain movies that prompted from him the accolades "moral nerve" and "moral courage." Both critics, of course, brought thoughtfulness to viewing and writing; but both had moral intelligence — an alertness to the phony and the pretentious, which each was intent upon exposing. The movies were for them what they are for many of us, an instrument of occasional self-consultation, a source of moral energy. In the words of Ruby, when she was a six-year-old New Orleans moviegoer (and herself on our nation's television screens because of her daily trips to and from school), "I went to that movie and afterward I kept thinking of it, thinking and thinking, and the next day it made me wonder what I should do, and would I be doing right or wrong." This personal, idiosyncratic reply, so patently, unashamedly moral in character, tells us what a movie can get going, but just as important, tells us that we all are — as the saying goes — children of light and children of darkness.

III

MORAL PURPOSE AND VULNERABILITY

IN writing *The Road to Wigan Pier,* his effort to comprehend the life of hard-pressed English miners during the 1930s, George Orwell had to struggle not only with the anger generated in him by the injustices he witnessed, but with his perplexity as he observed people struggle against great odds and sometimes emerge, not unscathed, but impressively thoughtful or sensitive or decent — able and willing to bear their heavy burden, yet demonstrate a constant, quiet dignity. "The truth is," he wrote, "that many of the qualities we admire in human beings can only function in opposition to some kind of disaster, pain or difficulty; but the tendency of mechanical progress is to eliminate disaster, pain and difficulty."[1]

I am not sure I agree with Orwell's inclusion of the adverb "only." I would once upon a time have registered astonishment rather than ironic assurance, and perhaps substituted "surprisingly" for "only." The "progress" Orwell mentions, after all, has not been without its concomitant, self-justifying ideology. We who live comfortably, relishing the benefits of that "progress," are apt to carry assumptions about what is possible for ourselves and what is not possible for the poor, benighted ones who lack our means, our achievements. Many of us who have benefited materially from progress have assumed, all along, that other advantages would also accrue — qualities of mind and heart analogous to the material achievements we now take for granted.

What might those qualities be? A personal stability? An inner contentment? A creative spark, a liveliness of manner, a forthrightness — evidence that years of relative serenity and well-being would have made their mark upon our emotional and moral development?

Orwell found the same grim living whether he traveled with London tramps, worked in the dirty, sweaty kitchens of Paris hotels, learned how hops are harvested in the English countryside, or journeyed to Wigan, there to go down into the mines with men whose "most noble bodies" he described for us, and whose quiet, even cheerful stoicism he found unforgettable.[2] Orwell, at times, put sociology aside. The moralist in him singled out some people (the miners, the embattled Spanish peasants and workers whom he saw fighting on both sides of the Spanish Civil War) for his admiration, commendation, even envy. At the same time he heaped scorn on others — who tended to be relatively well off: the Brookers, who ran a lodging house in Wigan, or the intelligentsia whose myopic shortcomings he delighted in anatomizing.[3]

Perhaps Orwell's view has to be approached with skepticism — whether it is "only" *in extremis* that we rise to heights, and whether those who witness "disaster, pain or difficulty" are prepared to specify those (presumably redemptive) "qualities." I continue to belabor this quotation of his because I have long admired his writing, his own qualities, and because I don't find it difficult to figure out which qualities he had in mind. They are qualities I have found in not only adults but children who have experienced terrible disasters, severe pain, almost indescribable difficulties. Whence their capacity to survive? I began to wonder two decades ago. Later, I found myself wondering whether my response was not a matter of condescension, of one person cleverly patronizing others. Finally, I now find myself trying to figure out how to account for some of those qualities, how they relate to the condition of people who are weak, who are defenseless, who are constantly in jeopardy.

There are, alas, millions of candidates in this world for the designation of severely destitute. The huge majority of today's children live in ways that American writers and readers would consider to be wretched indeed. More than nine-tenths of those people know Orwell's "disaster, pain and difficulty" as a constant and dominant aspect of everyday reality. In Rio de Janeiro,[4] such people seem to be everywhere on the streets of Copacabana or Ipanema, always ready to wash the car, polish the shoes, supply nuts or candy while one awaits a movie, or yes, inexpressively assuage one's conscience by receiving with expressed gratitude what has been begged for. One ten-year-old boy told my ten-year-old son and me, "anything you can spare, so I'll eat." While we were handing over some coins we looked nervously around, aware that others, equally vulnerable, maybe more so, would size us up as easy targets. The Brazilian boy himself, now marginally more secure, spoke with trenchant, unforgettable candor: "You had better hide; the whole world will be upon you — and then *you'll* have to beg!"

Orwell might have admired his wry sense of humor. To be chronically desperate, enough to beg, and yet to be able to extend one's understanding as that lad was doing — well, my son and I were abashed. Soon enough we smiled, followed the child's advice: into the hotel and safety. Our admiration came only in retrospect.

We often met the boy quoted above. He was persistent, plucky. Our friend, a physician who helped us constantly with our Portuguese, asked a friend who managed a Copacabana travel agency whether she knew the boy. Yes, of course, he was one of the regulars, a bold one, ever smiling — cunning as the animals in the jungle. One of many who recently had arrived in Rio de Janeiro or São Paulo from the rural interior. We listened to the travel agent explain a nation's recent economic history, with occasional critical asides (punctuated by a sweep of the arm) directed at "them" who lived "there," a looming favela to which the right forefinger pointed knowingly. The boy, he said, lived there, "without a doubt." The boy, he said, could not be trusted, however — nor can any of "these street children" (another sweep of the arm). "Most of them will die young. Mind you, they're lucky to be alive right now. If they're that boy's age, maybe ten, they've seen plenty of brothers and sisters die. The answer to all this is compulsory birth control — maybe sterilization. What else can our country do? There are too many people. We need fewer people. The women in the favelas must learn that lesson!"

I could imagine other ways of approaching the collective tragedy of all those favelas. I kept listening, but made a note to myself that this all-too-cordial and outspoken person was no match for the boy whose alternative way of seeing things had caught our interest. Maybe such a man (who, after all, ended up helping us meet the above-mentioned boy) serves as a handy scapegoat, so that one's own situation may seem, comparatively, more honorable. I've often wondered whether the intemperate wrath Orwell directed in *The Road to Wigan Pier* at those who lived better than the miner — including the socialist intellectuals who had dispatched him to write his story — didn't serve a similar, scapegoating purpose for an eminently decent writer who must have been driven mad by what he saw, and knew he couldn't change.

The boy had, in fact, told us in which favela he lived, and a friend of ours was able to be of immediate help in arranging a visit to the favela — because, in fact, her maid had once lived there, and knew a number of families still very much there. The families she knew were, however, residents of the lower part of the favela, the relatively affluent part, near the street. She reminded us that in Rio de Janeiro, the higher up a hill, the poorer the people, the more "difficulties" (her word brought to mind Orwell's use of it) the family would be having. Our boy, she suspected, lived near the top of the hill. "In your country," she reminded us, "the very rich would command the view that boy's family has, but here our rich prefer the ocean at their door."

She was right; with very little detective work we met the boy high up the favela. We learned his name was Eduardo. He himself asked us with simple directness, with no apparent nervousness, and certainly with no effort at (fearful) ingratiation, how we'd got there.

I was about to expain, when he smiled, and answered himself: "by car." He had, in fact, seen our car approaching earlier, and wondered who was coming to see whom. "A nice car," he observed. A few seconds (which can seem to be eternal) of silence befell us; then he said "rented." He wasn't asking, as someone certain of the answer but wanting to keep a conversational stew warm; he was declaring what he knew. I found myself bolder than I'd been in any previous favela visit, and I'd made many of them in the two years that had preceded this meeting. I said: "You know the Copacabana well!" He said yes, and then quite unself-consciously added, making me feel imprecise: "I know what the Americans do when they stay there."

Of course, I wanted to pursue that matter immediately, but I thought better of it. I was struck by Eduardo's terse but lively, and strangely affecting, manner of conversation, and I decided not to rush things, or quite possibly we'd both be reduced to banter. Perhaps I was taken aback by the thought that this kind of aplomb could prevail, here, high up on a cliff, the city spread below us as we stood at the door of a shabby lean-to, of mixed corrugated steel and wood, with many cracks and outright holes. Eduardo continued to stare at me, as I deliberated on how to change the tack. Suddenly his younger sister appeared, and he told her she must say hello to this American man and his son and their Brazilian friend. The sister did not oblige; she looked down at the ground, shuffled her bare feet. Eduardo told us her name, Maria, her age, five; told us she hadn't yet left the favela. He smiled at her, then smiled at us, then told her and us that she was on that last account "lucky."

How could I not feel that all of us well-to-do foreigners were judged by such a description of the little girl? Through my mind passed a picture of the Copacabana — Eduardo and countless other children roaming the streets, sidling up to Americans who, by the standards of Brazil's favelas, are fabulously rich, in order to sell something or be allowed to do something (wash a car, shine some shoes, go fetch a piece of luggage or a heavy shopping bag), or to be given money for doing nothing, for merely being there. But I had to turn to spoken words: "Yes, it's noisy and crowded in the Copacabana." But Eduardo Casseva was not about to ignore my effort to agree that Maria is lucky to have been spared the trip down the slope and across all those streets, after which the ocean stops the city. "She will go there one day," the brother predicted, "and then she'll tell me that she wants to keep going; then she'll tell me she's lucky, because she *is* going there!"

That was the longest statement he'd yet made — and next I saw his face fall. His eyes for the first time left his visitors, left Maria, left the area around their home, left as a matter of fact the entire favela — first for the Copacabana, distantly visible, and then for a second or so the sky, quickly thereafter to land upon us once more. I thought, too, that I saw a heaviness, if not a sadness descend on the boy's face and body. His face muscles slackened slightly; his mouth came narrowly open; his shoulders showed a scant but noticeable slump that reminded me of one of my first impressions of the boy, as he came toward us near our hotel: how straight his carriage was.

Immediately thereafter we were all diverted by a couple of cackling chickens, by the eagerness of both Eduardo and Maria to go see whether one or both of the two might have laid an egg. When the children returned with an egg their faces were both beaming. The egg would be the centerpiece of their supper. With it, we knew, would be bread, and the orange soda Brazilian children love so much. We learned that every Sunday, before church, their mother insisted that they collect the stray soda bottles, bring them to a place conveniently away from their cabin. Every Sunday, too, prayers were spoken for the chickens: may they keep providing eggs for this family. When Eduardo returned to the spot where his three visitors stood, he told us, right off, that the chickens were "paying attention to our prayers." Then he must have noticed a look of incredulity on my son's face, and maybe, across my face an overworked effort at sympathetic agreement on the efficacy of prayer.

His comment was, characteristically, brief: "God keeps His eyes on chickens, too."

We asked him if we might return another time, and he smiled Yes winningly. He was conscious of others, as he had been the first time we met him. Would we be making a number of visits nearby? I said no. I said I had made two friends in another favela, and there were just so many boys and girls I could visit, given the limits of time, and my continuing struggles with Portuguese, not to mention the busy schedule of my Brazilian friend, a pediatrician who was kindly acting as an interpreter and — I did not say so aloud — a fellow observer. I now began to explain why I wanted to come and talk, but quickly decided to ask the boy, instead, why *he* thought I was hoping to make more visits. Eduardo, however, was not going to fall for an American psychiatrist's open-ended questioning. Before I could inquire, he declared: "You want to know how we live here, yes? You will go home and tell your countrymen, yes?" Now I had to do the talking, and he listened quite politely as I explained my work, my intentions. When I stoppped, he decided we three needed reassurance: "No problem. We like the North Americans, and we like you." He looked at Maria, and she gave us a smile that was almost a match for his. We left soon afterward and as we made our way to the busy, lively Copacabana, my doctor friend called Eduardo a "born therapist." I wondered why he said that. My friend harked back to the boy's final, friendly remarks. Only now did I realize how nervous and confused I'd been up there, atop that favela; and how strangely quiet a time we'd had then, the noise of downtown Rio completely inaudible; and how strangely calming Eduardo's last words were. The succinct poise of his vocabulary had yet again aroused my admiration.

Over the weeks we got to know this boy and his family. The father of Eduardo was not the father of Maria, and neither father had been seen by either child for years. There were other children, two girls and a boy, in fact, ranging in age from six months to three years, but the father of those children lived with Eduardo's and Maria's mother. He, too, had a habit of leaving, but he came back a week or two after each departure, usually quite agitated and panicky. While talking about him, one day, I heard Eduardo's view of his entire family, its complex personal and social history: "I'm the oldest. My mother will be unhappy once in a while, and she tells me my father was the only man she loved. I had two brothers, but they both died very early in life. I remember the death of one of them, the second (I think I do!). I remember my father shouting, saying we were all going to die very soon, and he could hardly wait! I remember my mother trying to get him to stop talking about death. She was holding me right in his face, to prove (I guess) that I was alive, and I wasn't near death. I was crying, and the harder I cried the more my mother said I was alive, and the more my father said I was getting sick, and I'd soon be dead. My mother has told me several times of that day, and how she knew, then, what was in my father's head — that he'd leave us.

"I think my father died in a river. He was drunk. We were not here, no; we hadn't come to Rio yet. Her second man — she never married him — was no good from the start. She knew it. She told me. I remember that, too. I asked her why she wanted to stay with him, if he's no good. She said 'because.' She wouldn't say any more than that. When I tried to get the answer, she told me to go and play. I did, but my thoughts were still there, back with her. She used to do laundry for people, for the wives of all the police, the soldiers. My new father [his stepfather] had no work. He knew how to build houses, but no one wanted to build a house where they lived. People were leaving, to go to Rio, to go to Rio. I remember all my friends, one after the other, saying it: we're going to go to Rio.

"He took us. Before we even knew we were going, we were gone. Maria was born, then we left. Then *he* left — about two weeks after we got here. My mother and I built our house. If my new father had stayed with us, this house would be much better. It's as good as it is because my mother learned from him how to build, how to collect bricks and wood. For a while we had no place. We lived near a tree, and we were all very sick. I was sure Maria would die. So was my mother. Even now she calls Maria her 'miracle child.' It was Jesus who saved her, my mother says: the statue up there on the mountain. I once told her a statue can't save anyone, even itself. Didn't the priest say that someone was making marks, defacing the statue?

"It was the priest who got people to help us build, and maybe Jesus did save Maria. God told the priest, and he told others, and one day Maria had a place inside to sleep: the priest gave her a little bed. Maria thinks she may be a nun when she's grown up, if the nuns will let her come and stay with them, but I think they'll say no to her. They seem very rich — hard to get to smile and not very kind to us. They want us to pray to Jesus, but they make you want to go and say a dirty name, and you want them to be near enough to hear you say it.

"When she met Arturo, my mother changed. He's a boss. If he had a lot of money, he'd have all of the Copacabana licking his boots. He has to settle for us, my mother and Maria and me, and his own kids. There's only one way to live with him — try to beat him to the punch. I rush to do something I know he'll want me to do, and I rush to get everyone else to do the same. He looks around and he's surprised! I've cheated him out of his biggest pleasure! He gives me a bad look. Then he goes back to his Coca-Cola. He gets some free every day where he works."

The stepfather, Arturo, loads and unloads at a large Ipanema grocery. He is big, muscular, truculent in his approach to everyone, grown-up neighbors or even small children, including his own. He is conspicuously taciturn and subdued with us, and Eduardo is quick to take notice of that apparent anomaly — and quick to figure it out. Moreover, he is touching in his acknowledgment of our assistance of sorts to him: "I guess if you hadn't come here, I'd never have seen him be so silent when someone came to see us. Everyone else gets a big bark from him. He's the largest dog around! I tell my friends to watch out: mad dog! With you, he becomes a scared dog. Maybe, a watchdog who knows the difference between the cops and the robbers! My mother does the apologizing for him. She whispers behind his back that he does work no one else can do: everyone else would die, but his back will never die. When he comes home his back is sore, and he is cursing. He wants to give us the same treatment he's gotten from the storeowners! My mother says we should try to be good, and he'll stop. But *she's* good all the time, and he beats her. So, why wouldn't he keep on beating us? I'm away, cruising the Copacabana now, so I mostly escape him when he's worst, at night. In the morning he's up very early and gone before we rise. On Sundays, like a good dog, he nurses his wounds!"

This distance between father and stepson, and actually between mother and son, the result of Eduardo's excursions to the Copacabana every day save Sunday, has permitted him to become, by his own description, reflective about his family, himself, and not least, his future. (I have in this long statement of his rather obviously pulled together the gist of several days' conversation.) Eduardo's biography is, alas, essentially like that of so very many others the world over — the extremely poor peasant origins, the multiple liaisons of a woman who finds it almost unthinkable to live alone, and so will submit with little resistance to the brutishness of men, the fateful move into a city, and once there, the daily struggle for these humble, almost indigent people to get by. Eduardo's stepfather makes a pittance for the hard, hard work he does, the long hours he gives to that work. As for Eduardo himself, he has become, I suppose it can be said, a ten-year-old Copacabana entrepreneur. He moves with agility and resourcefulness from one everyday possibility to another — now selling shoelaces, now suggesting to passersby that they stop at this vendor's, purchase one of his fancy Italian ices, now asking to wash a car, now offering a well-off resident help with a package, a beach chair, while crossing the street, now simply asking a tourist or a wealthy businessman returning home to his grand, waterfront apartment whether a coin or two is ready for late afternoon distribution.

The boy is quite sensitive to others, partly as an expression of one or two of those "qualities" Orwell mentions: a subtle intelligence; a compassionate regard for others, even those who are rich and powerful and seemingly insensitive to his own kind; an alert sense of humor, always responsive to the world's ironies — along with the stubborn persistence of the lad, the ever-present modesty, and the astonishing "cool" he maintains, as he does his work, but very significantly, refuses without equivocation or hesitation other possible kinds of work, namely running errands for gamblers, hustling narcotics, or hustling himself.

Eduardo does not often discuss these criminal avenues to more cash. He is not one to take pleasure in virtuous self-display, or pious tirades. But the more I got to know about him, the more I learned of the choices he could have made but did not. When I questioned him, he spoke very thoughtfully, almost as if he wanted to distinguish himself not only from the gamblers and drug dealers and sex peddlers of Copacabana, but also from their self-righteous critics, who use such men and women as mere objects of denunciation. At ten, Eduardo did not look down on "these bad ones," even as, of course, he did have his own quite definite distance.

"I do not like to hear the bad ones pushed around in church by the priest," he told us visitors. My son asked him what the priest says. Eduardo replied that he doesn't pay attention to every word of the sermon; and in fact, he often dozes off all through the mass. But there are occasions when, during holy communion, Eduardo gets angry, wishes the priests would offer their hungry parishioners loaves and loaves of bread, rather than those tasteless wafers. As he is pressed about the priest's attitude toward the profane Copacabana world, we learn of Eduardo's own moral assumptions and purposes — what he believes to be "right," and what he believes to be terribly "wrong," and how he came to have and to hold dear those distinctions: "My mother won't let go of the church! She says that to us: I won't let go! I asked her why once, then another time, then another time, and always she comes up with the same explanation: 'Eduardo, it's all I have left of my earlier life; if I stop going to church I'll lose my memories.' She sits there, and it's the only time we see her cry! I think the priest knows he's got so many people there because every Sunday there are more tears in our favela than there is rain on the rainiest day of the year.

"When the priest calls everyone bad for what they've done this past week I think of him: What has *he* done that's bad? We'll never know! I don't like hearing our 'bad ones' being mentioned in church so often. Are they the ones who own Copacabana, Ipanema? They are kids, like me, trying to make some money, so they can eat, so their brothers and sisters can eat, and their mothers, and if they are lucky to have one, their fathers. On a day when I make nothing, or almost nothing, I wonder how long it'll be until I carry cocaine or let some weird man touch me. I'm afraid of going to jail — maybe that's why I don't, right now. No, it's not that, because there are days when I'm sure that in jail I'd at least get food and I'd have a bed and no water pouring in during the storm.

"I don't want to spend my life with people who have committed crimes. I agree with the priest: they're bad. I like walking around — being free. You see those soldiers, with their guns, their bayonets, and you know they're worse than my mother's man with beer in him. They are big cats in the jungle; he's a barking dog, and he'd run if anyone lifted a finger and told him to get away — anyone nearer his size than I am! When I am big (my mother says I'll be taller than this man of hers, because my father was taller than he is), I hope I won't have to lift a finger; I'll be glad that he leaves me alone, and if I can talk him into leaving everyone else alone, I'll be glad for everyone else. My mother told me when I was very small that my father told her to tell me when I got old enough to understand that the smartest person is the one who works for himself, if you can, and stays out of jail, and knows how to find one laugh for himself every day. One laugh is better than a lot of wine!

"That is what I try to do, hear a joke every day, and laugh, or make up one of my own, if I can, or just find something going on that seems funny, and then laugh and then say to myself, Eduardo, start whistling a tune, and keep laughing, and tell yourself you're still alive, and you'll be alive tomorrow. Beyond tomorrow no one knows. My mother says that all the time: beyond tomorrow no one knows. But now she really knows better; she knows that you can keep saying 'beyond tomorrow' for lots of tomorrows, and that's a life. Even in Copacabana they can't be sure beyond tomorrow — even there."

Eduardo is among Brazil's poor, yet he has not lost what I suppose can be called moral pride, a kind of self-respect that even a ten-year-old scurrying across the hot pavements of the Copacabana can manage to possess. But whence comes such a quality? Why is it absent in others? That second question begins to strike one as important, it turns out, when one finds oneself in the midst of people plagued by Orwell's "disaster, pain and difficulty." An eleven-year-old boy in an adjoining shack of Eduardo's favela has to experience, every day, excruciating pain (an injury never treated correctly). He has the same quite impoverished life to face that Eduardo has, yet the boy strikes one as not only petulant and demanding, but mean-spirited, gossipy, altogether unpleasant. Even Eduardo finds him grating to be near, and wonders whether it is the limb pain that has made for such a temperament. But that attempted explanation only tells us more about Eduardo's essential decency and charity; and when he proceeds to remind his visitor (remind himself, one wants to say, without condescension) that there are a number of children within easy walking distance who endure even greater, and more constant and disabling physical pain, and do so with far more stoicism and self-effacement than this grabby and talkative boy — well, by then it is, again, time to pause and wonder.

So doing, and on the well-known principle that misery loves company, the visitor asks the host what he makes of all this. Why is it that some people who bear awful pain turn out to be so very nice, whereas others turn out not so nice at all, or worse? Eduardo hesitates very little before responding: "A throw of the dice!" I wait for more. Nothing is forthcoming. I start all over again, declare my puzzlement at the outcome of lives, here in this favela and elsewhere. Eduardo shrugs his shoulders, and says he has given up trying to figure out people — though all the time he tries to do just that, as he asks for jobs, asks for favors with respect to where he can find what to sell, asks people to buy what he is selling, or just plain begs. He tells me that he operates "on hunches." Do I know what a "hunch" is? Yes, I say. When, he asks, do I use a "hunch"? I reply that, like him, I try to figure people out, and I tell him quite openly and with some conviction, and as well, a touch of despair, that I'm not sure I know how to do that work with any great success.

We continue our discussion, now with crayons and paper. I've asked Eduardo if he thought he could draw anyone, of any age, who is fairly "good," and by the same token, someone who is not "good" at all, or "bad." Eduardo lets me know that he can't quite see in his mind any one person who is altogether "good" or "bad," but he volunteers to draw "something." I sit back and wait; sit back and sip my Coca Cola; sit back and look at Jesus Christ, His arms outstretched, perched on top of a mountain whence He can see all of Rio and the Atlantic beyond; sit back, finally, and daydream and wonder how anyone, well educated or not at all educated, blessed with this and that "training" or without any training (hence also blessed?) can figure the riddle out — the reasons people end up as they do.

Eduardo has thrown himself into the drawing. He is no great artist, but he has an interest in using crayons and paints, and takes to them with special enthusiasm. He lets me see his work when he is through, first making this descriptive (and self-descriptive) comment: "I gave up on the idea of drawing two people, one good and one bad. First I was going to draw my stepfather; a lot of the time he's bad, but he can be very good to us, and one day I saw him crying, because he'd kept working, and he fooled his boss [who would have fired him instantly had he seen evidence of an injury, no questions asked] and he even fooled my mother, I guess. I saw that he wanted to show someone how bad his bruises were, but I knew that if I got too friendly, and told him I was sorry, and offered to help, then he'd blow up and start cursing me. He might even try to bruise me, to even things out! So, I just stood there, and I said nothing, and he wiped his face. Then he showed me his feet, and they *were* bruised! I got scared. I was almost ready to say something, when he told me he'd like to murder the guy who is his boss, the supervisor of loading. I told him I'd go and help him! That was when he smiled. That was when he said that if we killed one bastard, we might as well kill a few others, because it's better to die and do a lot of good for the world, not just a little! I sat down, and while he kept saying 'ouch' — I guess that was the first time he said it — we drew up our list. He felt better, I could tell. So did I. We compared notes on who should be on the top of the list, and we agreed: a man we both know, who used to live in the favela, and now has moved out, a pimp. If I was one of his girls, I'd give it to him — a knife."

A pause. I have not yet studied the drawing, but now think I have an idea of what I may see — a representation of evil, perhaps. I ask Eduardo whether he thought that he (or his stepfather or I or anyone he knew, for that matter) would actually be able and willing to plunge a knife into another human being. He is back talking in a second: "Yes, in the army you shoot, if there's an enemy to be killed. You have a bayonet, so you might have to use it." All right, the army is a special case — murder, as he suggests, becomes one's duty as a citizen. But are there any other circumstances under which he'd be similarly inclined to aim, to fire, or to plunge directly at, say, the heart? Again, he responds immediately: "If someone was going to kill me, or anyone else, I'd strike first, if I could."

Maybe I am pushing this matter further than I should — trying to stir up another hypothetical discussion of the sort people such as I spend their lives seeking. The boy sees some dismay in my face, realizes I'm at a loss to know what to say, and yet knows I'm trying to get at *something*. He then tells me what that "something" is! He takes his picture (Figure 1), shows it to me, and asks my question for me by answering it: "These people won't kill those people, but someone should. Since no one will, there will be lots of trouble every day for lots of people. My stepfather won't kill his boss, ever. I won't kill the pimp I hate the most. I'm afraid; from what I hear, he's already killed people, and I'll bet that guy who shouts orders at my stepfather would kill if he thought it would help him out somehow. He's a member of a bad gang. There is a Mafia here, just like in the States."

How does *he* know about the Mafia? What a naif this gringo doctor is! On the street one hears! He looks intently at the drawing, as if to say, tactfully, that it wasn't *his* idea to do it, and so it might be nice, now that it was done, to stop this apparently endless talk and use our eyes, not our ears. We both look at what he has done, and thus I hear his comments about what he has done (edited here from a conversation that lasted more than an hour), spoken with his usual animation: "I roped them in, all the people I'd shoot if only they were the enemy and I was in the army, and the officer over me said: fire! Here I am; I made myself bigger, because you always ask which one is me! [This situation had, indeed, come up before!] Anyway, I decided I might just as well make *myself* the officer. I'll never go to school, the way you have to if you're going to boss others, but this is only a drawing, and I might as well give the orders, since I'm creating the scene!

"The cemetery? They'll be buried there soon! No, not only them! It's like the big cemetery a few miles from here; it's more crowded than Copacabana in the late afternoon. They have traffic problems in the cemetery — too many bodies. They clear a lot of them out, I hear, and then new ones are put there, and people forget the dead after a while, and then another housecleaning! We all go there, so you can't keep these bandits separate from everyone else! In life they're not separate, so why should they be separate in death! If you ask me, the best you can do in the time you spend here — I mean, before you go to that cemetery — is to stay out of that gang, and stay here, behind the soldiers!

"My mother had a sister, and she came with us to Rio, and she had three men who loved her, but she couldn't have a child, not one, and they all left her. She used to live with us when I was a baby. She was very religious. She listened to every word of the priest and the nuns, a mistake. They told her she'd go to heaven, for sure — faster than anyone here in this favela, and all the other favelas. One day a gang of men saw her and they liked her. They took her and gave it to her, maybe 100 times, who will ever know? They found her near the church. She wouldn't go inside! She said she was too dirty! The priest tried to convince her to come in, but she kept shaking her head, and calling herself filthy, filthy, filthy. Then she hit her head against the door of the church, and she was right away out cold.

"Would you believe it, the priest didn't want to touch her! That's what his cleaning lady told us, later! He went to his maid and told *her* to take care of my aunt! He meant, let her live or let her die, but don't bother me with her, because she got herself into one big mess, and I want nothing more to do with the whole business. He must have called a nun on that phone he has. She came, and she nursed my aunt, and my aunt started talking, so they let her go. She got home, and she sat there, and then she just started crying, and she never stopped, not really, for the rest of her life. She didn't live long, after that day. She got headaches, bad headaches. On the last day of her life she called to me, and told me I should be good, and I'm the oldest, so I should watch over my mother, when the men she has go, and even when I'm big and have my wife, I should pay attention to my mother, and my younger brother and sisters, and she hoped we all live as long as she lived. She asked me if I knew what happened to her. I said I thought so, yes. She said the men were no good, but she wasn't worth much herself! I got angry, but she just smiled. She said she was glad to be dying, and she wasn't sure she'd go to heaven now, because the priest knew what he knew about her! I got angrier! She laughed. She said she wouldn't mind going to hell. Who knows: she might meet the priest there! Then, she said I shouldn't forget that Jesus could come back any day, and He could be anyone, He could be me or one of my friends, anyone.

"I didn't know what to say! I was scared. I could see she was even sicker than before! I could see that she wasn't going to be with us too much longer! I wanted to say something good, something that would make her better, something she'd like to hear and she'd smile hearing it. I couldn't think of a thing to say — and then, I just came close to her and I said it: Jesus could be you, if it's true He could be anyone; He could be you! I was scared for a minute I'd said the wrong thing, and she looked as if she couldn't even talk any more. Then she stared right at me, and she gave me the biggest smile I've ever seen on her face. She never spoke to anyone after that, and she died the next day. We got the priest and he wasn't very friendly to her body. I've seen him be nice to some dead bodies. He is a two-faced one, a double-dealer I hear people call him; and if Jesus entered *his* body, He'd find out quick it was a big mistake and leave in five seconds!"

He has never quite gotten that deathbed scene out of his mind — and a year had passed since the aunt had died, I suspect of an untreated cerebrovascular accident, secondary to the self-imposed trauma she administered to her skull at the door of the Catholic church, located at the foot of the favela where her family lives. In his picture he places his aunt in the cemetery, but she looks alive. There, a tall woman standing there, looking over the dead, looking at the alive ones — both those encircled evil ones and those huddled enforcers of the law who are firing away. I ask Eduardo again about the picture, pointing not too discreetly at the woman in the cemetery. I know who she is, but I want him to tell me more — and more and more: a hungry visitor, wanting to pick up anything, everything. Eduardo laughs, says he knows he should not put his aunt in the picture "like that"; he knows he should have "buried" her, meaning he should have shown only a gravestone. But he "just couldn't." Anyway, she's not dead, not until everyone forgets her — said his mother the day after the burial of her sister. Eduardo agrees with that remark heartily, puts his agreement this way: "I haven't forgotten her. She lives!" He has a wry smile as he says those words — wanting, perhaps, to go on record as still skeptical of the church's promises of immortality, and still more than skeptical of what he's heard in church about other Biblical promises, yet absorbed with his aunt, and her dramatic last days, and his intensely dramatic moment with her, and her continued presence among people, himself included. Lest I not fully understand, he offers this remark, this qualification: "She lives, if I live, and I do, and when I get serious I think of her."

Will any summary of this boy's "mental status" bring us closer to understanding what in his decade of life on this planet has made him what he is? There is no doubt that he is a living witness to Orwell's remark. The boy's "qualities" have been secured in the face of the awful wretchedness of a family's continuing ordeals. Those qualities are not hard to establish; they amount, in sum, to a decency which is lived, which is tested, which is rooted in a vulnerable child's purpose: to hold fast to a course. What course? A course that helps him avoid the most palpable tragedy he knows — that of imprisonment, and soon thereafter death: "They all die once they're locked up; they die without seeing the sun; they get sick and die."

Maybe he exaggerates with that remark, or means to speak symbolically. Maybe he uses fear to constrain various "antisocial" inclinations — none of which he'd be eager to share with the likes of me. Maybe an exceedingly long-range follow-up is required to get to the heart of this psychological and moral matter. After all, Eduardo may indeed falter, stumble badly, end up getting arrested, thrown behind bars — even shot. He knows nothing about the laws of his city, his country, but someone told him once that to beg is to disobey the law. All he can do, then, is to persist, hope, try all the angles a mind will let him try. But those angles are shaped by another angle — one of vision: the possibilities and restrictions, both, which a particular moral sensibility evokes in time. Whence this sensibility? Will it do to account for that sensibility by referring to early childhood memories, to those of a father, a priest, to encounters with one neighborhood (his place of residence) and with another (Copacabana), to encounters *in* those neighborhoods with friends and strangers — by referring to an assortment of mental pictures and sounds that have been fitted into a mode of moral analysis whose vitality and power are not too hard to notice?

More questions. Whence the clever humor? Whence the self-assurance he displays on the wanton streets of Copacabana? Whence his blunt earthiness? Whence his social acumen? This boy, essentially illiterate (a year of haphazard schooling in a church school), strikes not only an American visitor but his neighbors (including the priest) and those who know him in Copacabana (a store manager, a hotel official) as "bright." But his obvious intelligence only begs the question of moral purpose yet again: others his age are smart all right — cunning and manipulative and crooked and dangerous as can be. For Eduardo, "moral purpose" comes down to an often-professed desire to stay alive, to stay free, and to stay worthy of adults whom he has had occasion to respect, no matter how flawed, limited, inadequate they may be. Is he shrewd enough to realize that a relatively muscular conscience will allow his body's muscles to survive rather than die all too soon? Of course he shows an Orwellian attentiveness to the drama of everyday life, a charmingly Orwellian skepticism that masks a fervent will to penetrate this life's mysteries. How else regard his drawing? Oh, as an expression of fear, of anger, of guilt punishable by execution? The boy would be (has been!) the first to acknowledge, in his own sharp and direct language, how a child constantly resorts to words that convey his sense of his own weakness. "One bad step, and there's no more Eduardo," his mother has told him a few times when *she* has felt low in spirits. Is a child's sheer will to live, grounded in his moral guardedness, enough to settle our unease as to a satisfactory account of his moral purpose?

Perhaps another witness will help us. In 1980 I returned to Florida, where I'd worked many years earlier (1964 through 1966) with migrant farm children.[5] One of the children I knew back then — long since grown up and married and a parent — had recently been killed in an automobile accident. Also killed was his first son, twelve years old. John Thomas was thirty-two at the time of his death; his wife was thirty-one, and they had six other children, the oldest of whom, a daughter, was thirteen. The mother, Clara Thomas, had lost a number of other sons and daughters to miscarriages and the diseases that kill poor, malnourished children who receive scant if any medical care. Her oldest daughter, Martha Ann, is called Marty. She was the miraculous survivor of the car accident, and later I would hear from her about that tragedy.

The father, John Thomas, had told his oldest daughter and oldest son that as reward for some very hard fieldwork done they could have some good, cold ice cream, and maybe some french fries, which both loved, especially when salted liberally. They set out in a 1971 green Ford station wagon, their family car, used also for the long trips north to pick crops (as far as the vegetable farms of Delaware and southern New Jersey). The two children fiddled with the radio, which was impaired, but not quite broken. Marty describes what happened: "My father was feeling tired, but he was glad, because we had a few bucks salted away, he said. I asked how much, and he said fifty. That's a lot to save; usually we spend all we make doing the crops on food and gas, and sometimes we owe a lot. Daddy used to tell us, on bad mornings, that he'd been dreaming all night about dollar bills and the police and the people we owed to — and we'd know he wasn't going to smile all day. On that ride to get an ice cream he was like us; he was acting like a kid, laughing and joking and he'd see someone who looked funny walking, and he'd point them out — two guys who had heavy clothes on, and it was hot, and they were acting funny, daddy thought. He told us sometimes people go nuts, and they have to go into a hospital. (I think that happened to his sister.)

"Well, we were getting near the ice cream place, and my brother and I were fighting bad, real bad, like cats and dogs, my mother used to say when we fought like that. To tell the truth, it was stupid, real stupid; it was over which radio station we should try to keep playing. I was hearing some gospel rock, and I love that music; and he wanted his J. Geils, or one of those, maybe it was the Stones. I told him he was a 'damn Yankee.' He laughed. But he kept twirling the knob, and then when he'd get what he wanted, I'd mess him up, or the radio would, by going fuzzy on him. He was real bad upset, and I was, too, because when I got my music, he'd do the same to me, mess me up by switching the station. My daddy got mad at both of us. He said one of us would have to go in the back on the way home, if we didn't make peace, and keep it. So, we did. Daddy said the radio was no good, anyway; there was always so much static. So we sat there, and the next thing, there was the ice cream place. We got our cones, strawberry for me and chocolate for my brother, and daddy had an ice cream sandwich, and next door, we got our fries, and we started back. I began the trouble again; I did. I put the radio on, because I'd finished my cone, and I thought he wouldn't mind, my brother: he was so busy with his cone, and he's the slowest, the really slowest when it comes to eating ice cream. He just doesn't want to see the cone go empty on him! I was fiddling with the dial, and I caught Ray Charles, singing 'Georgia,' and I love him and I love that song, and that's when it happened, I think. The last I remember is Ray Charles singing 'the whole night through,' those words, and I was nibbling on my cone, and then I woke up, and my momma was there, standing over me."

Marty had been thrown clear upon the collision of her father's car with one that came right at him from the opposite lane, driven by a youth who was drunk. Her father and brother were not only killed instantly, but their corpses were badly burned. She herself was badly dazed, but not injured. A man who saw the accident knew whose car had been hit and where he lived. The police drove to the migrant camp to find Mrs. Thomas, who had no phone. I had also known Clara Thomas as a young girl; she'd been another of the children with whom I talked in the 1960s. I'd testified in connection with several legal cases involving migrants during the early 1970s, and so had kept in touch with both John and Clara, and with a public health nurse who had befriended them. It was the nurse who called me and told me of the tragedy, and I decided to fly to what I knew would be an extremely emotional funeral.

But fog prevented my arrival in time for the funeral, which had been held in a church quite familiar to me, a rural, hard-praying one, with no affiliation to an established Protestant denomination. When I came to the Thomas home, Marty was playing her beloved "rock Gospel" music, now with obvious sadness. She was alarmed when she saw me — a strange white man, whom, in fact, she'd met when considerably younger (aged three and four), and whom she now figured to be connected to the police, or the sheriff's office, or maybe a local newspaper, which was supposed to run a story on the accident, her mother had told her (because she'd been interviewed when she arrived at the scene, to find her husband and son dead). I chatted briefly with Marty, then sat with her mother for a few minutes, then left to talk with the nurse who had called me and a lawyer much involved in fighting on behalf of the interests of migrant farm workers in the Southeast. The nurse asked me how Mrs. Thomas was doing, how Marty was doing. I said I thought they were both "fine." The nurse volunteered that Marty was a very "strong" child. I asked what she meant — strong physically, strong psychologically? The nurse said "physically," and went on to tell me what a good, nimble worker this thirteen-year-old child had already become, especially at picking beans, a tough job. Then she had an afterthought: "She's a very thoughtful child." I wanted specifics and got few. I should have known better.

I decided to visit Marty and her family again. In the next two years I returned eight times for fairly extended stays (several days), and so doing, talked once more with other migrant children, each time with the subject of their moral lives in mind. Most of all I talked with Marty. Nor did Marty hesitate to talk — about her father and her brother of course, but also about her present life, her future prospects, her ambitions for herself. On my third weekend stay in Belle Glade, Marty was especially reflective. Could she have begun to put some emotional distance between herself and what she'd been through? "I know my father died with his heart feeling good," she said. Then she continued: "Sometimes his heart would be heavy, but not when he was in the kind of nice mood he had that afternoon, and not when he was pushing us for those ice creams. My mother used to tell us when we were real small, when we were kids just starting to know the world, that whenever daddy wants *us* to have an ice cream, it means *he* wants one! And she told us that daddy will only go get a cone, if he thinks he's on the high road. Well, I'd ask, what's the high road? And she'd say: 'Marty, the high road is when things are going just okay, just okay, and our heads are above water.' It took some more questioning, you know, to get it straight, because I'd wonder for a while where that 'water' was, and I'd still ask, sometimes, where the 'road' was, the 'high road.' But I guess I figured it all out, because I remember when I went to school for a while, when I was (maybe) seven or eight, I knew that the 'high road' meant a good time for me, and for all of us, because picking the crops had been going real fine, and we had some spare cash for candy and 'scream,' I used to call it.

"Like I said, he died fast, and he died happy. The same with my brother. I only wish I could have sat back and let him use that radio. But we never liked to listen to the same music, and I just pray that God will know that. He must, actually! He knows everything! He keeps track of all of us. A lot of the time I'll have my doubts about God, I admit. I mean, you wonder why the Lord will let someone get all tanked up, and drive a car at 100 miles an hour, and hit people coming back from getting ice creams! I cried all the time for a while, and I still cry. I think of my daddy, and my brother a lot. I miss them a lot. I hope I never forget them."

At such moments she would stop talking; her head would fall low toward her chest; she would fold her arms, and if she was sitting, cross her legs. If she'd start crying, she'd quietly unfold her arms and reach for a handkerchief, one of the two she owned, each a Christmas present from her mother and father. She had obviously treasured those two handkerchiefs, and had until recently kept them in a special place, under the mattress on the floor of the cabin where she lived. An aspect of the quality of "thoughtfulness" my nurse friend had mentioned comes across well in these comments, prompted by one day's use of the larger and prettier and sturdier of those two handkerchiefs: "I'd told myself I'd never really *use* those two kerchiefs, just *have* them; maybe when I grew up and found the man I loved, I'd give him one, and if he got sweaty, he could wipe off the sweat with the kerchief. Even then, I think I'd worry that the kerchief would get lost, or torn. My mother always said she didn't buy them for me to save them, but to do something with them — sneeze into them or clear my face of sweat with them! But I couldn't agree with her, and finally I just hid them in my shoes that I wear to church, and that way I'd take them out each Sunday morning.

"Since daddy died, and my brother, I use these kerchiefs all the time, and I don't worry about my future time. That's the wrong thing to do — always thinking about the future, so you don't do what you should do right now! The preacher said so at the funeral; he said we should live today as though it's our last day. I can't do what he said, not all the time; but since the accident I can do it more than before — like with using the kerchiefs. I wanted to give the two kerchiefs to them — one in my daddy's casket, and one in my brother's, but my mother said no, they'd both want me to use them, and where they're going, we hope, they won't need kerchiefs. If ever there was a good man, and he deserved to meet God Almighty, it was my daddy. When he was real sick with a bug, he still worked, and he tried to provide for us all the time; and he never drank, like a lot of people do. He said he'll take ice cream to beer and whiskey, and he'll take a 'sweet tooth' to a 'liquor-hungry tongue.' I hope he's happy, with God smiling on him."

I once stopped myself as I wrote some notes after a visit with Marty, and tried to figure out what it was about her that made others stop and take notice (not only the nurse she and I both knew, but the crew leader, one of the better ones, who "took" this family, among others, north each late spring to do harvesting, and also the minister who presided over the funeral services mentioned above). Even Marty's mother, who tried to be modest about all her children, observed that her oldest daughter was the "most helpful," a quality she attributed to her age: the one who had learned responsibilities before the others, and was old enough to shoulder them fairly well. But as the weeks and months after the accident followed one another, I began to realize, with each visit, that Orwell's conundrum applied here, too: a child who had surely faced "pain" and a terrible "disaster" and plenty of "difficulties" (part of them the inheritance of all migrant children, part of them the special presentation of fate to this child), but a child whose "qualities" were, even so, remarkable.

What qualities? A certain stoicism. A religious sensibility that wouldn't crumple under a tragedy that seemed senseless, and certainly hard to comprehend for those who believe that God "wills" what happens, that God "watches over" his people and "dearly loves" them. Also, a respectfulness of manner — without doubt toward older whites such as myself and the nurse, but also (I was told) toward others of her own race, her own age. Marty's mother Clara Thomas described her daughter as a "gentle soul," and even though the girl had been an unyielding fighter for her rights over the car radio, I certainly agreed.

Marty was also delightful to be with — courteous, hospitable, and though a mere thirteen, sensitive to moral and psychological nuances. Her compassion for others could easily be observed, and at times even seemed perplexing: "I saw my little cousin crying.

So, I picked him up — he's three — and I told him I'd hold him as long as he wanted me to hold him. He didn't stop crying, though. So, I tried to find out why he was crying, but he wouldn't tell me; he just kept on doing it, tears and tears and tears, until I wanted to go get him some water, because I thought he'd dry up. I didn't dare leave him. I just looked him over — no scratches or bleeding. I poked his tummy, and it didn't hurt. I felt his head and he didn't seem hot. (My mother does all that when we cry!)

"Finally I knew it was time for me to go. I didn't know what to do. I guess take him with me! But when I moved to leave, he screamed even more! I was ready to give up! And I did! I just started crying myself! I asked myself: Now Marty, what's the matter with you? But I knew: I felt sorry for that poor child, and I just wished I could help him to feel better. I want to be a nurse. I asked myself, while I stood there: What would the nurse do? But I couldn't come up with an answer for myself. I kept crying. I just sobbed like a little baby, like our sister Melissa did, before she just stopped one day, and she was dead. The next thing I knew that little boy stopped crying and he looked at me, and he asked me if I was all right. I told him I'd never be all right if he didn't become all right. Then he said he *was* all right, and all he wanted was for *me* to be all right! So, I said: let's both be all right! And we were!

"But I knew there must have been something that was bothering that child, and I told myself: Marty, don't forget that a few minutes ago you thought you had a little boy on your hands who was going to leave us here and go to the Promised Land. You'd better find out why he was crying so hard. So, I decided to ask, and I did, and I could see that he felt ashamed of himself, and he looked over at the table, and I don't know why, but I just knew. I saw this empty package of cookies, I saw the crumbs, and I just could picture him, gobbling them all up: You start, and you can't stop yourself, and you're doing wrong, and you know you'll pay for it, but you just keep on doing it, and then you're through, and now you realize what you've done, and oh, will you get it from your momma or your daddy! The kid saw me looking at the table, and he said he knew he shouldn't have eaten those chocolate chip cookies, but they're the kind with the big, big chips, and he never gets more than one, after supper, and he thought he'd just take his one right that afternoon, early — and then, like he said, the Devil got into him. But he was scared as he could be, because his father is a mean, mean man. I've seen him beat on those kids, and he beats on my aunt, until she's dizzy, and she's not even hearing you when you talk to her. So, I didn't know what to do; I just stood there — and then I had an idea. I said, come on, we'll fix everything up. I took him to my house, and I told my mother, please, we had to get some cookies for our cousins, and she owed me a dollar from a week ago — some of my picking money. She gave it to me, and I got the cookies for my cousin, and some for us, too. That night when I had a cookie it tasted real good."

This girl wasn't exactly an heiress. A dollar meant a lot to her. But one suspects she would have borrowed that dollar if her mother hadn't owed it to her, and she would have gladly worked a few hours in the hot sun, on her hands and knees, picking beans, in order to be able to get her cousin through his difficulty, and, so it turned out, *her* difficulty as well. I don't know how to "explain" such "behavior," other than to record her capacity for empathy, her tenderness and kindness, and — to approach the matter from another angle — her lack of self-importance or self-righteousness. We are, yet again, in the presence of a child who demonstrates a virtuous charity toward others, and even a confessional candor about inevitable failings: the power of that car radio.

One morning I heard Marty talk about the nurse whom we both knew, and again I was told by this girl that if she had her way, she'd also be a nurse. Marty told me this was no random thought. For "a year or two," she estimated, she'd been watching the nurse at work. She came to administer "shots" to the migrant children and for Marty the visits were instructive, but also, it seems, inspiring: "She gives the 'shots' without hurting people. Everyone thinks they'll hurt, but when she's actually with you, then you know there's no way that this lady will hurt you: *no way*. There will be times when my little sister and my little brother are all upset, and I have to feed them — then I'll think of the nurse, and try to be like her; I mean, easy with them, and nice to them, so they won't be scared, but you have to get them to take the food, and learn to clean up after themselves!"

Once she drew a picture of herself (Figure 2) as she'd like to be — wearing a nurse's hat and light blue uniform and badge, and ministering to some migrant children who have, she explains, become lost in a big field, where the crops are high and they are not; and so, having lost sight of their parents, they are sitting and crying, and she has accidentally stumbled onto them, and is preparing to help them find their way home. Such a portrayal of herself is, one learns, no random fantasy. She is not given merely to occasional gestures of concern for a cousin this time, a friend the next. She is, as her nurse hero said, "thoughtful" — and in two senses of that word: reflective and considerate. She managed to combine intellectual acuity with ethical awareness.

"That child is *innocently* good," a specialist in migrant education, who knows Marty, told me. How had she come to know the girl and on what basis had she come to her judgment? This woman, who herself is impressively able and kindhearted, cannot immediately answer. But eventually she has this to say: "I see a lot of kids like her; they've got a lousy future, and they know it in their hearts. I bring them books, and try to teach them how to read and write. Lots of them spend very little time in school. They're always on the move. We've found it helps if we try to catch them at home, in their camps, and work with them there, even if it's for brief times, and on the run — between their traveling, or after they've helped their parents by working with them in the fields. What I mean when I say 'it helps' is this: You can get them to pay attention, and they really learn something. When they come to 'regular school,' they feel strange, and they feel unwanted by the teachers and the other

kids, and I'll tell you something, lots of times they're right to feel
that way. You take Marty; she does wonderfully with books. She's
got an inquisitive head on her shoulders! She loves to hear us read
out loud to the other kids. But when she went to school last year,
she heard so many awful, insulting remarks from the regular kids,
she told her mother she didn't want to go to school. And, of course,
her mother needs her help with the younger kids, and out in the
fields, harvesting, as well — so she'll not push the girl to a place
where she doesn't want to be.

"If you ask me this girl, Marty (and she's not the only one here,
but she'd be special *anywhere!*) has a lot to teach those nice, well-
to-do white kids who look at her as if she's the scum of the earth.
She's a good person. Do we have good people all over the place? I
don't think so. We have a lot of people who are selectively good;
that's how I see it: they'll be nice to their own, they'll massage their
egos by helping someone who's up to their standards! Maybe I'm
getting cynical — in this job you do! — but there aren't many of us
teachers who have Marty's patience with children, and her affection
toward them. And no one is sitting around giving her credit for
being the person she is, or raising her salary for being the person
she is. She'd give a hand to anyone in trouble, a total stranger or a
next-door neighbor, a white kid or a black kid. When I read a story
about Florida's Indians, and what happened to them in the nineteenth century, I could see that kid perk up: Marty being herself!
She worried about the way the Indians were treated, but she was
cheerful: they'd pull through, she was sure. Well, *I* wasn't so sure!
But I wasn't going to pour out the statistics, just then. I did try to
find out why Marty held out hope for those Indians. I asked her
why she thought the Indians would pull through. She didn't wait a
second to answer me: 'Because they weren't doing wrong, and God
knows that.' Well, I had to stop and let that one sink in before I
could continue my class."

Perhaps Marty's conviction that God "knows" about the travail of
others — including migrant families such as hers — helps explain

a personal authority she seems to possess. She can cry with her cousin, but she also can be controlled, thoroughly watchful — taking in, it seems, every possible emotional and moral nuance. What she said she expected of history, with respect to Florida's Indians, is what she also expects of herself: that her destiny as a child of God will be realized, no more and no less. Such an expectation in others could be consistent with smugness, coy self-righteousness, outright arrogance. In Marty one saw a modesty — yet an almost unnerving composure.

Marty had no "great expectations." She has known the severest poverty an American child can know, not to mention racial prejudice. Such experiences do not make for swollen heads; and they are not often to be found in migrant camps. One sees plenty of sadness, and a good deal of stubborn persistence, and, true, moments of pleasure, of amused satisfaction in parents, of lighthearted frolic in children. But these are not boys and girls who declare themselves with pride, whose self-assurance survives the ups and downs that can visit any life, no matter how privileged. Marty had no big dream that would take her to college and beyond; she had small, everyday dreams, though, which in their sum, one begins to think, becomes a vulnerable child's almost defiant moral purpose.

Not that she would ever use such an expression as "moral purpose." She wasn't always sure at age thirteen that she was on the right side of things. Several times she had told her friends the nurse and the teacher that she wasn't sure where she'd like to live and which crops she'd like to learn to harvest especially well. Nevertheless, she could say this on the second anniversary of her father's death, her brother's death: "I remember them. I can still see my daddy and my brother joking while they tried to tell each other which kind of ice cream to get. We'll get to meet, I hope, on Judgment Day. In the morning, though, when you wake up, you can't just wait for Judgment Day! You have to help momma get breakfast! She tells us every day is Judgment Day! She tells us she could check us off, every day — how we're all doing — but it's up to God to say, and no one can be sure, and if you are sure, then you're in real bad trouble, and you'd better watch out, because He doesn't like us people speaking for Him, and saying what He's going to decide, and acting as though we're His crew leaders, and we're rounding up people to go to heaven, and people to go to hell."

When I heard her statement (it was interrupted twice by family diversions that prompted a change of subject), I realized yet again how eagerly children (and their parents) can sometimes connect the particulars of their everyday lives to the religious parables and paradoxes — which, of course, are meant to confront us in exactly that way, in the stomach and the heart as well as the head. The crew leader as the presumptuous spokesman for the Lord! Marty knows those crew leaders, all right, and alas, probably will know more and more of them as the years progress. Her vulnerability to their bold, sometimes brazen, sometimes craven greed for power is an unfortunate fact of life. Under such circumstances, she might have already surrendered herself, in one way or the other, to one crew leader, to a series of them. Had she done so, it would not be the first time in the history of American agriculture that such an event had taken place — a migrant worker, a child, used and abused by a man who makes a living by delivering field hands across the land, so that they can work, sunup to sundown, at the lowest wages, and often without the federal protection other workers get.

Marty has, instead, stayed close to such community as a migrant family can find for itself — a minister, a nurse, a teacher. Her mother has done likewise — tried to give her children some moral backbone, some personal independence, which will (she hopes) strengthen their resistance to predators and marauders. On the other hand, the mother is herself a migrant worker, is a poor widow, has a new boyfriend who drinks too much, has many children, has no cash reserves, has no property apart from a few kitchen utensils, a few pieces of broken-down furniture, and, yes, a mesmerizing television set. The mother is not the one who prompts this moral observation in Marty: "If my mother could only have a long rest. But she won't ever, she says, until she dies. She's told me once that she gets jealous, sometimes, of my daddy — that he's worked his burden, and now he's been called home, and she has to stay here and work hers, and only God knows for how long. She tells us lots of times that she's ready to give up. She looks at the television and asks why she's not the person on television, instead of herself! I know she'll snap out of that mood. If she doesn't, it'll be up to us kids. We have to keep going, until Jesus says okay, stop. Daddy didn't like to go to church, but when he did, and he heard the minister say that, he said 'amen,' I remember. He said 'amen' real loud."

As with Eduardo one bows before the mystery of Marty's life, while also trying to make sense of it. Marty may be whistling in the dark — trying with all her might to put the best light on a very grim time ahead. She may end up, years hence, desiring the beer and wine that many other migrants constantly crave. She may lose her tough, even fierce intention to make a go of things, whatever the personal cost, as a tribute of sorts to a God in Whom she strongly believes. Who knows, she may even lose Him — lose her faith in Him. But those of us who know her doubt it. She is a youthful version of other, older, penniless migrants who have demonstrated surprising doggedness, shown steadfast willingness to face down adversity, demonstrate pluck, whimsy, and made the outsider (and not a few friends, relatives, neighbors) take notice.

Nor will it do, again, to dispose of a Marty, of an Eduardo, by calling such a child "exceptional" or "special." We are all that, individuals with this or that distinctive quality. Orwell did, of course, select some of us as special for him, for others, and wondered how that outcome came to pass — the achievement of certain moral characteristics. He answered himself, it can be said, by positing "disaster, pain or difficulty" as correlates, if not explanatory variables, to use twentieth-century scientific words. Those of us who admire his way of putting things can follow his lead, try to find evidence to support his ironic connection. The evidence is not so hard to find in this world — where, in countless communities, honorable and decent people keep trying to make a go of it. Once we spend enough time with an Eduardo, a Marty, we need no further persuasion of the concrete human reality Orwell has in mind — that the truly vulnerable often enough do possess admirable "qualities." I don't think Orwell would want to claim an exclusive relationship of the kind he asserts — that *only* people in substantial trouble of one or another sort will end up with the qualities he almost takes for granted. I do think, however, that he would welcome any confirming impressions and even invite some speculations as to why this somewhat paradoxical element in our collective lives as human beings continues to endure.

Why, then, do some children who have so little seem also to have so much? Eduardo and Marty have moral purpose — even as they are in constant jeopardy of losing it. Is that assertion actually true — or does it betray a glib condescension? Isn't it ironic how some of us, who have talked proudly of a "value-free social science," can spot the moral jeopardy of others with great ease: How long can Eduardo last amid the moral anarchy of a contemporary Brazilian favela, not to mention the rich man's Copacabana district? How long, too, can Marty last amid the family deterioration, the social disorganization that afflict our migrant population? One can't predict the outcome for these children — or, for that matter, can't be a secure prophet with respect to any child.[6] One can only try to fathom how children like those two have managed so far to do as they've done. One thereby nudges theory toward human experience, hoping that the latter brings the former to life, and the former helps arrive at a persistent, comprehensible aspect of the human scene.

We all aim to survive, unless we've badly lost our bearings. Survival means eating, means reproducing ourselves — not only physically, but psychologically and spiritually. Survival means asserting ourselves enough to do these things — to claim our food, find our partner, make ourselves heard, understood. Survival means, as we've been told in this century, the energy of drives bursting within us.

If the theorists differ as to the origin of those "drives" (grounded in biology? grounded in a culture? where?), there is at least agreement among ordinary pediatricians that a child will not survive who can't find adequate food, and thereby (later) the energy "to love and to work," Freud's well-known twosome. Such being the common denominator, so to speak, of this life, one may assume, without too much fear of controversy, that extremely vulnerable children are those who cannot really take for granted too many meals in a given week (or a day).

Most of us in American pediatrics or child psychiatry have never, thank God, had to contend with such circumstances for the boys and girls we see. Our theories refer to "drives," and yet we don't stop and ask whether anyone who is in fairly imminent danger of starvation, say, is prompted by the same drives as those who finish a multi-course meal in a delightfully decorated family dining room and then retire to watch television (with its advertisements in the form of the truculent, competitive huckstering we've all learned to accept as our price for whatever we happen to watch). A starving child, someone with common sense speculates, is "driven" by the urge to get food. It is this fundamental psychological reality (an effect, obviously, of a widespread social and economic reality) which holds for most of the world's children. Orwell's "disaster, pain or difficulty" for such children (millions and millions of Eduardos and Martys) becomes this continuing vulnerability: the body's "instincts" pressing hard and long for a piece of bread — or yes, some water that will not kill one because it is fatally contaminated.

How do such children manage to accomplish that demanding, overriding task — to eat, to drink, to nourish themselves, to live in the absolutely fundamental sense of that expression? Eduardo and many other children have provided us the answer to that awesome question. All the time, in dozens of nations in all this world's continents save Antarctica, one can see them, hungry and malnourished and poorly clothed and to a pediatrician's eye sick in various ways — yet striving mightily to live. These children are indeed, as psychiatrists sometimes say about all of us, "drive-bound"; they will beg, borrow, steal, to eat, to drink, to live. Given that psychological and physiological condition in such children, whence Orwell's "qualities we admire in human beings"? Why don't such "qualities" dissolve in favor of an utterly rapacious "animality," or in favor of apathetic despair, a last-ditch self-centeredness? One assumes that Orwell would not find this unfortunate kind of inwardness nearly so odious in the poor as he did in those upper-class intellectuals he condemned so roundly, even intemperately, in *The Road to Wigan Pier*. Of course, plenty of boys and girls have in fact become morally destroyed as they try to stay alive. Copacabana has its share of such children. If rich men and women use them in various ways — for sex, to obtain drugs, as cheap and degraded labor — that is another story, not for this chapter of this book. To turn Orwell's remark on its head, we would have to wonder, and well we should, why it is that not a few of those who seem to have so little in the way of "disaster, pain or difficulty," compared to so many others, end up with rather few of those "qualities we admire in human beings," if with any at all.

Throughout history a significant number of children reared in luxury and privilege have demonstrated substantial egoism, insistent self-importance, pushy selfishness. Should we consider *them*, too, victims — in a jeopardy that rivals, morally, the kind an Eduardo must endure constantly: the perils, in their case, of a developing solipsism grounded in money and power? Should we mention "evil" as well as "good" in this discussion of the moral life of children: the "evil" of a child, Hank, learning to mouth racist remarks, the "evil" of a child living in prosperity, if not sumptuousness, and yet spoiled, spoiled rotten — utterly indifferent to others, even those near at hand, never mind the ones who live across the proverbial railroad tracks?

Such children are usually not "sociopaths" or "psychopaths." They are not without consciences. They obey the law and might even know how to *talk* a good moral line. Still, their self-centeredness has struck many a psychiatric or social observer as all too evident[7] — and one wonders whether the matter ultimately ought be left with cultural analysts and psychiatric theorists, or be considered a serious moral one. Of course our well-to-do suburbs also offer rather spirited and ethically sensitive children — even as one keeps remembering that among those who have known Orwell's "disaster, pain or difficulty" there are any number of thoroughly mean boys and girls, as morally stunted as their age-mates in Copacabana or various upper-class American enclaves. Meanwhile, the irony of an Eduardo's earnest decency, a Marty's, haunts us, as Orwell was haunted.

The common notion of "conscience" as a source of inhibition, of neurosis, of strictures against the appetites of human beings, though understandably useful and valid (when, say, Freud was describing what had happened to his uptight turn-of-the-century patients), doesn't quite describe what has happened to Eduardo and Marty and others, who call upon "conscience" for the very survival that their "instincts" or "drives" urge them to seek. In the familiar psychoanalytic imagery of our century, id and superego, the drives and the conscience, the instincts and the internalized demands of parental authority — all combine in extremis toward a common goal: to get through this very day, to eat, maybe to collect enough food for a few days, rather than part of one day. In a world where loss is the norm, where death is a continual presence, where there are few surprises and few expectations, where one's luck (bad) is already defined, where one's chances are slim — in such a world an Eduardo sets up the moral purposes not as antagonists of the "drives," or sources of psychological illness, but as important boosts to an everyday effort.

The Eduardos of this world don't live in the small, relatively isolated families that many of us upper-middle-class Western psychiatrists assume to be the norm for our various theories of child development. To work in one of the favelas of Rio or São Paulo, to spend a few nights with a family in one of them, is to be reminded how (unavoidably) provincial we all are. Eduardo would scratch his head as my son and I told him about the way we lived (at his constant behest, and often with our shyness, to say the least). We in turn had a bit of head-scratching to do as we observed a dozen people in Eduardo's home going through their daily and nightly rhythms. Every dawn in one room, ill protected from the outside, people huddle on the floor, some with a mattress, most with nothing between them and the earth. The earth is the floor. Soon thereafter a crowd of people begins to awaken, and wonder: What will this span of daylight bring in the way of food, water, illness, pain? No meal or even glass of clean water is taken for granted. Weather is an immediate experience — heavy rain outside becomes heavy rain inside, and the wind rushes through those shacks with an eerie, whistling imperiousness quite startling for someone used to closing a window, a door firmly. The sticky heat is everywhere, its powerful downward leverage on the emotions all too easily ignored by those who think of air conditioning as a necessity in a hot climate.

Suffering is also everywhere: in all children and all adults. In family after family the physician in me was always being addressed as I talked with people, or simply watched them move or remark to each other upon what was hurting them today. These are people who have no electricity and no sanitary facilities as we know and expect them. Outhouses or vacant land on the hill are where the body's products go. The word "privacy," so much a part of our political, economic, social, and psychological vocabulary (as it is part of contemporary psychiatry) takes on new meaning by its very absence in the lives of the vast majority of this planet's people. The celebrated intrigues of an oedipal childhood, the secrets kept and nourished, the rivalries harbored forever, all required privacy, dyads and triads, bedrooms and more bedrooms, days in which meals are served and nights in which dreams can unfold at leisure. For us of the Western bourgeoisie shame often makes for withdrawal into one's "private world," a phrase I heard again and again in the psychiatric wards where I did my training. To be sure, even in a mob the individual has a private world, his or her impressions, reactions. But the large, ailing, exposed, malnourished, hot, thirsty, jittery community of men, women, and children packed into a shack that is itself in severe jeopardy on the side of a hill is not the ideal place where some of the expected psychological fantasies and preoccupations are likely to flourish.

For Eduardo, and many others of his favela, each day brings a distinct possibility of death, and each day demands the strength of will to resist that antagonist. Disease and death are, in a sense, the equivalent of the oedipal father (for boys) or mother (for girls), the big and threatening presence that prompts one to take heed, and figure out how to conduct oneself. "Life is a jealous mistress," Eduardo was told by that aunt of his, and he didn't need a teacher or a child psychiatrist to explain the old peasant cliché, handed down from one generation to another. Such a mistress does indeed require each lover's unyielding devotion, rendered in the Copacabana hustle Eduardo and thousands like him know so well. Such a mistress requires mobilization of intellect, will, affect, and bodily strength. That mobilization, in turn, has its own requirements. One attends to the day's taxing demands, or gets closer to death itself. For these children death is a reality, not the "Thanatos" Freud had in mind when he mentioned his "metapsychological theory of the instincts." For these children the reality of tomorrow depends upon the effort expended today — begging and running those errands and washing the cars and shining the shoes, world without end.

Some of these children, under such circumstances, become Eduardos — dedicated workers in the vineyards of the rich who hold on for dear life to dignity, personal composure, even high-mindedness. These boys and girls possess a vitality that asserts itself in spite of hunger pangs, anemia, parasitic intestinal infestations, and a climate that can rob all one's energy. As one examines Eduardo's remarks, drawings, and paintings, and most of all the actions he takes, the manner he has with people, one notices repeatedly the moral aspects of his obvious determination: "I'd *better* bring home some money, or the baby won't eat too many more meals!" He chooses to articulate a hunger he knows well himself by resorting to a fragile infant's needs. One vulnerable child makes an effort to respond to an even more vulnerable child. That effort was prompted by conscience; and that conscience is rooted in remembered voices, moments, sights, events.

Eduardo remembers stray remarks made by relatives and friends, by the clergy, by people met in Copacabana, heard talking on buses to and from that part of Rio de Janeiro. He fits those remarks into a sense he has of what is happening and constructs for himself an obligatory rhythm, impelled by a mixture of fear and awe and anxiety and superstition and absolute dread, but also by nostalgia and yearning and affectionate sensations. He uses humor, especially, to weave the elements of that mental life into a reasonably coherent way of regarding the world. One minute he is superstitious, afraid that a run of bad luck will descend on him because he failed to cross himself or smile at Rio's statue of Jesus Christ; the next minute he is in awe of that statue, and turns meditative, even prayerful; at yet another time, his marvelous witty, ironic side notices something quite inconsistent, hypocritical, or fraudulent, and he feels much stronger, much more himself for having responded to it and arrested himself through perception, through language. An observed drollery has become his very possession, one source of a child's self-respect — something he, Eduardo, has made his very own in the act of description.

Tragedy is instructive, playwrights help us to realize. Tragedy can blind, can drive some to madness and acts of desperation. For these two children, as for others, tragedy becomes a handle for vision, for personal examination, for the momentary dissipation of fearfulness through bold moral confrontation. Eduardo observes the greedy nihilism of both the rich and the poor, and out of such a moral nightmare realizes his small daily victories by achieving distance. Marty will never forget that automobile accident: it sealed in her a sense of life's fragility and absurdity worthy of existentialists. Accidents can become moral incidents, as can the accident of fate. When a boy such as Eduardo thinks (in response to reality, not neurotic fantasy) that his odds for survival in any week are "maybe fifty-fifty," then a species of gambling fever may well be a psychological outcome: heads I must try something with all possible exertion, or tails I most certainly do lose. Such urgency turns moral, however, in our Eduardos and Martys. They have both acquired from others, and made their own, the commanding authority of God, or Christ, of His priestly representatives on this earth, of family members, of neighbors, of strangers, even — a nurse, a teacher, a person walking down the street whose casual remarks can evoke a spell of wonder or worry. Is it odd that children who may well be near taking the last breath, ask the questions we of our world know to be asked by our elderly, our terminally ill? Is it odd that children who are on the move a lot, and never seem welcome for long anywhere, may develop a habit of looking closely at the world, seeing through many of its duplicities and pretenses; or develop a habit, also, of seeking solace in another world, that offered by a religion or (also) by a drug?

For Marty, "we are here to prove ourselves to God." For Eduardo, "we are here to stay for a while, and if we're lucky, we'll leave people behind who like us, and when our name is mentioned, they smile and clap." Moral purpose has here become a Christian pilgrim's faith. Moral purpose has here become a stoic's resigned acceptance of the tragic possibilities both life and death offer us. Both Eduardo and Marty have lasted; both have had to witness more deaths than do many old people in our privileged world. The great irony is the liveliness of their minds, no matter how constant the jeopardy, the omnipresent pain of serious illness or injury. I will last, they try to say through word and deed. I will last for God's sake; or I will last because not to last is no fun, and besides, there are some amusing moments, and (who knows?) Jesus just might be around at the end, to share some stories with us; at least sometimes I really *do* think so, even if sometimes I sure don't. An edge cuts two ways, and these children live near or precisely on the edge. Having shunned (in fear, in disgust, in anxiety) the depraved life of which they see plenty, they seem to take the other way as an existential alternative, a moral inheritance.

The visiting doctor asks himself on numerous occasions whether Eduardo or Marty themselves have given any great thought to these matters which seem so puzzling, so vexing to an Orwell. One rainy night, with the glittering lights of far-off Copacabana visible below and the glowing statue of Jesus visible above us, we stood and looked and looked. We were atop the favela. Year after year new families have arrived, trudged higher and higher until, finally, there is some space for them to occupy. Beyond them is more space — though one day an end to that will come. On some stormy days muddy landslides already descend upon the upper hillside favela, and then death makes its persistent, powerful point. Suddenly a brisk wind came upon us. We stood there, feeling its lifting force, hearing it work its way through the shaky squatter shacks, whose loose ends were its quick victims. Then there were the human noises, children excited by the wind itself, by its assertion of ready mastery over a host of objects. A pause. Another gust, this one even brisker, more coercive. A tree bent. A dog barked, as if this stranger, the wind, were potentially dangerous. A word or two: some reprimands to children making light of something potentially not so funny. "They have forgotten," observes Eduardo, "what a wind can do up here — blow some of the favela away." He has not forgotten! Yet another surge of wind — quite strong, strangely exhilarating. The boy smiles now for the first time. He looks at me, starts talking, tells me of a passion: "I love the wind. When we first came here, it was the thing I noticed most, the wind. It cools us down. It dries us out. It gives us excitement. Do you hear them all? They are excited. It brings a change!"

Then a silence, a long one. I thought he'd continue; he seemed to be working himself up, getting into a declarative frame of mind. I was going to listen and listen, and yet again learn how his mind worked. But he'd had his say. He lifted his face. He turned his body so that it received the wind directly. He closed his eyes. A big smile came over his face. When one gust hit him head on, he laughed. After a few minutes, as suddenly as it came, it went: no more wind; a silence noticeable by virtue of what had preceded it. A wait. Now the silence is the winner; it lasts and lasts. Eduardo's body begins to relax. He relents from his pose, turns around, lowers his head, takes a piece of chewing gum from his pocket, puts it in his mouth, begins to work on it. He offers a piece to me. I say no. He says that he should remember by now that I don't chew gum. Then this fragment out of a life's store of memories: "My mother used to give us gum when she had nothing else. Once I asked her what would happen if she had no gum. She told me not to ask her that, ever." An embarrassed further pause. The boy then observes my discomfort, decides to help out. He tells me again how much he likes the wind. I agree. Now we are once more in agreement, so to speak — with respect to gum, no, but with respect to the wind, yes. Then this comment: "If I had a choice, to pick the way I'd die, I'd choose to be carried off by the wind over to the ocean. I'd be made clean twice before I saw His face." The boy saw me turn quizzical at the use of a possessive pronoun. He had figured out my mind's question — a general skepticism finding its expression in a grammatical worry. What is the antecedent Eduardo had in mind? In a quiet voice, a whisper almost, he tells me: "God's face." He has learned after only ten years on earth to stay alive, to master a modern city, to spar with death, even anticipate its arrival, contemplate its many possibilities: a grown mind's moral imagination at work in the continuing life of one of this earth's vulnerable children.

IV

ON CHARACTER

IN the Harvard College of the decade after World War II, Gordon Allport was a significant figure — interested always in connecting the newly influential social sciences to the ethical and religious concerns of earlier social and psychological scholars: William James, of course, and William McDougall, and further back, J. S. Mill or John Locke. I still remember a lecture of Allport's in 1950 in which he stressed the distinction between character and personality. He acknowledged Freud's perceptive, trenchant thrusts into the outer precincts of consciousness, but he reminded us what Freud could afford to ignore about himself and certain others: a moral center that was, quite simply, there. No amount of psychoanalysis, even an interminable stretch of it, Allport cautioned us — drawing on Freud's ideas on human development — can provide a strong conscience to a person who has grown up in such a fashion as to become chronically dishonest, mean-spirited, a liar. "Psychoanalysis can provide insight, can help us overcome inhibitions," we were told, "but it was not meant to be an instrument of 'character building.'" I found recently my old college notes, found that sentence. I had put a big question mark above the phrase "character building," as if to say: What is it, really? I had heard the expression often in the Boy Scouts, in Sunday School, and not least, from my somewhat Puritanical parents. They set great store by virtues they referred to as self-discipline, responsibility, honesty (often described as "the best policy"), and not least, the one my mother most commonly mentioned, "good conduct." Could it be that a social scientist, in the middle of the twentieth century, was mentioning such qualities in a college lecture — was, in fact, asking us to consider how they might be evaluated in people, with some accuracy and consistency?[1]

At that time such efforts were still being made, notably by Robert Havighurst and Hilda Taba and their colleagues at the University of Chicago.[2] But as I got nearer and nearer to becoming a doctor, then a pediatrician, then a child psychiatrist, I heard less and less about "character" and more and more about "character disorders" — elements of psychopathology that many psychoanalysts today connect with the vicissitudes of what is called "psychosexual development."[3] In his early productive years, before he turned fanciful — if not deranged — Wilhelm Reich greatly emphasized what he called "character reactions," the way in which each person works out his or her psychodynamic fate. "In the main," he once said, "character proves to be a narcissistic defense mechanism."[4] No doubt such a generalization can be helpful; we are brought closer to the subliminal workings of the mind, and to its historic necessities of symbolic expression and self-protection, in the face of turmoil generated from within, never mind the stresses that "life" manages to bring. But at some time, even the most factual-minded or dispassionately "rational" of psychoanalytic observers, eager to maintain a "value-free" posture, would be tempted to observe that there is more to the assessment of human beings than an analysis (even one "in-depth") of narcissistic defense mechanisms can provide.

Hitler's mechanisms, Stalin's, those of any number of murderers or thieves, surely offered what Reich called a "character armor" — as do, right now, the mechanisms employed by Mother Teresa's unconscious, and that belonging to Dom Helder of Brazil's Recife, or to such among us in America as Robert Penn Warren or Eudora Welty or, until her death recently, Dorothy Day. At some time the issue becomes decidedly moral — a "normative matter." If I may call upon Gordon Allport again, "character is personality evaluated."

How we go about making that evaluation is a matter of great import. The very word "character" may suggest a prescientific age; may remind us of pietistic avowals or moralistic banalities many of us have tried to put behind us; may bring up the specter of a word being used to protect the privileges of the well-born, the powerful — as if what is at issue is etiquette, polish, a specific appearance or manner of talking and carrying oneself. How much fairer, some say, to judge people through their academic performance, or through standardized tests: no risk of subjectivity, not to mention self-serving partiality. Still, it is not only Emerson, in another age, who suggested that "character is higher than intellect," and who observed that "a great soul will be strong to live, as well as strong to think."[5] In his long lyric poem *Paterson*, William Carlos Williams constantly distinguishes between the intellect (or for that matter, Art) and conduct — how we live our daily lives. And surely, to say it again, a century that has witnessed learned individuals embrace or apologize for Nazism, not to mention intellectuals preach uncritically the virtues of Stalinist totalitarianism, is not going to be completely uninterested in such distinctions as the age-old polarity of knowledge as against wisdom.

In my own working life the question of "character" came up in the early 1960s when my wife and I were getting to know the black children who initiated school desegregation in the South and the young men and women who made up the nonviolent sit-in movement. I remember the clinical appraisals, psychological histories, and socioeconomic comments I wrote then. I remember my continuing effort to characterize those children, those youths — as if one weighty, academically acceptable adjective after another would, in sum, do the job. Ruby was from a "culturally deprived," a "culturally disadvantaged," family. Tessie's grandmother was illiterate. Lawrence was counterphobic, suffering "deep down" from a mixture of anxiety and depression. Martha "projected" a lot. George was prone to "reaction-formations." Jim seemed to have a "character disorder," even a "borderline personality." Fred might well become psychotic later on. Meanwhile, these youthful American citizens were walking past grown men and women who were calling them the foulest of names, who were even threatening to kill them — and such hecklers were escaping sociological and psychological scrutiny in the bargain, while any number of judges were ordering "evaluations" by my kind to be done on sit-in students who were violating the (segregationist) laws, and who were thought to be (and eventually declared by doctors to be) "sick" or "delinquent" or "troubled" or "sociopathic" or "psychopathic." A historic crisis had confronted a region politically, and, in so doing, had ripped open the political, economic, racial aspects of our manner of judging others — the direct connection between those previously mentioned "principalities and powers," and what in our everyday life is "normal" or "proper" behavior. One day, as I mumbled some statements suffused with the words of psychiatric theory to "explain" a child's behavior, my wife said, "You are making her sound as if she ought to be on her way to a child guidance clinic, but she is walking into a school building — and no matter the threats, she is holding her head up high, even smiling at her obscene hecklers. Last night she even prayed for them!" It was my wife's judgment that the six-year-old, Ruby Bridges, whom we have called upon as a witness earlier in this book, was demonstrating character to all the world.

As part of my investigation into the moral lives of children, I asked (in 1980) the principals of two public high schools — George Washington Carver High School in Atlanta and Highland Park High School near Chicago — and one private boarding school, St. Paul's School near Concord, New Hampshire, each to select "two teachers qualified to judge character." These teachers would, in turn, select four or so students who, in their opinion, possessed "character" or "high character." When two of the principals asked what I meant by the word "character," I replied that he had asked precisely what I was trying to find out. I told the principals that I wanted to speak with all the students at once, not individually, at each school; and that I also wanted to meet with the two teachers at each school together.

I went to St. Paul's School first. The headmaster had arranged for two teachers to select four students, and I met the students in a classroom a good distance from the headmaster's office. We were, in a sense, free — no classes, no one to interrupt or keep an eye on what was to be a full morning's discussion. I told the students, two young men and two young women, that I wanted to explore what "character" meant to them, and we were, with no hesitation, off and running.

The word was not a strange one for these students; they had heard it used repeatedly, they said, though none had ever really stopped to think about its meaning. Early in the discussion, one of the young women said, "We talk about 'human nature' or 'personality' or 'identity'; I suppose in the past they talked about 'character.' " These students were quite articulate, as they sifted and sorted among themselves. In no time a whole school was being morally scrutinized: the "jocks," the "beautiful people," the "social butterflies," the "freaks," the "party people," the "grinds," various teachers, and the "goodly heritage," a phrase many who have gone to St. Paul's have heard again and again.

Much time was spent struggling with the question of arrogance, with the temptations of self-importance and self-centeredness — a personal hazard these four were not loath to acknowledge. They were in a school known as one of the best in America. They were, in different ways, doing well there — one academically; one as a scholar-athlete; one as a person trusted and liked by a wide assortment of classmates. Yet they worried that their success was a temptation to "become stuck-up," as one put it. Self-righteousness and self-consciousness were elements likely to shut a person off, making that person less responsive to other people. Gradually, how one responds to others took on high importance. One of the young men put it in this way: "I tend to be a private person. I like to take long walks by myself. At times I don't want company. I want to hold on to my individuality. But I like to be with others, too. I like to be a *friend*. I'd like to think that if someone were in trouble, he'd turn to me, and I'd be there, and I'd put that person's trouble above my needs, including taking a solitary walk!"

Other topics came up frequently: the tension between loyalty to one's friends and loyalty to one's own memories, habits, yearnings; the tension between one's competitive side and one's regard for others; the tension between one's wish to win and one's willingness to help others. The word "honesty" was mentioned over and over — an Augustinian examination, done with today's psychological panache: Who is "really" honest, and for what "underlying" reasons? Moreover, does it "pay" in this society to be honest all the time? When do honesty and self-effacement turn into "masochism"? When does pride in one's convictions turn into bullying egotism? If you really do have "a sense of yourself," are you not in danger of being smug and self-serving? When does popularity reduce one's individuality to the point of belonging only to the herd?

Such questions were asked quite earnestly. When pressed by one another (I ended up being mostly a listener), the students offered lists of the traits that constitute "character": a person who sticks to a set of principles; a person who can risk unpopularity, yet is commanding enough to gain the respect of others; a person who has the courage to be himself, herself; a person who is open-minded, who plays fair with others, who doesn't lie and cheat and, interestingly enough, deceive himself, herself. These students had a decidedly dialectical turn of mind: "You can try to be a better person, but it's a struggle. You can be humble, and that way, intimidate people. You can use humility. It's hard to know what's genuine in people. Sometimes people pretend to be something, but they're really just the opposite. They flip and they flop. I don't like the people who are sanctimonious. They lecture others, and people take it, but it's out of fear or there is guilt, and it's being exploited. Every once in a while, I prefer someone who puts his cards on the table and shows he's a real pain in the neck to these holier-than-thou types. Character doesn't mean being a goody-goody person! If you're that kind of person, there's a lot of meanness, probably, inside you, or competitiveness that you're not letting on about to others. Maybe you don't know about it yourself!"

These youths were, obviously, what we now call psychologically sophisticated. Yet, they were (thank God) not eager to have all human behavior a matter of psychology or psychopathology — or sociology, either: "There are reasons we end up being one kind of person or another kind of person, but when you actually become that person (when you're nice to others most of the time), then that's a true achievement. A lot of people don't become nice, and it's no excuse to say you had a bad childhood or you never had the right luck. I think you have to take your troubles and overcome them!" The Puritan spirit lives still in the woods of southern New Hampshire, no matter how often references were made — and they were many — to "adolescence," "identity," Sigmund Freud's ideas, the latest notions of what "motivates" people, what makes us "anxious" or "strung out" or "ambivalent."

More than anything else, these four youths grappled with what used to be commonly called "the meaning of life" in philosophy lectures. One of the young men said this toward the end of our meeting time: "What matters — don't you think? — is what you do with your life. I've tried to be independent, to have my own thoughts, but to listen to others. I hope to live comfortably, but I won't be greedy and selfish. I don't know what our responsibilities are — to ourselves and our friends and family and neighbors, and to others in places abroad I'll never even see. Even today, this is a big world. What are we supposed to do? We're lucky to be here at St. Paul's. We have such a good life. What do we owe others? Isn't that 'character' — what you decide to do for others, not just for yourself?"

The "great suck of self," Walker Percy calls it in *The Second Coming* — the inevitable pull toward our own thoughts, our own wishes, our navels. Adolescence is not the only period of self-absorption, as these youths seemed already to know. For them, one is likely to be neither bad nor good. For them, character was no rigid, categorical trait. For them, character is not a possession, but something one searches for: a quality of mind and heart one struggles for, at times with a bit more success than at others. Not one of these four students wanted to spell out a definition, set down a compulsory series of attributes, offer a list of candidates. One heard from their mouths expressions of confusion, annoyance, vanity, self-satisfaction, self-criticism, self-doubt, self-assurance. One heard, maybe most of all, tentativeness — reluctance to speak definitively about an aspect of human behavior one student kept describing as "hard to pin down," but also as "important to consider when you're thinking about someone."

The two teachers I met at St. Paul's School, a middle-aged man who taught math, a young woman who taught English, had met, discussed the subject of "character," and added to one another's notions, so that, in the end, a written statement was available:

— The aggregate of distinctive qualities belonging to an individual.

— Moral vigor or firmness, especially as acquired through self-discipline.

— The ability to respond to a setback.

— The ability to form an attachment to ideals of a larger community or organization than oneself, and to exert one's influence for the good of the greater body.

— The possession of a sense of humor that allows one to see that there is more to life than living.

— The ability to be an individual in a crowd of people.

— A sense of self that has been found through experience.

— The ability to allow others to be individuals, even though they may be different.

— The ability to disagree with others without condemning (or losing respect for) the individual one disagrees with.

— A sensitivity toward the feelings of others.

— An understanding of the wholeness of other people's person-
alities or character (even when it is different from one's own).

These two teachers had thought long and hard about a vexing
subject — whom to choose for my interviews, and why? A very
bright person, involved in many activities, able to speak coherently
and easily, headed straight for Harvard? A quiet person who defers
to the ideas of others in a classroom, does well, but "not all that
well," yet often seems to reach out for others, not to save them,
but simply "to do a good turn"? A marvelous athlete who also is a
leader in many ways during a school year? A hardworking youth
who is most often self-effacing, yet has managed to stand up once
or twice on a matter of ethical principle?

In Highland Park, north of Chicago, a somewhat different arrangement had been made. The principal of this suburban high
school had selected two teachers, as I requested, but they had picked
four students each — seven girls and one boy. We met in a room
across the hall from the principal's office. Twice the principal asked
how we were doing, offered water, tea, coffee — in general, showed
a distinct, active interest in our discussions. He himself had thought
about the word "character," and as with so many of us, found it a
bit puzzling and elusive. So too did the students with whom I spent
a winter morning. Several of them said that character had a lot to
do with personality; in fact, declared "a good personality" or "well-
rounded person" to be equivalent descriptions to "good character"
or "high character." Two young women dissented, however: "Character has to do with honesty. You can be popular, and have a shrink's
seal of approval, but not have character!"

We fairly quickly got into a discussion of ethnic and racial tensions — in the school, in our society as a whole. At St. Paul's it had
been the cliques that seemed to threaten individuality, hence character. At Highland Park High School these students seemed to view
social divisions as having to do with class and race: Italians and Jews,
"working people" and "wealthier people," blacks and whites.

I was given some outspoken lessons in how family life affects one's situation in school, and not least, one's character: "It all depends on who you are! Some kids want to go to an Ivy League school; that's all that's on their minds. They put up a good front, to show they have 'character'; they join clubs, and have all these hobbies and interests, so as to impress the teachers and the people who read college applications. Some kids have to work while going to school. They try to get a good deal, a job that pays well. They're making contacts even now for later on. It's built into their 'character' that the world is tough, and you have to know people to get ahead. A lot of the black kids are here because there's a military base in the school district. They come and then they go. It's hard to figure them out. It's in their 'character' to stay away from us whites. There's a lot of tension among us whites. Go into the johns, and you'll see a lot of writing! [I went, and I saw the ethnic slurs in both the men's rooms and the ladies' rooms.] But a lot of the time we get along pretty well. We've got brainy ones here, headed for college since they were born, and don't get in their way, or else! We've got kids who will work in a store or factory, and not be ashamed. They see the world differently. They take different courses. They have their own code."

The speaker is a wry, outspoken, somewhat detached young woman, bound for college, but "not a fancy one." She is neither Italian nor Jewish, but Anglo-Irish. She had made a virtue out of marginality, and the others in the room seemed a bit deferential: "She isn't pushed around by anyone. She's her own person. She can mingle with anyone. She doesn't put on airs with anyone." The associations moved relentlessly from social situation to moral conduct — not the first time, or the last. "You have to know where the person is coming from," I was told several times. Explain! "Well, if you've got a lot going for you, then you can be more relaxed. True, you can be a tightwad and be rich; but it's easier to be generous if you've got a lot behind you!" On the other hand, one student insisted, "there's still room for being poor and good in this world!" She persisted: "I know some kids, right in this school, and they're not here now, they weren't chosen to be here, and they're from pretty poor families, compared to others; their fathers just get by, make a living. And they would give you the shirt off their backs, those kids: that's character. And they wouldn't go talking about what they've done, bragging, and showing off — that's character! Some people, they know how to play up to the teachers, and they get a big reputation, but what's the truth about them? What are they like when no one is looking, and what are they like when no one is listening?"

We went round and round. Class and character. Egotism and character. Psychology and character. Smartness and character. Motivation and character. Caring and character. Manners and character. To be stuck-up. To be considerate. To be a help when a person needs help — a flat tire, a car ride, a pencil or piece of paper, a loan of money, a sympathetic ear. To take risks, extend oneself to others, brave social pressures. Grade-mongers. Leaders and followers. Hypocrites. People who have one or another veneer. The "way-down-deep truth" of a person. A final test of character: sickness, financial straits, a disaster. Character and mental health.

Part of *Ordinary People* had been made in Highland Park. The students had watched the filming, and they wondered: If one is hurt, bewildered, "seeing a shrink," can one have the "mental peace" to demonstrate character? Can one escape consumerism, selfishness — develop "an ability not to be absorbed with objects?" And at some interesting and suggestive length: literature as a means of understanding character, as in *To Kill a Mockingbird* (Atticus had character, he was open-minded, stood up for what he believed, no matter the risks and costs, and so was a "moral man"); or as in *Macbeth* (Lady Macbeth was a "bad person," a "bad character"). And politics: Lincoln and Eisenhower and Truman had character; Johnson lacked it, as do Nixon and Carter. "All politicians probably lie," one student observed, "and maybe all people do, but some just keep on lying, and you can't trust them, and you don't like them, and they're just no damn good, and you can tell, after a while, even if they tell you they pray every other minute! The truth about a person's character eventually comes out, eventually."

Such faith was not universally shared. There was much talk of appearance as against reality: the way people present themselves to others, as opposed to some inner truth about each of us. In contrast to the students at St. Paul's School, these Highland Park students were distinctly more interested in the relationship between a person's social, economic, ethnic, or racial background — and that person's behavior, hence character. And it did come down to that, they all agreed at the end: "You are the way you act — in the long run." What did that qualification mean? Well, it goes like this: "Some people can put on an act. But if you keep your wits, and keep an eye on them, you can find out the truth about them. If they're good people, kind to others, not just wrapped up in themselves, you'll find it out. If they're putting on a production, you'll find that out." No one, in that regard, seemed to have any doubts about his or her ultimate psychological acuity — or about the long-run dramatic capacities of one or another individual.

There was, as we were ending, a spirited, occasionally tense discussion of tests, grades, the criteria used by colleges and graduate schools to evaluate people. "I know kids who get all A's and would murder their parents, their brothers and sisters, if they stood in their way," one youth offered. Yes, but there's plenty of nastiness to go around, others said, even among those who do poorly in school. What should committees of admission do? How does one make a fairly accurate moral judgment about a person? Numerical rankings may not tell enough. Multiple-choice questions may not do justice to life's strangeness, the complexities and inconsistencies and contradictions with which we all struggle, though some with more decency and integrity and generosity of spirit than others. But how do we arrive at an estimate of a person's essential kindness toward others — in the face of thousands of importunate applicants, each putting on the very best faces possible? Don't interviews have their hazards, the unpredictable variations of mood and temperament,

The Drawings

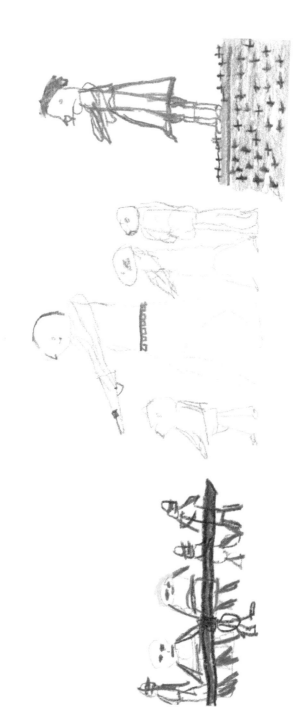

Figure 1 (p. 108)

Figure 2 (p. 121)

Figure 3 (p. 233)

Figure 4
(p. 262)

the nuances of subjectivity that can, alas, of a sudden, amount to outright prejudice? We ended on an eclectic note — the desirability of taking a lot into consideration when accepting people for a job, a place in college, and, yes, when judging that elusive concept "character." The last person to leave the room, the young woman who spoke least, said that she thought "character meant being kind and good, even when there was no one to reward you for being kind and good."

The Highland Park teachers, like their students, were acutely aware of the divisions in this society. Actually, the teachers were themselves a bit split. The assistant principal, a man, was quite in touch with the more academic students of the school; whereas the woman teacher was very much involved with those students who were working at jobs while trying to get through Highland Park — headed, mostly, for what many social scientists would call "service jobs," or membership in the "working class," or the "lower-middle to middle-middle class." The two did not argue, however; in fact, they mostly echoed the sentiments of their chosen students: "Grades aren't the whole story, by any means"; and very emphatically, "Character has something to do with moral life."

Both teachers worried about class — expressed concern, for instance, that "mere etiquette" can deceive, or insisted that human scoundrels, like wolves, find sheepskins ("social veneer") to wear. I had heard practically nothing about class-connected deceit at St. Paul's, but I heard a lot about it at Highland Park — and character seemed to require, teachers and students agreed, an absence of such a tendency. Moreover, psychiatry and psychoanalysis were even more prominently mentioned at Highland Park than at St. Paul's — a way of getting to the "deeper truth" about people, hence to a judgment of their character. Disturbed people were described as less likely to show high character. When I mentioned Gandhi's personal eccentricities, his moments of cruelty, vanity, thoughtlessness, the students were ready, all too ready, to take the clue, the hint, and write him off as sick. When I reminded them that he was, nonetheless, an impressive moral leader, the students worried about the burdens placed on his family, and about his own psychiatric burdens.

If I had a little trouble persuading this group of students and their teachers that, neurosis or no neurosis, a person's moral motives can affect his or her character, they had no trouble persuading me that a neighborhood, a level of income, the possession of a given nationality, can all affect a person's character. The teachers especially emphasized the distinction between the quietly considerate person, as against the demonstrative, if not flamboyant, performer of public good deeds. "Some students want to get an A in character, too," one teacher said, as we broke off, a reminder that not only can life be unfair, but virtue can be unfairly perceived — when, in truth, sins are being shrewdly masked. As Flannery O'Connor observed, through the comic irony of a title to one of her stories, a good man is hard to find.

At George Washington Carver High School, in Atlanta, I had quite another discussion, with the principal ready to point out the extreme hazards to what he called "character formation" well before I saw (in a room that belonged, really, to his office suite) the four children (two boys and two girls) and two teachers (both women, one who teaches math, the other, biology). "There is a problem with drugs," he explained. "There is a problem with poverty, with terrible poverty, with welfare homes, with absent fathers, with unemployment all over the place." He gave me a lively lecture on the school's history — once a "dumping ground for school failures," now a "place of hope," much connected to businesses that offer promising black youths a great variety of jobs, a chance "to enter the mainstream." In time I was able to begin talking with the four selected youths, though not before being told emphatically: "Character is something you have to build, right here is this school, every day. You have to lay down the law, and see that it's enforced. Character means discipline and hard work and looking to the future and getting there!" Of the three school leaders, Carver's principal was the only one to volunteer (or hazard) such an explication.

The students were averse to this line of reasoning. These were young people who were determined to find jobs, determined to be hard workers, strong parents — and not reluctant to explain why such a commitment was connected to a definition, in their minds, of the word "character": "A lot of us, even here, with the principal and the teachers bearing down every minute on us, have trouble reading and writing. We're not going to college, most of us. We're going to try to get a job and hold on to it! It takes character, I think, to do that — not take the easy way out and drink or use drugs or say the white man is on our backs, so what the devil can we do! To me, character is being stubborn. It's staying in there, it's getting out of a hole, and breathing the fresh air, and not falling down any more."

My wife and I had spent three years in Atlanta, talking with youths such as these — young black men and women trying, in the face of adversity, to forge a better life for themselves.[6] These were more outspoken and self-assured individuals than the ones we had known in the early 1960s. They were quick to describe themselves as "job-hungry" and as full of determination, willfulness, hopeful anticipation. They were not, though, uninterested in some of the refinements of psychology I had heard discussed in New Hampshire and Illinois: "There's success and success. It's not only getting there, it's *how* you get there. If you have character, that means you keep trying, no matter how hard it is, and you don't lose your soul while you're doing that. You have to say to yourself, 'I'll go so far and no farther.' You have to draw the line, and if you do, and you can hold to it, you've got character." Nods all around, followed by smiles of recognition as the temptations are mentioned: white devils and black devils who offer serious distractions in the form of drugs and booze, bribes and payoffs, an assortment of "tricks." These street-smart kids have lots of savvy about Atlanta politics, Atlanta vice, Atlanta hypocrisy, black and white alike. Their moralism and self-conscious, urgently stated rectitude is hard earned, yet not entirely invulnerable, and they seem to know it on both counts.

One pushes the word "character," gets responses that are connected to hardship, ambition, the requirements of people living on the edge. They show little interest in metaphysical or metapsychological speculation. Character? Why, J.R. in *Dallas* lacks it, utterly; Dr. King had it, that's for sure. Character? A lot of big shots may seem to have it, but too bad more people don't know who is scratching whose back. There's a woman who works in a Howard Johnson's motel, and she lost her husband from cancer, and she has five kids, and she has two of them out of high school and in good jobs, and the other three are headed that way, and she doesn't stand for any foolishness, none, and she takes those kids to church every Sunday, and they pray hard and long, and she has character, in case anyone wants to know! Not in a school that bears the name of St. Paul, and not in a school where Catholics and Jews seem ready to square off at each other all day, every day; but in Carver we heard about the church. Each of these four high-school-age Americans goes to church on Sundays, and if there is reluctance sometimes (the joy of a late sleep), there is, after all, no real choice: "We have to go. Our mother says we have to go, and once we're there, I don't half mind! I like it there. I'll make my kids go, too."

Much talk of "uplift." Much reference to "building" oneself into "a stronger person," getting "on the map." How? There are auto repair shops. There are radio and television repair shops. There are cosmetology shops. There are dry-cleaning shops. There are tailoring and sewing and shoe repair places. There is a big airport, and people work there — on engines if they are on top, otherwise as cleaning people or doing errands, or driving buses and taxis, "lots of things." If you get one of those jobs, and you hold on to it; if you get yourself a girlfriend or a boyfriend, and they become a wife or a husband, and you become a father or a mother, and you "stay with it," and are good to your family, earn them a living, take care of them; if you remain loyal to your church, and pray to God when you're weak; if you don't forget your people, and try to lend a hand to the ones who didn't make it, who stumbled and fell and are hurt and sad and who are wondering what the point of it all is, and maybe have done wrong, done it too many times — if all that is "inscribed on your soul," then, by God, you have character, and it's important to say "by God," because it's "His grace that does things."

"I'm not as small after church as I am before church," one of these four told me. As for "good manners," they aren't superficial at all; they tell of something very deep down, no matter what so-called depth psychologists have to say, not to mention those who make of them religious figures: "You can tell a person by how he speaks to you. If he's respectful, then he's good; if he gives you the shoulder, then he's bad. I don't care if someone has a lot of bad in him. If he keeps it a secret from the whole world, then he's 'way out front. If he shows his bad self to everyone, he's putting it on us, man, and it's hard enough without that — another hassle to deal with. My grandmother tells us: 'Keep your mouth shut if there's no good to come out of it. Keep your mischief to yourself. We've all got it — but some of us don't show it off.' She's right; she has character."

Some other virtues that bespeak character are punctuality; how you carry yourself; an ability to laugh, when there's a good excuse for crying or shouting or shaking your fists; how you speak — with clear enunciation of words, so that others may hear you; self-respect, as measured by neatness and choice of clothes, as well as respect for others, as measured by a smile, a please, a thank you; obedi-ence — to your elders, to the law, to your own self-evident ideas of what is right and wrong. "We all stray," said one of the young women, "but if we try hard not to keep repeating ourselves, and if we're not afraid to learn from our mistakes, and if we're willing to work hard, and sacrifice, then we have character."

The two Atlanta teachers were tough-minded, outspoken, a touch contemptuous of anyone wanting to offer sympathy, never mind condolences. They were demanding, insistent, forceful women: "Let these kids work hard, and better themselves, and be good members of their families, and they'll show character; that's how, the only way!" They spoke candidly, bluntly, unapologetically: "We chose the best we have to talk with you. We chose the smart ones, the ones who could talk with you and get themselves across. We have others here who would tax your patience and understanding. Maybe they have 'character,' too. I don' think character is the property of the lucky and the smart and the successful, no sir. But to me, character means an active person, who is ready to face the world, and make a mark on it. That's why I chose these kids. They're ready, they're ready to turn their backs on all their troubles and be good — be full of action. 'Never be lazy,' I tell my kids at home, and here in school. There's that expression: going to meet 'the man.' Well, I say we can become 'the man' ourselves. We can take control of our own lives, be our own masters. It may be preachy of me to talk like this, but we've got to pep-talk ourselves, and then get on with it! I pray to God — we need His help badly — that more and more of these kids at Carver will get on with it."

On the way home, back North again, I took out my books and papers: notes to write, ideas to savor, comparisons to make.[7] They made me remember the wonderful message that Kierkegaard gave us more than a century ago: "Morality is character, character is that which is engraved (χαράσσοω); but the sand and the sea have no character, and neither has abstract intelligence, for character is really inwardness. Immorality, as energy, is also character; but to be neither moral nor immoral is merely ambiguous, and ambiguity enters into life when the qualitative distinctions are weakened by a gnawing reflection."[8]

He was a great one for leaps, the nineteenth-century version of Hamlet, the melancholy Dane. I wondered on my flight home whether Kierkegaard might somewhere in this universe be smiling, be assenting to the message, the slightly hectoring statement delivered by that mathematics teacher, and later by her tough, occasionally very tough, principal, who told me that he had "a lot of bad characters" to deal with, but damned if he couldn't "take them on," "turn them around," "convert their wasted energy into useful energy." It all sounded slightly like the noise of strained braggadocio: I'll talk big, and hope for the best. It all sounded exaggerated, romantic — like Kierkegaard. It all sounded pretty good, though, to those four young people and two of their teachers.

V

YOUNG IDEALISM

Aɴɴᴀ Fʀᴇᴜᴅ in a letter warned against an inclination she had observed in the 1960s "to idealize idealism in the young."[1] She was not playing with words: "There is no reason to gloss over the emotional conflicts which dispose some young people to become full of self-sacrifice. In psychoanalysis we know that the most generous and self-denying people can be the ones who are struggling the hardest with their own desires. I am, I realize, not saying anything that is new, or hasn't been emphasized in our field for over half a century, but I still find it surprising when a colleague is unwilling to turn over the coin, as we say, and look at what is *not* so obvious. It is not only our patients, I am sure, who struggle with alternations of greed and asceticism, and who sometimes make even the beneficiaries of their good deeds feel puzzled by the intensity of their moral life."

I sent Miss Freud a description of a young man I had come to know in working alongside the civil rights activists of the 1960s.[2] I had kept in touch with this exceptionally earnest, decent, hardworking man, and had found him to be almost provocatively persistent in his quiet, dedicated, unostentatious willingness to sacrifice what I saw as his own life's interests in favor of trying to further the aspirations of others. Here is a drastic condensation of his words, spoken in April 1972: "You're right, I'm twenty-six, and that means I'm not eighteen. But you mention my age as if you're a judge, and

you're ready to remind me that my parole is going to be ended
soon, if I don't watch out! If I told you I was leaving here [a town
in the southern part of Georgia] for Atlanta, and I was going back
to school, maybe law school, you'd have a look of pleasure on your
face. You'd say that I was shaping up at last, that I was *growing* up
at last, that I'd finished one of your psychological 'periods,' and now
I was 'mature,' or about to be whatever that word means.

"That's what I want to know, what *does* it mean to be 'mature' ?
Do you stop asking that, when you become a professional man, like
you — who is supposed to have the answers, all the answers in his
well-trained head? I know (you're right) that I'm taking a psychological risk — because the older I get, the harder it'll be to leave
here, and go back to school, or to get a job in some company, or
teaching in a school down South, or maybe, back North. But the
truth is, it's never me, talking to myself, who wants to leave here.
It's always someone else — people who come visit me, or write me
letters. They all are family or friends, and they all say they're only
trying to be 'helpful,' but sometimes I wonder if it's *me* they want
to help, or *themselves!*

"One of my oldest friends — he's now a lawyer in a big-deal New
York City law firm — came down here to visit me. He wanted to
introduce me to his wife, and he wanted to tell me about our roommate, who got killed in a car accident on the old Merritt Parkway
in Connecticut. We had a nice time. They were very moved by all
the hospitality the people had shown them. We should have stayed
here, and not gone to Atlanta 'to get away.' I'm not here because I
love the poverty! I'm here to work against the forces that keep the
poverty unchanged. So, I was the one who suggested we drive up
to Atlanta and spend a day or so there. It's an interesting ride, and
besides, I wanted to have a few good meals in those Atlanta restaurants. Here it's hamburgers and cheeseburgers and french fries
and Coca-Cola, and lots of days, I just eat to keep going.

"When we got to Atlanta we were all different people. Even
before, the change had started. My friend started noticing those

'pretty homes,' those so-called antique shops — lots of them phony, I thought. His wife wanted to stop everywhere to 'pick up' this, or 'look at' that, to the point that I was getting to dislike her — even though I'd already decided, before we left, that I liked her a lot. Then, there were the incidents with the people we met — the waitresses and the store folks. My friends were used to being waited on, right away, and they were used to *getting* people to wait on them, right away, if there's a wait. So, that's what happened: they'd make it clear that they wanted someone to wait on them — and I'd go crazy. I'd be ready to choke them! But I'd say nothing, not a word. And the result was — as you can imagine — lots of silence on my part. I just kept wishing we'd never left home. In fact, I remember thinking: the southwestern towns of Georgia *are* my home, and these people aren't friends coming from my home; they're old friends who are beginning to seem like strangers — because I'm at home here, and they aren't, and the differences between the way they think and act and the way I think and act are driving us apart, 'way apart!

"It got a little better in Atlanta for a while. I guess I was happy to see all those tall buildings, and feel the fast pace of life there. I don't really know if that's why I *was* happy, or whether I was desperate, because of our drive — what had happened — and so ready to try anything to prevent a disaster, even a fight. All I know is that we checked into a fancy hotel, and I decided I wanted to take a long, long bath, not one of those fast, efficient showers. I wanted to sit, and to think! I wanted to soak in the hot water (it's not so easy to come by where I live!), but I also wanted to think, and I mean think, plenty hard. So, I told them I was tired and I needed to take a nap — just after we had breakfast. My friend had snapped his fingers at a waitress, and she didn't seem to mind at all, and they got on nice, actually, but I was furious, and then right afterward, I got depressed, the usual sequence! Then they both had to have the *New York Times*, and you'd have thought they were heroin addicts facing the possibility that there might, there just might not be a fix nearby. I suggested the *Wall Street Journal* because a stack of them was right there on display. They bought one, but that wasn't enough, so they asked, and they were told that they'd have to wait for a few hours, and you would have thought the world had come to an end. I tried to joke with them. I said there was television in the rooms, and that TV news is the most up-to-date. I said the Atlanta papers carry *New York Times* stories and columns. But it was like offering ice cream and cookies to drug addicts: they weren't interested. They said they were going to look elsewhere, and that's when I bowed out with my story of feeling exhausted, and went upstairs. 'Are you all right?' When they asked me that, I could hear my answer, but I never spoke it: 'I was, until you two came to visit me!'

"I sat there in that tub and thought about my life. I thought about the past, and I thought about the present; and I sure thought a lot about the future. I asked myself what kind of a person I really was. It was funny, sweating in that hot, hot bath. I got distracted, every once in a while, by the comfort — the hot water itself, the smell of the luxury soap oil, the soft, thick facecloths and towels, the huge tub. I'd ordered some coffee from room service, and I just sat there, drinking and thinking — a real plutocrat! Most of all, I asked myself: are you an honest person, or are you a faker, a hypocrite? Are you pretending to do some work for the poor, but really putting on a show, to impress others, or are you really putting your life on the line, because that's what you want to do, and where you are is where you want to be?

"How do you ever get the right answer to those kinds of questions? I sat there trying to say the truth. I was actually talking out loud. The maid knocked on the door, and I was startled, then I was afraid they were coming to get me and take me away to a mental hospital! But I realized she was just doing her job — to see if the room was ready to be cleaned. I just went on talking — as if my conscience was one person and my mind that weighs things, sifts them through, was another person. Maybe there are two or three more people

inside me, for all I know: my dad, who is a judge — and it's hard
not to hear *his* voice, if you're one of his four sons; and my mom,
who is always trying to help people out, but she has a pretty good
life up there in New England; and my old girlfriend, who left me
(left here!) because she just couldn't take this life any more.

"Don't ask me what I decided. You use the word 'conclude'; you
ask 'What did you conclude?' I'm not the kind of person who knows
how to answer a question like that! Have you ever thrown it at
yourself, and people who work nine to five in banks and insurance
offices and law firms? Have you ever asked them to think about
their lives, and 'conclude' something? I'm sorry! I don't mean to be
testy! I feel on the defensive — and I did that morning. I was ready
to decide that I'd been living in Georgia too long, and the time had
come to leave, to take a long, long furlough.

"It's a war, fighting sheriffs and cops and crooked county com-
missioners, and the one or two rich businessmen who really call the
shots in any town. I've found myself pressuring them and threatening them and bargaining with them, and I've begun to see that
I'm not completely different from them — no sir! I enjoy pushing
them, and kidding with them — the give-and-take of being a small-
town power broker! I get a little something for 'my people,' and I
go back and tell them what I got, and why I couldn't get one more
thing, not one more, and they look up to me as if I am God Almighty.
And it isn't only because I'm white and they're black. I've seen black
organizers like myself strut around just as proudly — and get plenty
of adulation. We're smart ones! We've gone to college. We know
how to talk straight with those big shots, and we can command their
grudging respect, and why wouldn't a poor black tenant farmer, or
a black who washes the floor of a store and cleans the seats in a
church — why shouldn't all the blacks in the country be grateful as
can be about what we do for them?

"Sitting there in the tub I was trying to find out what I'm doing
for *myself!* What are your motives, Jimmie boy, I kept asking. To
tell you the truth, I couldn't come up with *any!* I drew a cold blank!

I kept speaking out loud to myself, and I still couldn't hear myself say anything — other than a lot of the usual stuff: to help the poor, and to live up to my ideals. Okay, I said, what *are* those ideals? I was a schoolboy, by then, reciting: giving so that you'll receive; loving, so that you'll receive love; following the teachings of Jesus, even if it hurts — all the Sunday school lessons I could remember, especially the Sermon on the Mount and the Prayers of St. Francis of Assisi, both of which my mother and father used to mention all the time at home.

"But I'm not Jesus or St. Francis, that's for sure! I'm a guy who likes to stay in a nice room in the Hyatt Regency Hotel, and likes nice food, and nice clothes. I like to travel, too. When I was in college I dreamed of going to Europe every summer — each time a different country. And look where I ended up, for six summers in a row! It's so damned hot down here in July and August, and the humidity is awful. I'd never think of buying an air conditioner, because none of the people I work with have one. They don't seem to mind it; I do. There are days when I'm not even lusting after a woman in my head, but just sitting or lying still and thinking how great it would be to have one small air conditioner, that I could fit in a window and then plug in. Once I lost control. I told a couple of friends — two black mothers who work with me — how much I'd like to have an air conditioner. Do you know what? I heard they were going to take up a collection to get me one! Oh God, I had to stop *that,* fast! I knew I had to lie! I knew I did! I had to 'save face,' as they'd say in Asia, and I had to 'save face' for them, too! I told them I was allergic to air conditioning! When I heard myself saying that, I decided I was really mixed up. I began to wonder then what in hell I was doing, and who was fooling whom in that little town!

"But there, in Atlanta, I decided I wasn't a nut, not really. I remembered all our struggles, all our losses — but our victories, too. We 've become an important part of that county. People listen to us — and I mean poor black people, never mind the rich white ones! I love the people I work with; I think they're fond of me.

What more can you ask? Well, I can answer that: a wife, children, and 'a regular job,' My mother, who taught me a lot of the 'idealism' I'm supposed to have (she was always telling us 'idealism is important'), *my mother* is the one who wrote me a letter a year ago and told me she was praying for me, in church, that I 'find myself,' and that I 'get a regular job.' I wonder what Jesus said, listening to her prayers! I felt like writing her back and asking her if Jesus ever held 'a regular job' — or ever 'found Himself.' Jesus, the migrant preacher, who became so unpopular and disturbing to everyone big and important that He got crucified! It's amazing how we use Christianity these days — to help us become real solid burghers! I don't usually think of God as getting a laugh out of our shenanigans, but when I got that letter from my mother I thought again that God must find us all pretty funny.

"Anyway, I got out of the tub, telling myself I was going to stay a little longer down here — maybe until I'm thirty, I don't know. Why 'until thirty'? I was being ironic. That's supposed to be the magic cut-off year! We're allowed to be odd, off the beaten track, until then, aren't we! Maybe when I *do* turn thirty, I'll write home and tell my mother that I *have* found 'a regular job,' and this is it, right here. She doesn't even dare write me about her *other* worry! I know it, though. It's mine, too: how do you meet a girl you might want to marry if you're a white upper-middle-class kid, who's gone to Harvard, and yet you're here, spending all your time with poor black people, and the only two other white people are a married couple, and sure, you have girls you know all over, from New Orleans to Nashville to Atlanta to Florida to Washington and parts north, but that's just it: they're all over the place, and not right here with you. One girl I used to like 'back home' came to visit me, and I'll tell you, she freaked out after the glow of being Lady White Bountiful began to wear off. Listen to me talking! You get harsh and cynical being an idealist!"

I was eager for Miss Freud to read this young man's statements because I had always been impressed with his courage, his candor, his intelligence, his competence as a political activist and community organizer, his steady capacity for self-observation, and not least, his considerable sense of humor. Perhaps he made *me* anxious and apprehensive about my own values, not to mention social attitudes, economic viewpoint. I kept having the fantasy that *he* would be helped, were he to talk with one or another of the psychoanalysts I knew and admired — an old supervisor in Boston, a good friend in Atlanta, and especially, Miss Freud herself, who had, after all, maintained a long interest in the psychological vicissitudes of altruism. In her most influential book, *The Ego and the Mechanisms of Defense*,[3] she devoted a chapter to "A Form of Altruism," and another to a powerful evocation of the mental life of young people, buffeted as they are by the turmoil of the adolescent years. One of the best-known passages in that book goes as follows:

Adolescents are excessively egoistic, regarding themselves as the center of the universe and the sole object of interest, and yet at no time in later life are they capable of so much self-sacrifice and devotion. They form the most passionate love relations, only to break them off as abruptly as they began them. On the one hand, they throw themselves enthusiastically into the life of the community and, on the other, they have an overpowering longing for solitude. They oscillate between blind submission to some self-chosen leader and defiant rebellion against any and every authority. They are selfish and materially minded and at the same time full of lofty idealism. They are ascetic but will suddenly plunge into instinctual indulgence of the most primitive character. At times their behavior to other people is rough and inconsiderate, yet they themselves are extremely touchy. Their moods veer between light-hearted optimism and the blackest pessimism. Sometimes they will work with indefatigable enthusiasm and at other times they are sluggish and apathetic.

For the young man whose words appear above, whom I had known since his own adolescence had by no means ended, the "lofty idealism" never seemed to yield, even with the approach of age thirty. Nor did the apparent capacity for "self-sacrifice and devotion." Many times, as I noticed those two qualities, yet again, in this person, I began to wonder whether he wouldn't end up, in the sum total of his life, refuting Miss Freud's comment that "at no time in later life" are we capable of showing so much of such inclinations. Several times during her various American visits I discussed with her the subject of altruism and idealism in the young. Eventually we talked about this youth. Always Miss Freud cautioned against regarding the young man's outbursts of anger as necessarily "pathological"; and too, she shunned that word as a suitable one to explain his willingness to endure relative isolation, loneliness, a low standard of living. Even the obvious moodiness I reported did not deter her from the following comments, made as we sat at Yale University's School of Medicine in 1971: "I have never been in your South, but I would imagine the stresses on these men and women are quite severe. I assume you have asked yourself why such people have sought out such a situation for themselves, and continue living as they do. I am sure that in each person's life you can find the reasons — but that holds for all of us, doesn't it! There are satisfactions to be found in helping others — and conflicts are thereby solved, at least temporarily. No, I am not saying that these young people are specially conflicted. No, I would have to see them for some time, and compare their difficulties to those we all carry with us through life.

"I have seen some professional people — nurses and social workers and doctors — whose lives are constantly stressful, and I would say, *sacrificial* in nature: they give of themselves all the time to others, and the rest of us are somewhat perplexed, or in awe, or made to feel skeptical or even angry, as if we're receiving a moral rebuke in the nature of an example — lives being lived so honorably and with such concern for others. Perhaps our response tells us something — that there is an element at work of pleasurable self-righteousness which aims to accuse the rest of us. But I know some young people whose idealism seems quite honest and humble — not intended as a rebuke to others, merely as an expression of their own interests and concerns. In these cases, I think there is an interesting psychological (no, I did not say psycho-pathological!)

process at work: the young man, the young woman becomes 'one' with the people being 'helped.' This is a complicated psychological development, as you know, and involves several of the ego's mechanisms of defense — identification and projection, for example. I have worked with several people who have been able to immerse themselves in the lives of others, do an excellent job of attending their needs as doctors, lawyers, nurses, social workers, and not become resentful or bitter or moralistic — a sign that there isn't as much 'sacrifice' on their part as you or I might be tempted to suppose. On the contrary, there are considerable satisfactions: the person is laboring hard, of course, but manages to be healing himself, or herself, because those being assisted include the one who is also doing the assisting."

Miss Freud's shrewd observations made me go back to examine once more the conversations I had recorded with a number of politically active youths in the American South. Here, for instance, is what the above-quoted young man said on his thirtieth birthday: "It was just another day for me. You can't take birthdays too seriously here — because the people themselves don't. They have a tough time, and they keep going. They're not self-centered enough to dwell on birthdays and anniversaries and memories of this and memories of that — not the way we do. They don't wake up on their birthdays expecting a tableful of presents, and later, some fancy cake and ice cream, and maybe flowers. These are people who are lucky to have a hearty meal once a day. They're used to lots of fat and lots of starch and lots of sugar. The diabetic you talked with — well, after you left she asked me how she was going to be able to afford the kind of low-carbohydrate, high-protein diet you kept telling her she should go on. She can't afford to go buy the lean meat you mentioned; she buys 'streak-o-lean,' which is mostly fat, with a sliver of meat running through it.

"I used to hate the very sight of that 'streak-o-lean.' I felt like vomiting — but I couldn't let on; I tried to smile when I saw the stuff. One day I was invited for supper at a tenant farmer's house.

I hoped and prayed they'd serve me corn and tomatoes and french fries and bread and Coke, and maybe a donut. I'd seen them eat that again and again. But would you believe it — they got 'streak-o-lean' because *I* was coming: to give me some meat. 'Streak-o-lean' in my honor! Well, I said my prayers, the way I used to do when I was a kid, and I sat there and ate it all up, and then I asked for seconds! I just decided that people have gone through awful things in this world — so much misery and torture and concentration camps; and so it damn well wouldn't hurt me to eat what was given me, and be grateful to be there, having a good time with such good and decent and generous people.

"In a matter of months the strangest changes took place in my eating habits. I began to *like* 'streak-o-lean,' and *like* all that fried, starchy food. I once asked myself if I was conning myself, but I had to conclude that I wasn't doing that. I don't know how to describe it — but I've become immersed in this life, in the lives of the people I work with. I feel part of their existence. I really miss them when I leave; it's as if a big part of me is gone, and I'm floundering and helpless. When I come back, I see not only 'them,' I see myself: I'm reunited with what has become my life — me here working with people and getting a lot from them, not just trying to be of help to them. I went up to Atlanta once, to get catalogues from Emory, and to look around for a place to live. I thought I'd try graduate school; I thought I'd work myself out of the South, back to New England, in stages: first Altanta, then a leap North. But I didn't last but a couple of days. I wanted to go back to south Georgia. I was homesick! I missed my friends, my own small community of people here! I don't blame you for looking closely at me! Sometimes I'm confused myself about why I feel like this! When I was driving back it all of a sudden came to me: I've put my whole life into this work, into these families, these men and women and children I live with and try to teach. But remember, they teach me, too — and to leave them would be to leave a lot of myself. It would be like starting in all over again as a person!"

He went much further, acknowledged his seemingly "mystical involvement with this community," then apologized for using such an expression. But he was entitled to be respected for his judgment about himself, and a year later, as Miss Freud heard the remarks above, and more along those lines, she was inclined to nod with deference and agreement: "There are young men and women who become, in their minds, so identified with certain people [that] their sacrifices and personal renunciations are felt to be pleasurable — because meant for themselves as well as others! When this man tells you he feels 'lost' in Atlanta, he is telling you that in his mind he has not left the small town where he works. When he helps others he does more than try to get food for them, or jobs. He has renounced a substantial portion of himself — surrendered himself to their lives. This is an altruism some of us see in patients who are not working in your American South!

"It can happen that the people who see anger and hatred in others are struggling with those emotions themselves; but it can also happen that people see in others their own dependency and weakness, or they appease their own self-criticism by the protection of an identification with people above or beyond criticism. This man is a harsh critic of his country, and he has had his bad spells with himself — when he has felt 'low' and 'moody.' But if he has joined his own instinctual life to that of these poor black people, then he can feel at peace with himself, buoyed up even, as he does his work, and he can also feel that he is receiving as much as he is giving, because what he gives he gives to those whose collective fate he has joined to his own fate. You and I may worry that he is not living as we might want to live, but he knows what happens when he goes to Atlanta, and why — and so he is glad to be back 'home.' My hunch is that when he was a child, in his first 'home,' he learned how to defend himself against a severe conscience, and he learned how to express his feelings of weakness — perhaps by investing his energy in the trials of younger and weaker children or animals. But we would have to know more about him than we do now, if we were to trace the origins of his altruism."

Miss Freud has speculated elsewhere at considerable length on the probable roots of altruistic behavior. In *The Ego and the Mechanisms of Defense* she observes that "it remains an open question whether there is such a thing as a genuinely altruistic relation to one's fellowmen, in which the gratification of one's own instinct plays no part at all, even in some displaced and sublimated form." She goes on to observe that "masochism" can provide "another and easy route to the same goal" of altruism — compared, that is, with the person who uses, as she puts it, "projection and identification [as a] means of acquiring an attitude which has every appearance of altruism." The problem with a judgment of "masochism," of course, is that the person who renders such an estimate may be offering a social and cultural bias, rather than a strictly psychoanalytic evaluation.[4] The young man whose remarks appear above learned himself about that kind of unfortunate mixup when he heard his life being described by his own college roommate, directly to his face: "My old buddy, my organic chemistry lab partner (we were both going to be doctors, and neither of us is!) came to see me, and he looked around this town, and he started giving me a real shrink job. He said I was in 'trouble.' He said I was 'trying to be a martyr.' He said I'm 'some species of masochist.' I guess I was supposed to be surprised — and then change my ways. I was hurt. I wondered why a good friend would want to talk like that to someone who's trying to do the best he can, even if it's not in the most conventional setup — a bank, a law office, a doctor's office. I tried to play it 'cool.' I knew that if I got excited or started arguing, I'd only confirm what he said in his mind. Actually, I wasn't interested in proving him wrong. I wanted to find out if he was right! I said: 'Let's talk about the whole damned business — my masochism!'

"He began the way you'd expect — that I'm isolated down here, and I live in a 'shack,' and I drive a beat-up truck, and I wear old clothes, and I've submerged my own life in the life of this very poor community, and there must be some 'psychological reason' that I've done so. I said I'm sure there is! There's a psychological reason for everything everyone says and does! There must be, I guess — if you're a twentieth-century rationalist, that's what you have to believe! But when you start down that road, you're not alone. Everyone is walking with you — including my old college roommates and all their friends and all the people who study 'masochism' and write articles and books on the subject!

"I started thinking, as we talked, about *his* life — all the stresses and strains on it. For years I'd heard him tell me how he hated taking lots of economics and political science courses in college, but he had to do it, to get into law school; and how he hated those three years there, but it was necessary if he was going to have a good job; and how he hated being in "a big corporate firm,' and being 'a cog' there — long days and plenty of nights and even weekends of poring over books and briefs and tax laws and torts and liens and God knows what. This guy, who used to play the saxophone, and who loves jazz, and who wanted to take a lot of courses in fine arts, because he loved looking at prints and at photographs, has now ended up with a huge collection of jazz tapes (one of the biggest in the world, he tells me!), and with a fantastic 'system' to play them, but he 'practically never' has the time to listen to all that music. He forgets what I remember — all his complaints of no time, no time. I used to hear him complain in college, and I believed what he always said in the next breath — that there *would* be time, eventually. Always it was the next hurdle, and then the next one after that! *Then*, he'd have time. But he's too honest, at least with me; he keeps telling me about what he'd like to be doing, and what he can't do 'yet' — until I'm now wondering when that 'yet' will finally come. When he's in an old-age home, if he's lucky to survive the rat-race?

"He has called his life a rat-race dozens of times. This isn't just me, the social rebel and civil rights freak and silly southern romantic, and masochist talking. Give him a beer, and he's his own worst critic. He's not yet 'lost' and 'brainwashed,' he'll tell us, his old friends, when we're together for someone's wedding or a class reunion. He sees it all clearly — the drudgery and the narrowing of the people who submit to the drudgery. But he's got to submit! He doesn't say that outright. He only tells you why he has to submit; he gives you his laundry list: the debts he still has from his education; his wife and his son, and the second child on the way; the education those kids will need — and how they're going to have a trust fund to pay for it, so they won't be 'mortgaged' to the 'incurred costs' of going to college and graduate school. (He's already decided both of them are going that far, right through graduate school!)

"There's a lot more! My friend ends up describing his whole life, and I can just visualize it — a very nice apartment in a very nice neighborhood, and a fancy car in a garage, and the rent for the garage more than the rent most people in this country pay for where they live. It's a great life, I'm sure — but that's not what I hear all the time from the guy who's living it, or from his wife, either. She's always complaining; every time we meet she has something that's worrying her, or making her as anxious as hell. Now, she's trying to get her son into a fancy private school; and it's so competitive, they're 'pulling strings,' she says: one of their friends is on the board of trustees. She gets migraine headaches. She carries some medicine around with her all the time. She told me, two years ago, that sometimes she wishes they'd just 'quit' and go live in a small town on the coast of Maine. I'll never forget that talk. She just poured out her resentments — all she puts up with on New York's fancy East Side; and she kept saying how 'simple' she wanted her life to be, and how the happiest time they'd ever had was the month of July the year before, when they 'escaped' to Maine, and they both fell in love with the coast up there, and they swore they'd go back every year, but they haven't been able to return yet.

"I reminded my old pal about what he'd said, what his wife had said. I asked him why the fantasy of Maine is 'normal,' but the reality of my life here in Georgia is 'sick.' He got annoyed at first.

He said that he wasn't calling me 'sick,' he was just saying that I'm living like a poor southern tenant farmer, when I could be living a comfortable life up North. I didn't have to be a lawyer like him, he kept saying; I didn't have to fight it out to be a member of a Wall Street law firm. But to go to an Ivy League school, and work hard there, and make Phi Beta Kappa, and then to turn down everything because one summer you do volunteer work in the civil rights movement, and then you can't seem to break away, and here you are, and it seems as if you'll be here for life, and you're not married yet, and you can't very well meet many 'eligible women' doing the kind of work I'm doing — there's something 'off track here,' he put it. He didn't want to judge me; he kept telling me that, and he freely admitted that his own life is full of 'tensions,' he knows it, and he's not pushing that life on anyone.

"That was the drift of our talk — one of the longest philosophical hassles I've ever had. I recall those all-night 'soul sessions' we had in SNCC during the Mississippi Summer Project; but I was a college kid then, and it was all so abstract and remote: we were talking about 'life,' not our lives. I think we assumed that this was a very important interlude in our lives — that we were down South to do a necessary job, and then we would get back to the big job: to plow ahead as college graduates. Instead, I stayed and stayed, and now I am: well, an oddball, my friend is saying — a masochist, even.

"He may be right! I don't deny that this life isn't always fun. I have a rough time on certain days. The people aren't only poor, they're scared — and they're as scared of us organizers as they are of the sheriff or the big shots who own the county or oversee the way it's run. We're a small bunch here, and we get ingrown and we get into trouble with each other. We're human beings, and we're in a fight, you could say, and we get tired, and we get low, and we don't behave as we should! We're a band of brothers and sisters, as corny as that sounds. We're a great help to each other. And we leave here every once in a while, when we know the tension is high, and we need the old R&R — a little rest, a little rehabilitation in Atlanta or Florida. We go home, too.

"It's during those times, actually, that I feel *more* determined about this work. I take one look at the life in Fort Lauderdale or Palm Beach, one look at downtown Atlanta, and those fancy suburbs north of the city, or one look at the Philadelphia 'Main Line' where my parents are living now, and I'm ready to come back to this place. Is that 'masochism'? Or is it someone who's doing work he likes with people he likes, and in a place where the living is the way he likes it — a small-town pace, where you know everyone, and by God, even the ones you're working against will say 'hello' to you, and 'good morning,' and 'so long.' "

Many evenings with such a young political activist bring up a number of recurrent themes, often best posed as questions. Is idealism best regarded as a passing phase in some young people — normally ended by the demands of yet another "stage" in an escalator-like life? Why do some youths persist with their idealistic preoccupations or affiliations for long stretches of time, whereas others shun idealism altogether, or are exceedingly limited in the amount and duration of commitment they make to any effort that can be described as idealistic? Without question, there are childhood sources of altruistic energy — and yet, why in some do those sources become an aspect of a particular, idealistic life, whereas in others such sources are "left behind," as it were? Surely, in that last regard, many of us clinicians have seen patients whose "masochism" or whose capacity to "identify" or to "project" have not prompted in them the altruism Miss Freud has tried to comprehend.[5]

Such questions and the reflections they suggest only beg the mystery of the individual. Yet, we have not always given the intellect its due in this matter, nor the moral influence exerted by various teachers and mentors, never mind parents. Idealism is not always or necessarily the result of a mind yielding to the continuing sway of infantile conflicts. Youths can respond to the persuasions of books and teachers, to the examples set by historical figures (or contemporary ones) as well as to the more personal influences psychiatrists are understandably inclined to notice and reckon as important if not decisive. If the ego has "mechanisms of defense," it also has properties that may be described as perceptual energy or a capacity to think and not only to use language, but respond to its power and suggestiveness. Moreover, the ethical life of a young adult can be strongly influenced by adults quite unlike well-remembered mothers and fathers. The moral transformation of a black hustler and prison inmate, haunted by a desperate childhood, into the person Malcolm X is not by any means a singular historical or psychological event.[6] As with all of life's many ironies, some of the more unpromising childhoods on this planet (so far as auguring for a later idealism goes) may well be the surprising preludes to a later earnestness if not tenacity of good will. One can even go further, cite the significant and enduring (or so it seems) good intentions and good deeds of men or women who don't in general qualify for the comprehensive description of "good persons."

I met two nuns in Brazil who work with the poor in one of Rio de Janeiro's favelas. Several times they told me of a woman who was especially generous to them, eager to help their work with impoverished and often homeless children through steady contributions of money. I met this woman and talked with her again and again during one Brazilian winter. She was a young person, a prostitute. She worked the Copacabana area of Rio. She told me of her daytime job as a hairdresser, her evening work with men. She was neither bold and tough, nor sentimental, nor self-pitying. I found her almost casual candor engaging — and cumulatively provocative, unnerving. She had an eye for the social world around her, and an ear for the emotional nuances expressed by the women and men she came to know so briefly, so intimately. In a strange way it was those well-to-do people who inspired her generosity, her idealism, more than the plight of the young *favelados*, whose collective life she knew, of course, so well out of her own experience as a child:

"When I stand and work on those women, on their hair, and listen
to them talk and talk and talk — about their pets and their clothes
and the shade of lipstick that suits them best — I want to wring
their necks one minute, but the next I am filled with tears for them.
I want to go and do something that will make me believe it's possible
to be different than they are!"

She stopped talking and looked into the distance of the Atlantic
Ocean, far below and quite clearly visible on that crisp winter day
from her home high up a favela. I wanted to pursue what she had
started, but she would not oblige. In fact, she gave me a look of
contempt, I thought, even as I was asking the interpreter to ask her
to expand upon her evaluation of her customers at the elegant Copacabana hotel. She already knew, as I spoke in English, what I
had in mind! She was an authority of sorts on greed — its daytime
workings in wealthy, idle wives of rich Rio men, its nighttime workings in those men themselves, and now, its workings in a poking,
prying Yankee who kept following up, hungrily, every possible conversational lead. Soon she had to excuse herself: The sun was going
down, and — well, "I have to see some people; I have appoint-
ments." The interpreter and I drove her back to the Copacabana.

A month later, in another conversation, she took the initiative,
brought up the subject of her response to the women whose hair
she fixed: "Two days ago I stood there and soaked a woman's hair,
rinsed it and rinsed it, and juggled two lotions, and I thought to
myself: Kill her, kill yourself afterward, and at least you'll have done
some *real* good in your seventeen years of life. You'll have taken
away one bad, bad, bad person from this earth. You'll have pushed
someone toward hell, where she belongs. You'll go there with her,
and you can have the joy of watching her burn while you do —
that's what I kept thinking to myself. I'm amazed that I finished
working on her — and she was alive. She smiled and told me I'm
a 'dear' and gave me a huge tip, and I put it in a separate place in
my wallet. I don't let her money touch some of the other money I
make. There are a few nice women who treat us all well, and who

are as unhappy as we are about what goes on here in Rio. One of them brings food to the street children. I feel like refusing her tip. I asked her once to give my tip to the street children, and she wouldn't hear of it. I was going to go right over and give the money to some children who hang out near the hotel, but then I decided that I need the money for my own brothers and sisters, and her money I can use and feel clean, so I'd better not give it away!

"Some money I get — I want to throw it into a garbage can, or I want to send it out to be washed and dried and folded and returned to me in a plastic bag that says 'clean' ! That woman's money is the worst; she is the worst; that morning was the worst. Why? I don't know how to answer! Maybe it was me; maybe I was just having a bad day. She was her usual self, stretching out on the chair, yawning and sighing, scratching skin through her expensive dress, moving her gold bracelets up and down her arm, staring at all those diamonds on her ring, telling me about the latest French movie she saw, telling me who came to her house for dinner and what they ate. One of the men she mentioned I know!

"That's it — when she started talking about him I got hot, and I felt murder in my fingers. I was afraid of them! I was afraid they'd take over, they'd do what *they* wanted to do, and we'd both be on our way to a meeting with the Devil! But the fingers were obedient! Too bad, I thought, as she talked about that party and him; but I'm glad now, because without me my family would be out on the street begging, or dead. She called him 'perfect'; she called him 'a perfect guest'; she called him 'one of the finest men' she has ever met. I stood there, listening and remembering. My body remembered! This lazy man who expects everyone to do something for him, me included! As I combed her hair and heard about the food she served to him, I thought of him, and the way he gives orders. He gets excited snapping his fingers. I think he loves the sound of his own fingers more than anything — more than *anyone*. I asked the woman what his wife was like. She said it's a pity, because the wife has some trouble with her lungs: she can't breathe sometimes. It's called 'asthma.' She has to take medicine. He's supposed to be so worried about his wife. He calls her twice a day from his office. Once he told me to be glad I'm healthy, and that's what I remembered when I heard his wife is sick. The night he told me about his wife, I had trouble breathing myself! I coughed and I felt my lungs closing down, but I kept taking the air in and letting it out, and so I was all right.

"I take his money right to the nuns. I tell them to give it to the kids who are the worst — stealing from hotel people and living on the streets and sleeping in alleys and always trying to sneak food out of stores. The nuns ask me where I get the money — each time the same question. Each time I say I found it. They believe me, though they smile! The Mother Superior says I'm lucky, because God is using me for the sake of the nuns: I find the money and turn it over to them, and they give it to kids who need it. Then *I* smile! I feel good! I almost convince myself that God wants me to go and do that animal a favor, and get paid by him, twice a week, before he goes home or goes to that woman's parties, so that some kids won't go without supper. While I'm with him I think of some of the kids I know who beg for a living. When he takes off his clothes I think of the kids; when I go near him I think of the kids; when he's making his noises I think of the kids; when he leaves I think of the kids — and I run, I run as fast as I can to the nuns, and all the way I'm thinking of the kids.

"After I leave I always go to the Copacabana beach, to one place there, where it gets rocky. I go and sit on a rock, and let the water clean my feet. I forget the kids, and the hotel and the machines we have for the hair of the rich ladies; I forget all the men and the nuns, too. The only thing I think of — well, it's the story I heard from my mother before she died, that Jesus loved all the poor, and He even loved the women who got into trouble, and He looks after everyone, and so I think of Him, looking after me. Then I'm ready to leave the rock and go to the sand and put my shoes back on and start in all over again. Once a man saw me, and he was rich, I knew, and he wanted me to do him a 'favor.' But that's one time I'd never do anyone a 'favor,' because it's the only time I'm clean. Jesus can't follow you around all day. If you get His attention for a couple of minutes, that's enough. I hope He does forgive me."

I found it rather too easy for my own thoughts to fasten her and her behavior down tidily, knowingly, firmly. Even as she told her story in fits and starts, now pausing for a swig of orange soda, now stopping altogether in order to chase a chicken out of the hut or warn the youngest sister, aged seven, not to touch (in the midafternoon) some food that she will serve as supper, I found myself rushing headlong into a series of psychological categorizations: She is plagued by anger, by shame, by guilt, hence her regular episodes of charity. I decided, eventually, to go seek out the nuns. She said it would be fine if I did so. There were four of them, two of whom knew her well, and one especially well: Sister Ruth, an energetic, rather punctual and austere person who spoke notably precise Portuguese, even to a foreigner's ear. She knew what I had come to learn: "I have talked with this child — she is not yet eighteen — many times, and I have tried to encourage her to go to school, and learn how to become a nurse. She loves children. She helps so many of them. She would be a wonderful nurse in a children's hospital, or maybe, a teacher. She laughs at me, though. She says she has taken care of children all her life, and she's had enough of them. Her mother died three years ago, but before she died she was sick for a long time, for many years. There's never been a father of any of those kids. The mother had three boyfriends, I believe.

"What is right in God's eyes? Every day I pray to Him for guidance! I'm not sure what I think and what I say is what He wants me to think and say! When a pretty girl comes to me with all those *cruzeiros*, and says she wants me to feed other children, I look at *her* long and hard! I ask myself: What is she doing? Why? Then I ask myself, what are you to do? Why? All those questions! I have no correct answers, only prayers we've said, and more prayers as we try to follow His example. He never turned His back on anyone.

He was ready to forgive everyone. He opened His arms to all the hurt and troubled people, and He promised them the highest gift possible, a room in His heavenly mansion. Shouldn't we try to have His spirit, to follow His spirit, when a child tries to show her love of others? Or should we sit her down and question her and question her and, finally, tell her to leave and to take her money with her? She comes here with kindness in her heart. Her voice trembles when she describes what she has seen in this city, little boys and girls sleeping in alleys, and eating food they have taken from garbage pails. She is not one to throw money at us and say: here, do this with it, or that with it. She tells us, each time, her story — a scene she's witnessed and can't get out of her mind. This *attention* she gives to the children — to us that is a sign that her heart is part of His.

"You asked why *she* should be giving so much to charity — and why we accept her gifts. Yes, her own family needs all the help she can give it. We have a soup kitchen for the favela where she lives, and we feed her brothers and sisters, along with all their friends. You're right, in a way: She could keep all the money she makes, and get her family a better home, and some good clothes, and take them to the market and buy them all the meat they want. Sister Maria and I have talked with her about that choice many times. We have sat in this room and prayed together, she and the two of us. And we here have discussed this by ourselves — and had a disagreement or two! This is a girl who has known such terrible pain and suffering. Her mother's boyfriend frightened her into having sex with him regularly. She was only twelve or so. She poured the story out to us. Her mother never knew. She has known poverty, like all the rest, and hunger, and she has somehow survived. She has faced death several times — disease and two miscarriages. But she is meant to survive! She is tough — like some of the old women of our favelas who seem beyond life and death: here to stay and stay. We call them God's witnesses. Through their eyes, He sees His beloved poor.

"We disagree with you, I think, about the poor. We do not think they are doomed. We do not feel they are to be pitied. We agree with this child — that her pity belongs to the women whose hair she washes and sets, and to the men who buy her and buy her and buy her for their pleasure. God save them! As for this girl who does their bidding, God will save her! We are not being as 'other-worldly' as you suggest! Of course we agree, it would be better for our young friend if she never again went with one of those Copacabana men — even quit her hairdresser job. We have offered her a job with us! We'd love to have her helping us with our kitchens; we have seven of them, and hundreds of mouths to feed, and she'd be wonderful with the children. But she refuses us.

"There is something mysterious at work in her. No, not psychological; we don't see her as needing one of your Brazilian colleagues! Why? Well, we've asked her if she worries about her life. We've asked her if she wants to change it in some way. We've told her we can help her change it. She says no, no, no. Would you have us grab her and hold her here — kidnap her and take her to a mental hospital? Two months ago seven of us spent a day discussing this problem. You see what one person, touched by Christ, can do to the rest of us!

"No, we came to no general agreement. We agreed to continue our discussion — and to pray, always, for His guidance. I am sure that this child of God is troubled, as you say, and I'm sure she sins daily, as do we all. But she provokes us all to amazement and confusion, as Jesus did when He walked the earth, and as He still does, and I think we all have to remember that He warned us He would not come to us in a quiet and easy way. He would constantly trouble us, upset us, challenge our ideas and our notions of what is good and bad, right and wrong — as this strange girl does. We see many children who come to us for food, and in their eyes there is not only the stare of hunger and destitution; over and over there is a 'grace' we find hard to forget on their faces. You ask what I mean? I don't know how to answer your question. I have no scientific proof — and here you are a doctor, and even your translator is a doctor! But when you meet children who are ready to thank God, not just us as sisters, as His Servants, then you're in the presence of 'grace.'

"My brother is a lawyer, and I visit his home, and I see the children in his neighborhood. So many times I have driven to see my brother, and I get out of my car and I try to talk with the children, and they seem so surly, so stuck on themselves. Oh, yes, not all of them — you are right to caution me. But enough of them! Besides, almost all those children ask me, as soon as I meet them, where I live, and what I do! They want to investigate me before they even say a decent hello and talk about the weather! I have never heard such questioning from our poor ones; they say hello and they look so eager, so anxious to help, so open. Yes, they have a 'motive,' yes they hope for good! But then isn't being hungry part of the grace that is theirs — enabling them to be sensitive and kind to visitors?

"I can see I'm not winning you over to my theology of everyday life! Even so, we must at least bow, both of us, before this one riddle you yourself are trying to understand — how it is that a girl who has had such a terrible life can manage to be so kind and generous to others. If it is not God who inspires her generosity, her idealism, what else might it be that does? Not this child's father, and not her mother! Not the examples of other men and women in this neighborhood, who don't (you can be sure) lecture their children on the virtue of giving to others! She is the oldest, and so there was no brother or sister to teach her anything. One of us said: She is crazy, as so many of the saints of our Church have been! We are *not* recommending that she be considered for beatification, but we know that the Church is not the only path to true goodness, or sainthood, for that matter.

"No, no — I don't mean to deny her selfish side! We are all sinners, surely! She is a difficult young woman! She is stubborn. She is demanding. She is, actually, as imperious at times as those women who go to the Meridien to have their hair done. She has

observed them keenly, and caught some of their moral disease —
the terrible pride that goes with ordering people around all day.
She comes here and starts ordering us around! 'Here, take this, and
please give it to the hungriest of your children,' she'll say. When
she says 'please' she is polite. But she can also be a trifle impatient;
she can omit 'please' and omit 'thank you' from her remarks. And
she's tough, of course: If anyone tried to push her, she'd fight back.
I risk pride myself: We humble ourselves when she comes, and
then she glows, as if she's finally found people who listen to her
and don't try to order her around. She's so used to being ordered
around, it's natural that she'd find it tempting to order others around!
She'd make a great Mother Superior! She'd have us all on our toes!
But she'd have us living in a favela ourselves — as generous as she
is! We're not ready for that! Because we've all had such protected
lives, even before we entered this order of the Church, we are afraid
to surrender ourselves to God. She has nothing to lose. She is ready
to give everything — the daily 'take' she's glad to have and even
more glad to be rid of! That is grace! We in this community have
not yet come to that level of achievement!"

In many years of talking with children and adults all over the
world, I've never met the equal of that Sister for shrewd theology
and psychology — rendered, my interpreter said, in the plainest,
least pretentious language. There is no doubt that the young woman
we were discussing has a vexing mixture of psychological traits. She
is, indeed, high-handed in her own way. She is also more than a
bit perverse — willing to set aside for a Catholic charity money that
might enable her brothers and sisters to live better; though, in
fairness to her, she keeps them, by favela standards, quite well. She
can be, too, almost ruthlessly split in her loyalties — unwilling to
say goodbye to a life she considers sordid, and unwilling to profit
personally from that life, or yield to it in some important moral
sense. But she *does* yield to that life. I have wondered, after many
conversations, whether she is as disgusted or outraged by her activity

as she sometimes claims. She is quite attractive — tall, with long brown hair, hazel eyes, and a vivacious if not flirtatious manner. She watches intently, and that can, of course, be flattering as well as intimidating. She knows she is interesting to men, and doesn't try to interfere with the consequences. She likes learning about the way rich women and rich men live. I begin to realize that she is far angrier at the rich women than the rich men. Maybe "underneath," where some of us seek a larger truth, the reverse holds — a terrible anger at not only the men she "sees" two or three times a week, but the awful trio of men (maybe more, in truth) to whom her mother allowed herself to submit.

In any everyday sense, all this gets worked into a philanthropy that is ironic yet startling, wise, honorable in its declared intentions. Anna Freud wondered "whether there is such a thing as a genuinely altruistic relation to one's fellowmen, in which the gratification of one's own instinct plays no part at all, even in some displaced and sublimated form." Miss Freud has declared the matter "an open question," but she knew how often a youth such as this Brazilian woman struggles with shame and sorrow as a prelude to compassionate regard for others. Of course, to recognize the psychological sources of a form of behavior is not necessarily to denigrate the behavior. The psychological observer gratifies various instincts, as each of us does, needless to say, in the daily course of our occupational lives, to say nothing of the activities, hobbies, or charitable interests we pursue. Christian theologians or apologists have known this for many centuries — and so modern psychological knowledge does not unnerve those Brazilian nuns, who are constantly marveling at a great psychological (and they would say spiritual) mystery: how goodness can, and does, emerge from a world saturated with sinful possibility.

In January 1980, I asked the nuns to reflect upon Miss Freud's "open question," and they were inclined to side with the skeptics. One after the other, but not in a Calvinist fashion, they reminded me of "our fallen state." Among the clergy of the Catholic Church, especially its Mediterranean division, sin does not inspire a raging, demanding moralism — an effort at scourging in the interest of salvation. These nuns were relaxed about the lusts that work away in us — and inclined to consider that anything we do, however kindhearted, partakes in some degree of sinfulness. Their benefactor was not unwilling to be confronted by the Mother Superior, later in that month of January — with a doctor at hand listening: "If you are asking me whether I feel selfish, like the women I denounce to you, then I can see I'd better say yes, because you are wearing a smile on your face, and I know what that says about your own opinion! I think some days that I'd like to be as clean as a bird flying overhead, but then I see the bird come down and eat garbage, so I realize that it's foolish to try to build a wall around yourself. Sometimes I'm ready to buy revenge, if only I could! I mean, if a man came to me and said he'd kill everyone whose hair I've set, and every man I've tried to please this past week, or month, I might say yes, go ahead, and I'll pay you what you want! That is a terrible thing to say, but it is the truth of how I feel. But I change my mind, usually. In the favelas we have worse — people who kill other people. And look at me, saying I'm tempted to hire a killer! I asked one of the nuns if she has ever wanted to kill anyone. She said she didn't think she has wanted to kill, no, but she has been *very* angry at times. She said she has to pray for a long time, to quiet down her anger. I don't pray much. I think when I leave here, after giving my donation, I'm quieted down!"

This young woman is a loner. I felt that her sympathies were often abstract as well as concrete — choosing to quarrel with a terrible social order that made her, among others, its victim, rather than emphasizing a compassionate response to Rio's many favelas, with their thousands and thousands of ailing children. All the more ironic that my physician friend and translator should introduce me to a well-to-do young woman and a well-to-do young man, cousins, whose idealism on behalf of the very same (Brazilian) *favelados* seemed specifically connected to particular boys and girls, particular families, all of which those two youths virtually adopted, nourished, tried to strengthen in countless ways. Not that these two youths were without their emotional struggles. Miss Freud mentions in her written discussion of altruism the "similarity between the situation in altruistic surrender and the conditions which determine male homosexuality." I have heard others in psychiatry and psychoanalysis indicate a view that stresses the significance of that connection — an expressed solidarity with the poor and the unfortunate as a "displacement" of an earlier felt kinship with brothers or sisters, "underneath" where, naturally, the probing physician would discover all sorts of rivalry, envy, hostility, competitiveness, jealousy.

The young man of the two was not a homosexual. He is now married and the father of two children, and he has continued his philanthropic idealism as a teacher. Still, as one talks with him, one hears the image of brotherhood coming up, and one suspects him, as the oldest of four brothers, to be a possible candidate for that last-mentioned category of Miss Freud's. The "homosexual" energies she had in mind are part of everyone's psychological nature, though we all vary in the significance of those energies to our daily mental activity. The issue, by and large, is not one of overt homosexuality; rather, a question of how children come unconsciously to deal with certain people of the same sex, and how that kind of learning influences the nature of later lives.

Here is how the young man describes his becoming a teacher: "I was slated to follow my father, become a partner with him in his business. I didn't have it in me, I guess! My father spent half of his time when I was a kid trying to toughen me up. He kept telling me this is a tough world, and you have to be tougher than everyone else, and I should ride my bike until I'm real tired, and then push myself, and ride farther, and come home so tired that I feel refreshed. I've never felt *that* tired! I've felt so tired I'm ready to collapse, and I have collapsed!

"He always made us boys argue with each other at the table, and in sports he loved to see us beat one another. He said it's great to win, and bad to lose, and we should just as well practice on each other, because later on, that's what everyone does, tries to beat the next guy. My brother next to me [one year younger] listened to my father and followed his orders. I think my father wished he had named him 'Junior,' not me! Pedro is a tough, tough soccer player, and he wants to start his own business — make soccer equipment and sell it all over Brazil. He's tough with my younger brothers, too. He orders them around; then they come to me and I tell them to relax and not be scared. My mother helps out, too. She says our father's bark and Pedro's bark are worse than their bite, but those boys are only nine and eleven, and it's scary to have *two* people on top of you all the time.

"When I was through with the university, I wanted to be either a doctor or a teacher. I wanted to go to the west and work with our native people, the Indians, or to the north, and help the poor to live better. My mother told me not to say what's on my mind to my father: 'Give him time, and he will adjust to you!' I said no, he'd never 'adjust' to me — only to Pedro. But she had faith in Father, and she had her own way of 'bringing him around' — that's how she says it! When she really wants him to stop and reconsider a decision, or change his ideas, she starts getting sick! She has asthma, but only at certain times does it get very bad. Then Dad becomes worried, and he tells her she's right, she's right, no matter what she says. Then she begins to get better! But she's not pretending. She *does* become sick! She looks weak and she stays in her room, and the doctor comes, and gives her a higher dose of medicine and she carries the inhaler around with her, even when she goes to the bathroom. She brings my father to his knees — at her bed. He listens to her at last!

"It's all wrong — our family: the squabbles, and my father lording it over us, and my mother manipulating him with asthma, and my brother Pedro trying to be Tough Man Number Two! Sometimes

I'm more afraid of him than of my father. My father is my father: When he sees one of us crying, he stops and feels sorry for us. Pedro sees tears as a sign of contemptible weakness, and he's ready to go right for the jugular. He mocks us! He says we're 'weak' and 'frightened' — even our younger brothers. *He's* frightened, I have figured out, but if I told him so, he'd go berserk, I'm sure.

"They sent me to a psychiatrist, you can see! It was a teacher at school who called up my mother and told her I'm in trouble. Why? Because I worry too much about the little children in the lower grades — whether they'll get hurt. Because I'm always criticizing rich people, and I'm from a rich family, and so is everyone else who goes to that [private] school. Because I say things in class that get the teachers 'upset,' and 'stir up' the children. One day in Latin class we were reading Cicero, and I thought he wasn't as good as the teacher said he was. She'd already told us about the slaves in Rome, and all I did was ask whether Cicero ever spoke against slavery. She tried to explain that you have to realize what the times were like back then. Then I said (I'd raised my hand!) that if you think like she was telling us to think, you will never want to change anything, because you'll always be talking about 'realizing' this and 'realizing' that — the 'historical perspective' she says it's so impor-tant for us to have. She thinks of us as a little bunch of Ciceros, ready to run the whole show and write orations to compliment each other, and to attack anyone who's against us. Maybe that guy Catiline was wrong, but Cicero wasn't the friend of the poor Romans, or the slaves; he was a big shot, and we should be able to ask any questions we want about him!"

Such talk, delivered with vigor and intensity, soon enough brought the speaker to a prominent psychiatrist's Rio office. The doctor saw the youth many times, saw his mother, saw his father, even asked to see his brother Pedro. All those meetings prompted the doctor to suggest that the "problem" wasn't any one person in this family, but everyone, even the small boys, who were quite anxious and apprehensive a good deal of the time. Their older brother, willing

to be quiet and submissive and "passive" in response to such behavior, turned into a quite different person when his younger brothers were noticeably under attack (as he saw it) and in distress. He
rallied to their cause as a fighter at the dinner table, and as a warm
and loving protector elsewhere. Often he looked after them, coun-
seled them, played with them, read to them, even went to buy
them clothes, games, athletic equipment. They were, in a way, his
children, as his parents and Pedro quietly recognized. His love for
them was not only evident but intense and absorbing.

Once he told me this: "I think of those boys all the time. I don't
want them to be as fragile as I am, psychologically. I want them to
be strong and confident — but that won't be easy, given our home
life. I wonder whether it's even good for them that I am so tender,
so affectionate with them. I'm afraid that the result is a weakness
on their part — they cry easily, and they run to me when they feel
'nervous.' If I weren't there, maybe they'd have toughened up, and
become smaller Pedros by now — that's what he says! But I love
them more than myself, I think. It's strange to say it like that, but
I would gladly die for them, and I would gladly sacrifice my own
happiness for theirs. If I sound like a doting mother and father
both — I guess I am that! Neither of my parents has much time for
those boys. My father wants to make a million American dollars a
day, and my mother is so worried about her own health that anyone
else's, even the health of her children, doesn't attract her attention."

This young man's psychiatrist was quite sure that his patient would
have an exceedingly difficult adult life — even with the help of
psychotherapy. It wasn't hard for either of us doctors to see the
"masochism" and "passivity" in this fellow; nor did we fail to discuss
at length his strong ("homosexual") attachment to his two brothers — a psychological "orientation" that did, indeed, seem to get
further connected to the world's weak, hurt, ailing people. He was,
it could be said, a "maternal" young man, whose "latent homosexuality" provided much of the "psychic energy" for his overall "attitude of benevolence," which was described at a psychoanalytic

conference as a "firm sublimation." A solidarity with younger brothers had become a solidarity with *favelados;* it extended even to Roman slaves. Eventually this same young man would go through years of psychoanalysis — and become a decent, conscientious, able teacher in an elementary school. He would also take under his wing, in his late teens and early twenties, the children of a particular favela: bring to them all sorts of sports equipment, clothing, food. They were, it was not hard to see, kin to him in the tradition of his two younger brothers: boys (mostly) whom he tried to protect against the cruelties of a city, a whole social and economic system. Miss Freud's mention of (unconscious) "homosexuality" as a common aspect of altruism came to mind again and again as I watched this young man's idealistic nature emerge and persist over the years.

He himself tried to do justice to his philanthropic nature one evening when he was given a medal by a grateful Catholic Church in Rio: "I am honored to be here, but the evening belongs to the children and their parents. We are here to view their work [at crafts] and to see them perform [at sports]. But I want to thank you all for what you've just said about me — the good words. I don't deserve such praise! I'm only trying to spare some children some of the pain they'd otherwise have to bear. Even so, there is still plenty of injustice in their lives, and maybe only when they meet God will they be rescued from the injustice of their fate. If it is any comfort, I know some rich children, who also have suffered a lot. My heart went out to them, and it goes out to all of you here. We need to link arms and all be brothers and sisters — no matter who our parents are and where we live. To me, bringing some soccer balls here, or clothes, is a selfish act! *I* feel better. *I* feel stronger and a better person. *I* feel the love you offer me; I see it in the eyes of the boys as we play soccer together on the field over there. So, may God bless you all, and forgive me for being unable to stop coming here and soaking up your kindness and love!"

A touching and fine statement, well received indeed by his young friends, who looked up to him with enormous respect and gratitude — sometimes, too, with surprise that turned to a kind of awe: Why does this rich man pay such affectionate and continuing attention to us? One fourteen-year-old boy, pressed to answer that question, shrugged his shoulders, said he hadn't the slightest idea why, but added: "Please God there will always be a few like him." Then the boy reconsidered, observed this: "Maybe God touches some people; maybe He makes them good — I mean, better than others. He must try to keep some people good. Most people here get into trouble. But the priest is good, and so is our friend we love who just spoke. He loves us, and we love him. We love the presents he brings us, too! He knows that. He loves to bring them to us. That's what makes him so special, that he gives us lots of things, but he won't lord it over us afterward!"

I discussed with Anna Freud youths such as this Brazilian one, and a number of American young men and women whose idealism was impressive to behold. Once, bluntly, she asked me the "question" she declares unanswered in her book — whether there is any altruism that is "pure." Is idealism or altruism always a mode of contending with a person's felt inadequacy, weakness, worthlessness, or a person's responsiveness to others? I was hard put to answer her categorically; I tried to sift and sort, to evade a blunt yes or no. But finally I decided, after looking over many pages of summary notes, that I would vote with those who see sin everywhere.

Not one young idealistic person I have worked with has ever claimed immunity from lusts of various kinds; has ever denied envy, rivalry, ambition. The sin of pride (narcissism, we call it) is a commonplace in these talented and kindly people. As Dorothy Day, who lived one of the most altruistic lives of this century, said when asked about her own motives and purposes:[7] "We reach out to help others as a statement of our own need for help. We are all beggars and sinners. We are all in more jeopardy than we dare acknowledge. When I offer bread to the hungry, I am feeding my soul's hunger — its 'long loneliness' I once called it! When I offer clothes to those who lack them, I am making myself feel more protected from the nakedness of so many moments — when we feel that nothing is between us and the devil! When I offer someone a place to stay, I am reminding myself how homeless we all are — unsure on many mornings or evenings, of where we belong in God's eyes!

"Lots of young people come here and expect me to be as pure as a fresh snowfall, and always sweet-talking, and full of love for everyone I see. We sit down and talk, and I tell them I get angry at a lot of the people who come here, and I get angry at some of the people I work with, and most of all, I get angry with myself, for good reason, on many a morning! I also tell them that it is *us*, who run the 'hospitality houses,' who want to feed the hungry, who cook and serve, who are the ones in great need, even in great trouble — and so it is a favor these people are doing us by coming here and taking from us what we have to offer. This is not easy for some young people to understand: the reciprocity of giver and receiver, the two sides of the same coin, the help the helpless offer to the helpers. But when a young volunteer — on leave from a college, maybe — *does* begin to see what that means (the giving to us by those who are down-and-out, and supposedly with nothing to give anyone), then it's a real breakthrough for the young man or the young woman. A *spiritual* breakthrough (I don't know much about psychology, so I can't talk about psychological breakthroughs!).

"I often hear the young, who stay with us for a while to work, say that they've just begun to realize what being idealistic is all about. Then I'll ask them *what* they've 'just begun to realize.' And often what I hear will go something like this: 'Oh, until we came here we thought being idealistic meant being anxious to help others — willing to sacrifice your own desires or interests, at least part of the time, in favor of doing something for someone else.' Then, the person will tell me of their earlier life. 'That's how I was brought up — to be compassionate to people who aren't as lucky as I am,' the person might say. And more: 'I have to admit that no one ever taught me to think of compassion as a full-time job! That's why I was stunned when I first came to visit the Catholic Worker people here. I kept asking people how long they'd been here, and how long they were going to stay. I'm embarrassed even to think about all that now — how rude and presumptuous I was. When I didn't get definite answers, I got annoyed at these people, and began to wonder if they were "all there" — if there wasn't something a little "confused" about them! It took me weeks and weeks to begin to look away from "them" and toward myself. That's the big problem with a lot of us in this country — college kids like myself who have been brought up to be kind and thoughtful, but always within limits: There's a world to conquer, too! We always feel sure about ourselves — it's the other people, who are different, who might possibly be troubled or confused!'

"We might pause then — or I might hear more: 'But at last I realized that you can't have everything (I'd been taught, mostly, that you can, if you work hard and you're fairly smart), and that if you really want to help others there's exactly one place to start: with yourself. For instance, the more I tried serving food here, and got no "thank you's," the more frustrated I became. Then I found myself getting tired, and more tired, and finally so tired I thought I was sick. I went to see my doctor, and he told me I was basically all right; but he thought I was "depressed." Who, me? Yes, you, he said, then I tried to figure out why; and eventually it dawned on me, with a little help from a long talk with Dorothy [Day], that I was really quite put out with these poor, sad people who come to us for lunch. Why? Because they weren't being *grateful* to me; they weren't *thanking* me; they weren't getting down on their hands and knees — through a smile — to bless me as a wonderful, wonderful person!'

"Again, there's likely to be a pause, and then I'll hear more: 'To me, I started understanding, idealism meant being rewarded, being elevated by others. I *was* angry, and I *was* depressed — because I wasn't getting my due from those "street people," those "city hoboes" and "drunks" who were getting this high-class waitress service out of me, and even so, remained sullen and grumpy and absorbed in themselves! Well, I tried to change a little! I tried to be more casual. I'd been hovering over these people, waiting for them to smile their gratitude at me. Instead, I simply tried to be friendly toward them — and not expect any big bonus in return. The result was amazing — a big bonus in return! What bonus? The bonus of people treating me as a friend — someone who's nice enough to be helpful, but isn't trying to get a moral or psychological receipt for every bowl of soup or cup of coffee handed out. Since then I've gradually relaxed when I'm on the serving line — or any time I try to help people in trouble. I try to remind myself that ego trips are for some other place and some other time. If you're trying to be idealistic you are trying to extend yourself to others, I'd remind myself. You can't deny yourself, but you don't have to keep patting yourself on the back! The point is to feed others here, not feed yourself on their dependency upon you and your friends who are working here!' "

Dorothy Day believed this kind of self-awareness to be one of the more constant signs of a robust idealism — evidence that a given egoism has managed to see beyond itself, to appreciate its stake in the dignity of others. Arrogance and self-importance are not confined to obviously greedy or bossy people. Dorothy Day confessed her inclination to be self-righteous or unthinking as she faced the inevitable burdens of her kind of idealism, and so it has gone with many others, by no means her equal in commitment. Idealism can generate moments of despair, but sometimes there is a subsequent burst of energy and enthusiasm — the consequence of realizing that generosity has its restorative possibilities as well as its frustrations.

During the civil rights days of the early 1960s, I reported on another aspect of despair among idealists, a "weariness." Years later, as I kept up with some of those youths, I began to realize that some of that exhaustion and moodiness[8] was actually an aspect of the disillusioned idealism Dorothy Day had described. Danilo Dolci, another extraordinary fighter on behalf of the world's needy and defenseless people, told me of a "lowered morale not connected,

seemingly, with any objective turn of events" — a "personal melancholy" he called it[9] that "lifts at a certain point." The idealistic
activist has to find out what he "wants" out of his work. Dolci didn't
have in mind a psychiatric inquiry — at least not necessarily such
an inquiry with respect to one's purpose. He had in mind this chain
of events: "In our work we are trying to change people — the way
they live in their communities. To change a social system, to introduce a new politics — this can be heady for the ones doing it, the
organizers, the fighters. They are human, and they want recognition.
But what if they don't get, at first, what they think they ought to
get? They pout! They become disillusioned — and that's good: to
lose one's illusions! It is dangerous to walk the earth among others,
and not see oneself through their eyes. So often those we try to
help see us as needy in our way as they are in theirs. If we but say
yes, that is true, to ourselves — then they will see that we have
done so, and the air will be less charged, and our spirits higher."

Some of the disillusioned idealists I had known in, say, 1964 or
1965, ended up a decade later still trying in one way or another to
further the moral principles that had prompted the earlier journey
South — whereas, of course, other men and women said a firm
goodbye to such social idealism. I would not dare generalize about
the psychological difference between those who went from the civil
rights movement to a migrant legal services career (after completing
law school), and those who went from the civil rights movement to
a legal career on Wall Street in corporate taxation. But one of those
who took the former path pointed out to me, in a conversation held
long after the Mississippi Project, the influence that may make a
critical difference: "It's over a decade since that time in Mississippi.
I never thought I'd end up being a lawyer. The year 1976 seemed
then like the year 2000 seems now — 'way off. Most of us left the
South by 1965; the job seemed done so far as we were concerned.
We went back to our lives. I finished college, and then took time
off again, only it wasn't to do 'good,' but just to travel and think. I
felt I was spoiled rotten to be able to do that, bum around, hitchhike

through England and Scotland. In Glasgow I saw the terrible slums, and I was just made sick. The old refrain started again in my head: Why is it that so many people are poor, and meanwhile others live like fat hogs, wanting more and more, and to hell with everyone else? I tried to get a job in one of the community service centers in a Glasgow slum, and while I was being interviewed I thought to myself: this is stupid. Go back home and do what you want to do here back there! So, I did go home.

"But when I got back I still wasn't sure what I actually wanted to do. I began to think I was sick in the head. I mean, I went to see a psychiatrist, and he told me I had 'problems,' and it was up to me if I wanted to work them out. If I did, he couldn't see me, because he was filled up, but he'd send me to someone. I told him I'd think about it — what I did want out of life. I decided to go see a shrink; then I changed my mind. I applied to law school. Then I almost withdrew my application, because I kept thinking I should go back to Mississippi, and try to do some kind of volunteer work there. You can see, I was in real bad shape! Then, I met someone! She was going to law school, and she was two years younger than I — reminding me of all the time off I'd taken.

"She changed my life. She kept reminding me that I'm me, that there's no point in trying to be someone else — such as one of my classmates who's a lawyer working for Gulf Oil, or another who's working for American Airlines. I began to realize that I didn't want to stop criticizing what I didn't like about my country; I wanted to find a way to help others improve their lives — and that way, I'd be improving my own life. Maybe if I'd wanted to give up my values, I'd have gone and spent years with a doctor figuring out why I get so upset when I see poor people getting a raw deal — here or abroad. But I'm not anxious to lose that side of myself. Besides, I'm in this rut for life. I just think I was destined to be this way. My father is a math teacher in a junior high school who still worries about some of the poor kids he teaches. As much as he wanted me to go to an Ivy League school, and go into a profession like law, and make a million, he also wanted me to cry for the poor people, the way I saw him doing. My mother fought with him, and now she fights with me and my wife. She'd like me to be a real cool, rich lawyer, and I never will be one, and she's angry as hell. But she couldn't nag my father to change, and she can't nag me to change. And guess what! My wife nags me all right, but in the opposite direction from my mother. My wife nags me to be even more generous with my time and energy at the migrant legal services office. She's so damned involved with all these poverty law issues. I'm used to being nagged, though! I almost *need* to be nagged. That's what I've begun to realize — that I wait for others to push me, then I get going. No wonder I'm trying to help people who are being pushed around all the time."

Had he, in fact, gone into psychiatric treatment, he might have prompted his doctor to reflect on the nature of his "passivity," his "masochism," his "identification" with the humble and humiliated of this earth. Nor would he have been an easy person to treat. He concluded that his difficulties were not those of a "personality" in distress — but rather of a moral sensibility opposed to the workings of modern corporate America. He despised totalitarian governments, had grave suspicions about statist socialism, but abhorred an America in which so much wealth existed side-by-side with a poverty that touched the lives of millions.

It was these difficulties, he would eventually decide, which kept troubling him as he tried to figure out how (and where and with whom) to live: "My parents believe in psychology. They've wanted me, for years, to see a shrink. They think that if I do, I'll settle down. I think my father has this scenario in mind: I'll go to a doctor, and then I'll stop worrying about the poor, the migrants. I'll leave that shoe-string 'welfare law place' (he calls it!) in Florida and go get a solid job in a solid firm. But my father doesn't want to see how much of *his* father is in me. My grandfather's life as a labor organizer somehow got worked into my life. *That* is the 'childhood influence' I can't seem to shake off, and don't want to shake off —

my grandfather fighting the scabs and preaching the old Wobbly slogans about 'equality' and 'justice.' "

I have noticed, again and again, that those youths who are openly troubled about their commitment to reform as against their desire to live comfortable, respectable lives, are the ones who seem to last longest as active idealists, though not without substantial mental anguish. Such youths state the obvious about themselves — that they simply cannot or will not shake off a youthful idealism in favor of various "practicalities," various "adjustments to reality," as pressed upon them by parents, friends, former college classmates, new acquaintances. Nor are such young idealists only to be found in the more obvious places — among our migrants, among our Indians. Any number of dedicated idealists straddle the world of commerce and philanthropy, and make a constant and personal effort on behalf of poor people.

If some old civil rights volunteers content themselves with a check or two to a group or two, a vote every two or four years, a signature for this or that cause, others of that 1960s American cadre still seek opportunities to tutor children on weekends, to take active part in reformist politics, to volunteer their professional time as doctors, lawyers, business consultants. We do not read often enough, if at all, about those such as John Sawyer who lived in a "Freedom House" in Mississippi in 1964, and twenty years later, in 1984, was a banker, yes, and a lawyer, yes, but also a constant friend to community groups in New York City, to the extent of carefully choosing his regular job so that his Harlem work and his Bedford-Stuyvesant work would not suffer. "It's a fifty-fifty commitment," he shyly says — and observes that his "contacts" in one world "most certainly help" his reformist work in another.

Perhaps I should offer a respectful emendation to Anna Freud's analysis of young idealism. There is, at least in some of us, an intense idealism that doesn't yield its energy, later in life, to competing interests or obligations. Youthful idealism has become, for certain men and women, a much-valued moral habit. Without it some middle-aged persons, even relatively old men or women, feel anxious or inadequate — or yes, even fearful. Nor do these much older men and women deserve to be called "chronic adolescents" because they persist in feeling many conflicts Miss Freud accurately ascribes to some adolescents. Perhaps our age, which has allowed for serious sexual crises in later life, serious conflicts as to life's purpose and meaning, serious conflicts in one's career, will begin to take an interest in how the idealism of some young people persists and alters in the face of life's opportunities, hazards, obstacles.

The middle-aged migrant legal services employee who speaks earlier in this chapter (a brilliant Yale Law School graduate) expects never to be free of his conflicts. He respects constitutional authority, yet rebels hard against various aspects of the "establishment." He recognizes his self-centeredness, yet he yearns to extend himself to others different from himself. He can be hopeful one minute, despairing the next. He craves possessions, the artifacts of our materialist culture, yet can be dissatisfied with this side of himself. He loves the nation to which his heart and soul belong, but he also often criticizes that nation. He works as a community advocate, yet is himself a solitary figure — often desirous of long walks in suburban woods or country fields. Moreover, like other Americans, he struggles with his personal and familial commitments — his wife and two children on the one hand, his "mistress," as he calls his work, on the other hand.

Youthful idealism has its roots in all the emotional, moral, and social complexities this life can present to anyone, be he or she rich or poor, black or white, citizen of an industrial or a "developing" nation. The ambitious theorist, striving to find a categorical "type," whether psychological, sociological, spiritual, or philosophical, has his or her work cut out: Any moral drama has an astonishing range of characters, one finds. The early experiences, the earnest expectations and fearful worries, the sturdy or fragile loyalties and allegiances of these young people are perplexing, even confounding and maddening in their range, depth, diversity. "I give up about these kids," the black civil rights activist Robert Moses said to me at the "orientation session" (in Oxford, Ohio) for the Mississippi Summer Project in 1964. He couldn't quite figure out the motives of some of the college students who had flocked to that Project from all over the country. At the end of that summer, let alone in future years, Robert Moses would be equally exasperated: "I *still* give up!" He immediately added this comment: "Some of these kids defy my hunches or past experience. I suppose it's good they do! I hope they'll continue to surprise us!"[10]

At another moment, as Bob Moses and I remembered yet another of those 1960s volunteers, and did a "catch-up" on her 1980s life, he said, "I'll be damned" and I thought the same thing, and then he turned an expression of surprise into a literal-minded self-arraignment: "I should be damned! I never would have anticipated that outcome. I thought she was being a 'young rebel,' reacting against her stodgy background. I was wrong. I didn't know enough, I guess — or didn't have the time (to be more charitable to myself) to get to know enough."

VI

SOCIAL CLASS AND
THE MORAL OTHER

IN Charles Dickens's novel *Little Dorrit*,[1] published in 1856–1857, a scene takes place (toward the end of the story) that illustrates, casually and in passing yet with remarkable vividness, the moral crisis that can confront someone who attributes his own shortcomings to the imagined power of another person. William Dorrit had earlier served time in debtor's prison, but by this stage of the narrative he has made his way out into the great world. Carefully concealing his earlier poverty, Dorrit seems to have attained the pinnacle of affluence when he is visited, unexpectedly, by the son of his former warder at the Marshalsea Prison, Young John Chivery. In brief compass, Dickens captures every turn of Dorrit's emotions. The suddenly alarmed Dorrit responds to Chivery's innocent visitation, first in terror, then in anger, then appeasingly, then suspiciously, then ingratiatingly, then with munificence in offering a virtual bribe for silence: "a little — hum — Testimonial . . . to be divided among — ha hum — them — *them*." Here is Dickens leading up to that moment, then letting its effect be realized:

The aforesaid grandeur was yet full upon Mr. Dorrit when he alighted at his hotel. Helped out by the Courier and some half-dozen of the hotel servants, he was passing through the hall with a serene magnificence, when lo! a sight presented itself that struck him dumb and motionless. John Chivery, in his best clothes, with his tall hat under his arm, his ivory-handled cane genteelly embarrassing his deportment, and a bundle of cigars in his hand!

"Now, young man," said the porter. "This is the gentleman. This young man has persisted in waiting, sir, saying you would be glad to see him."

Mr. Dorrit glared on the young man, choked, and said, in the mildest of tones, "Ah! Young John! It is Young John, I think; is it not?"

"Yes, sir," returned Young John.

"I — ha — thought it was Young John!" said Mr. Dorrit. "The young man may come up," turning to the attendants, as he passed on: "oh yes, he may come up. Let Young John follow. I will speak to him above."

Young John followed, smiling and much gratified. Mr. Dorrit's rooms were reached. Candles were lighted. The attendants withdrew.

"Now, sir," said Mr. Dorrit, turning round upon him and seizing him by the collar when they were safely alone. "What do you mean by this?"

The amazement and horror depicted in the unfortunate John's face — for he had rather expected to be embraced next — were of that powerfully expressive nature that Mr. Dorrit withdrew his hand and merely glared at him.

"How dare you do this?" said Mr. Dorrit. "How do you presume to come here? How dare you insult me?"

"I insult you, sir?" cried Young John. "Oh!"

"Yes, sir," returned Mr. Dorrit. "Insult me. Your coming here is an affront, an impertinence, an audacity. You are not wanted here. Who sent you here? What — ha — the Devil do you do here?"

"I thought, sir," said Young John, with as pale and shocked a face as ever had been turned to Mr. Dorrit's in his life — even in his College life: "I thought, sir, you mightn't object to have the goodness to accept a bundle —"

"Damn your bundle, sir!" cried Mr. Dorrit, in irrepressible rage. "I — hum — don't smoke."

"I humbly beg your pardon, sir. You used to."

"Tell me that again," cried Mr. Dorrit, quite beside himself, "and I'll take the poker to you!"

John Chivery backed to the door.

"Stop, sir!" cried Mr. Dorrit. "Stop! Sit down. Confound you, sit down!"

John Chivery dropped into the chair nearest the door, and Mr. Dorrit walked up and down the room; rapidly at first; then, more slowly. Once, he went to the window, and stood there with his forehead against the glass. All of a sudden, he turned and said:

"What else did you come for, sir?"

"Nothing else in the world, sir. Oh dear me! Only to say, sir, that I hoped you was well, and only to ask if Miss Amy was well?"

"What's that to you, sir?" retorted Mr. Dorrit.

"It's nothing to me, sir, by rights. I never thought of lessening the distance betwixt us, I am sure. I know it's a liberty, sir, but I never thought you'd have taken it ill. Upon my word and honour, sir," said Young John, with emotion, "in my poor way, I am too proud to have come, I assure you, if I had thought so."

Mr. Dorrit was ashamed. He went back to the window, and leaned his forehead against the glass for some time. When he turned, he had his handkerchief in his hand, and he had been wiping his eyes with it, and he looked tired and ill.

"Young John, I am very sorry to have been hasty with you, but — ha — some remembrances are not happy remembrances, and — hum — you shouldn't have come."

"I feel that now, sir," returned John Chivery; "but I didn't before, and Heavens knows I meant no harm, sir."

"No. No," said Mr. Dorrit. "I am — hum — sure of that. Ha. Give me your hand, Young John, give me your hand."

Young John gave it; but Mr. Dorrit had driven his heart out of it, and nothing could change his face now, from its white, shocked look.

"There!" said Mr. Dorrit, slowly shaking hands with him. "Sit down again, Young John."

"Thank you, sir — but I'd rather stand."

Mr. Dorrit sat down instead. After painfully holding his head a little while, he turned it to his visitor, and said, with an effort to be easy:

"And how is your father, Young John? How — ha — how are they all, Young John?"

"Thank you, sir, They're all pretty well, sir. They're not any ways complaining."

"Hum. You are in your — ha — old business I see, John?" said Mr. Dorrit, with a glance at the offending bundle he had anathematised.

"Partly, sir. I am in my" — John hesitated a little — "father's business likewise."

"Oh indeed!" said Mr. Dorrit. "Do you — ha hum — go upon the — ha —"

"Lock, sir? Yes, sir."

"Much to do, John?"

"Yes, sir; we're pretty heavy at present. I don't know how it is, but we generally *are* pretty heavy."

"At this time of the year, Young John?"

"Mostly at all times of the year, sir. I don't know the time that makes much difference to us. I wish you good night, sir."

"Stay a moment, John — ha — stay a moment. Hum. Leave me the cigars, John, I — ha — beg."

"Certainly, sir," John put them, with a trembling hand, on the table.

"Stay a moment, Young John; stay another moment. It would be a — ha — a gratification to me to send a little — hum — Testimonial, by such a trusty messenger, to be divided among — ha hum — them — *them* — according to their wants. Would you object to take it, John?"

"Not in any ways, sir. There's many of them, I'm sure, that would be the better for it."

"Thank you, John. I — ha — I'll write it, John."

His hand shook so that he was a long time writing it, and wrote it in a tremulous scrawl at last. It was a cheque for one hundred pounds. He folded it up, put it in Young John's hand, and pressed the hand in his.

"I hope you'll — ha — overlook — hum — what has passed, John."

"Don't speak of it, sir, on any accounts. I don't in any ways bear malice, I'm sure."

But nothing while John was there could change John's face to its natural colour and expression, or restore John's natural manner.

"And, John," said Mr. Dorrit, giving his hand a final pressure, and releasing it, "I hope we — ha — agree that we have spoken together in confidence; and that you will abstain, in going out, from saying anything to any one that might — hum — suggest that — ha — once I —"

"Oh! I assure you, sir," returned John Chivery, "in my poor humble way, sir, I'm too proud and honourable to do it, sir."

Mr. Dorrit was not too proud and honourable to listen at the door that he might ascertain for himself whether John really went straight out, or lingered to have any talk with any one. There was no doubt that he went direct out at the door, and away down the street with a quick step. After remaining alone for an hour, Mr. Dorrit rang for the Courier, who found him with his chair on the hearth-rug, sitting with his back towards him and his face to the fire. "You can take that bundle of cigars to smoke on the journey, if you like," said Mr. Dorrit, with a careless wave of his hand. "Ha — brought by — hum — little offering from — ha — son of old tenant of mine."

Little Dorrit has been described as a novel about the various confinements of the nineteenth-century industrial order.[2] Along with the Dorrits' rise in society comes a new supply of constraints, intimidations, insecurities, and outright prohibitions. In the Marshalsea there had been fear and degradation; but in the high society to which the Dorrits "escape," they adopt pretense and deceit, even terror. For William Dorrit the sight of Young John Chivery is a breakthrough of memory, a "return of the repressed," as Freud would say. Beyond that, though, Young John represents irrefutable evidence of the power of the past.

At first — while the servants are present — Dorrit acts polite and guarded, but the moment he finds himself alone with Chivery he displays a frightened man's rage at being exposed, put at risk. What risk? the reader asks, for the reader knows, and Dorrit has every reason to know, that there is in actuality no risk at all. Nonetheless, a decent friendly visitor is instantly transformed into a threat. Chivery's willingness to leave ("I wish you good night, sir") eliminates any rational possibility of external danger, but Dorrit embarks at once on another tack: benefactor to the poor. Still, despite his burst of generosity, he is reduced to asking his visitor to tell no one what he knows of the past of the Dorrits, groundless as William's apprehensions are. Young Chivery professes himself "too proud and honorable" to tattle. Dorrit still does not trust him and listens at the door after he is gone.

Here, as elsewhere, Dickens shows no interest in explicit psychological interpretations. He is telling a story, he wants the reader to be carried along on the wave of life. Yet in this brief incident (it takes up only four pages in a novel of some nine hundred), we are offered a virtuoso's analysis of a complex yet common mental phenomenon — the creation of the *other* as a way of protecting, and of concealing, the secret wishes of the self. The old *them* (the prisoners of Marshalsea) must never be allowed to mingle with the new *them*, members of England's high society. The new friends — Dorrit presumes — would never accept his former plight with compassionate understanding. Such a presumption cannot be dissevered from the person who chooses to make it. Yet Dorrit has to live his life among the denizens of a new world, and he cannot easily tolerate the resentment he must feel at thinking that his comfortable and influential friends would never accept him if his past were ever to be revealed.

What is one to make of this mixture of vulnerability, shame, rage, and defensiveness? Dorrit tries bribery, tries petulance, tries cajolery, and at last tries lying. The man of money and position becomes a child who tiptoes, who peeks and listens in hiding. In the language of the clinic, an element of paranoia emerges as an aspect of an episode of regression, and Dorrit is on his way to becoming a prisoner once more. And now we obtain final confirmation of the hold "many of them" have on him. Dorrit, sitting with his face turned away from the Courier, gives away the cigars as the pretext for a lie about Chivery's identity. He, who tried to placate and thereby banish "them," is now reduced to lying to his own servants so that they will not become judges, potential receivers and keepers of the truth, the dangerous truth. Dorrit looks to Chivery like the luckiest man in the world, right at the top of the social system. Chivery looks to Dorrit like a Trojan horse, dangerous enough to bring on a psychological shudder — and profound insecurity as a consequence.

The great Victorian storyteller and moralist was no stranger, obviously, to the intricacies of psychology. Such a moment in *Little Dorrit* justifies D. H. Lawrence's assertion that "the novel is the highest example of subtle inter-relatedness that man has discovered."[3] The "inter-relatedness" evoked in a scene like this one is stunning in its moral penetration, in its insistence that we have ingenious ways to fend off or reverse the accusations we level at ourselves. Dickens shows us that a man of great means can also be as vulnerable as a child. Mr. Dorrit's visitor, to repeat, is no potential rogue. But a man who arrives as a friend is regarded instantly as a threat, even an enemy. A person on the top of a ladder is afraid of his footing. He may, somehow, some day, lose his standing, be sent hurtling down — again be a member of the ordinary citizenry, or of the wretched mob residing in Marshalsea Prison.

For Dorrit, self-respect means a social station untroubled by the stains of memory. The presence of John Chivery brings poverty back to consciousness, and the result is an acute sense of imminent jeopardy. No one is standing nearby, ready to condemn Mr. Dorrit, or even report his actions to yonder big-shot world. No one outside of himself, that is. His mind, however, is seized by a kind of panic — the terror that goes with self-accusation. The charge is at best deception, at worst betrayal. He has been told loud and clear by some judging voice in his head that he ought be on constant guard, lest he be discovered. Dorrit's money and personal freedom are beyond anyone's reach — at least at this page in the novel. He is arraigned by shame, sent scurrying, psychologically, by a sense of helplessness — a chronic acquiescence to the social intimidation his world exerts on him. Dorrit's low regard of himself (shame), and all-too-high regard of others, induces him to act, to deceive, to cover his tracks. He is undone, accordingly, by a nervousness that is far more persuasive than the merits of the situation.

The next step is that of the subjective emergence of a "them" — the creation of the moral Other. But the "them" he wants to placate is, he realizes, more elusive than any enumeration of prisoners would suggest. Thousands of pounds sent to Marshalsea by its former inhabitant won't stop him from regarding himself as, forever, tied by fate to "them." Generosity extended to a "them" is patently self-serving, hence the donor's apprehensiveness. Like a child he hovers, spies, peeks, listens under cover, holds his breath. His own "Courier" becomes an instrument of his social insecurity — a means by which his mind gives symbolic expression to its moral unease. With his back turned to the Courier he gives away the cigars and tells another lie, hoping to conceal his former helplessness from his present servant.

Many children anywhere and everywhere can be observed choosing similar forms of placation in their continuing struggle to live relatively comfortable emotional lives. Here is a reverse of the *Little Dorrit* episode — a Brazilian child's self-definition linked to his view of the Other: "When I see boys of my age coming out of the hotels in Copacabana, or the apartment buildings, I think of how lucky they are, and I wonder if they *know* how lucky they are. My friend Freddy says they don't. They just go running to the next game they're going to play, or to the car that's waiting, with the chauffeur standing, and he opens the door for them, and smiles (some chauffeurs bow), and then the door is closed, and they sit and wait until they get to where they're going. Freddy says his grandma prays in church for those rich kids! She's sure they'll all go to hell, and burn there for a thousand years; and we'll go to heaven, and Jesus will sit down with us and give us a big feed, and tell us He knows all the streets of Rio, and not once did a hotel let Him come inside and go to a room and get a night's sleep!

"I laugh when Freddy talks like that. Poor Freddy: his mother died when he was born, and his father disappeared, and his grandmother gives him big Jesus talks one minute, and the next she's coming after him with a mop or, when she's really crazy, with a machete she brought with her when she came to the city. She wants him to go back north and cut sugar, but he's left her house, and he'll never sleep on her floor again. He goes to see her, and he says he can see in her eyes when she's ready to go off — she gets a mad look, and he points to the sky and says He's there, Jesus! It always works: she stares and stares, and he slips away. Sometimes she catches on to him, and swears at him as he's running. But sometimes she not only stares, but sits and speaks to God. She hears Him talking, and she answers Him. Freddy hid once and heard her telling Him all her troubles. Later, she told the priest she saw God, and the priest took her and screamed: he put his hands on her shoulders and shook her hard. He said she had the devil inside her. But a nun told her if she keeps seeing God, they'd investigate, the church people! Maybe Freddy's grandmother knows a good thing, and is trying to get it!

"No one says Jesus loved the rich; even the rich don't say He loves them! Even priests in Ipanema, who love the rich, and get new cars from them, don't dare say Jesus was all for them. Freddy and I wait outside their churches. We beg on Sundays; it's the best day. Outside church is the best place. We hear the talk inside. It all sounds good, until you remember that Jesus said there's the good and the bad, and the ones who are on top, all of them, will end up where I am, sleeping on some garbage pit, with the fires going all the time, and no fire trucks to come and put them out.

"I'm still not sure why it takes this whole life here to prepare you for the next life! What if it's the other way around — that we're here because we flunked some test in heaven, and so we're sent to shine the shoes of the rich, and pretend to cry when they leave church, so they'll soften up, and throw you a few *cruzeiros!* I got Freddy to ask his grandmother about this idea, that we're the ones who got thrown out of heaven, and that's how we got here, and the old lady went wild. She was ready to kill me! She said she'd spend the rest of her life trying to track me down, so she could kill me! I told Freddy not to worry: I can take plenty good care of myself, and besides, no one's going to tell her where I am, because she'd give herself away: People would be sure, then, that she's lost her head, if she has nothing else to do but chase a kid all over this city.

"Most people don't want to be bothered with someone like Freddy's grandmother. They don't want to be bothered with anyone who gets in their way. That's what Freddy and I have figured out: if you stand around and beg, or push people to let you shine their shoes or carry their packages or wash their cars or help them clean their house or move — then they just want you out of their way, and it takes a few coins to remove you, so they give them to you. Please, don't bother us, they'll say. Or, they'll say okay. That means: I surrender, or you've got me, so here's the payoff, a bill, and now disappear!

"I told Freddy once, we should pray for all of them; that his grandma is right — they're all going to hell in a hurry, and it's up to us to be nice, because they don't know how to be nice, only peel their money. They have clips, the men, gold clips, and I'd love to get my hands on those clips. I'd cash them in, then we'd all eat everything we've ever wanted. They'd be invited, too! I'd never want to keep anyone from a feast, if it was mine — if I bought the food, and I cooked it in a fire I'd made, in a place where I'd spent the night. Freddy says no one who's rich would ever eat with us. But you can't be sure. A rich kid once gave me a watch! He took it off, and gave it to me. It wasn't the best watch! He probably had five others. He probably wears his gold watch on Sundays to church. But he gave me the watch, and I told Freddy you can't be positive about all of them — only try to guess which one is like you. What do I mean like me? I mean, someone who's just trying to get through today and tomorrow, and he doesn't really have a grudge against people, against everyone. He'll be nice, if the person he meets is nice."

This Brazilian boy's thoughts, culled and edited from many conversations, came to mind as I read *Little Dorrit* again in 1980, in preparation for lectures I was to give that year on Dickens's later work, the so-called social novels: *Hard Times, Bleak House, Little Dorrit*, and *Our Mutual Friend*.[4] *Little Dorrit* is filled with people whose personal insecurities compel them to hide behind conventions, condescensions, prejudices, not to mention lies and dishonest business dealings. Again and again thoughts of the Other rescue one or another nervous soul: it is *them* who are pitiable, pushy, lacking in manners, style, deportment; it is *them* (when things get really tough, inside the head, for the ambitious and the greedy!) who are demanding and manipulative and insolently craven. Yet, the boy Manuel, only twelve, seemed to offer an opposite way of dealing with others, not to mention his own hard-pressed self. Whereas William Dorrit sensed peril almost everywhere, this boy of Rio de Janeiro's late 1970s streets laughed as he contemplated the world around him, including the important (and self-important) world of Copacabana and Ipanema, where he had occasion to keep close watch on "them."

For Manuel Silva (his mother's last name; the father left home before the boy's birth), the presence of others, well-dressed, well-groomed, well-off, and in health quite well (he himself limps and has poor eyesight and terrible asthma and chronic dysentery and multiple skin eruptions, sores, infections) does not seem to cause him fear, worry, resentment — even, it seems, envy. I have pressed this lad, and the interpreter with me — both of us a bit incredulous: Somewhere within there must be malice prompted by desire. And why not, given a "street urchin's" down-and-out life? Instead one hears a child lost in innocence, it seems; and captured by religious rhetoric, it seems. "He is too nicely spoken," the new interpreter says, her choice of English itself rather arresting. He is "holding back," the doctor thinks, or "unaware of other feelings," or saying what he has learned will please us. Our lack of confidence in him, our rudeness and skepticism toward another are, in this case, not that of a child. Still, we kept up our keenly interested watch, and we settled for an easy explanation — a bright child's natural charm and witty spirit.

Yet, over the weeks it became clear that this boy who spent half the week sleeping on a mattress of his mother's favela shack, and the other half huddled with friends in an alley near a church at the edge of Rio's Ipanema section, deserved a less patronizing, more respectful inquiry from the two adults who kept wanting to know what he thought and why he thought what he thought. We began to appreciate his moral seriousness — its expression in the child's observations of other people. Talking about them, he told of himself. Perhaps two perplexed outsiders were able to help Manuel by pushing him hard with questions: "When I answer your questions, sometimes, I hear myself as if I was someone I don't know! I think you are trying to discover what I think of everyone in the world! But I only know my friends here. You ask me about the people we meet, but we don't know them so well. We can tell, right away, if someone is mean and stingy; they don't have to *say* no, their faces send us the signals. Do you know what happened last week? I saw a man walking down the street, and he had on shoes that cost a lot of money, a lot; and he had on a suit that was expensive. He had on a silk tie. He wore a gold ring and a gold watch. He had a shiny leather briefcase. I told my friend David that the man was a lawyer, or a banker. But I said we should ignore him. I didn't like his eyeglasses; they were cold. I mean by 'cold' that they were not the kind of glasses a man who gives to us kids would wear! The glasses had gold parts, holding them on the ears — and no rims. It all happened so fast, but I'm taking so long to tell you!

"My friend David ignored my advice. I saw the man look at us, and he turned away as if we're trouble, dirty trouble. So, I said, 'wait,' but my friend approached the man and I got mad; I pulled him away, and said no, he's not the one. The man heard me, and he stopped, and came to us, and he asked me how I was so sure. I didn't know what to say. I smiled. David spoke. He said I'm a good judge of people! The man said no, I wasn't! He took out his wallet and gave us a load of *cruzeiros*. He didn't even count them! Then he whirled around and he ran off. Yes, he did run — as if he was late. No, he wasn't scared of us. Or wait, maybe he was. I don't know! I think he was angry at me. He was trying to prove David right. But if I hadn't stopped David in his tracks, if I hadn't said to him that we had a real tight-ass one, and let's not waste our time, then I think we'd have gotten the cold shoulder. That guy was trying to prove that no one in the world, *no one*, can get his number — not if he doesn't want to let the person get his number!

"I think we bother a lot of rich people! They'd rather we disappeared. But they know there are too many of us! If you try to be friendly, they're even more upset! There are some people who would rather that we go up to them and be coughing and even choking and crying, and then they'll give you a coin. The worse off you are, the better they feel! If you go up to them and smile, though, and try to be polite and friendly, they'll hold their noses and look at you as if you're a filthy animal, or sometimes, a dangerous animal, and they walk faster and faster and faster, and that's when I know they're scared, a lot scared, and it's best to move away, right away. That

man who showed me up — I wanted to tell him thank you, and say
I'm glad you got to have the last word, but he was too fast. I wish
everyone would be like him: My friend and I would have some more
money in our pockets, and lots of people would be pleased with
what they've done. But I still don't think I'd want my sister to be
his wife, even if she'd live like a movie actress. She'd win money,
but he looked like the kind of man who reaches for his belt, or has
vinegar and pepper on his tongue, always. My sister cries enough
when someone says she's done something wrong!"

I began to wonder then whether a perfect stranger, after all, wasn't
getting perhaps too bad a time of it — a street kid making a somewhat presumptuous sidewalk psychological appraisal, prompted by
a strong need to condemn another: The lean, fat-cat capitalist as a
touchy, combative hustler, ready to take on anyone, anywhere, even
a Manuel aged twelve standing in ragged clothes and without shoes
in front of a rather grand apartment house, near which are parked
an assortment of European sports cars, each imported at the cost
of a fortune in government duties. But the child resisted the "them"
I seemed to have in mind for him, if not myself. He had an instructive, a startling inclination for (tolerance of) the specific. I asked
what it was about Rio's fast-walking, well-dressed businessmen or
lawyers that gave him his psychological clues, and he gently cor-
rected me, maybe reprimanded my lazy or self-indulgent or briskly
ideological mind in this poignant and powerfully stated manner:
"Each of them is hard to figure out. I've made other mistakes than
that one! If I never made mistakes, if I could size up everyone
walking in and out of the Copacabana hotels or the homes and stores
in Ipanema, I'd be in big demand. I could sell washing machines
and furniture; I could get people to buy the clothes in the store that
hired me to spot people and persuade them! When my grandmother
[his mother's mother] was dying, she told me she had a message
for me, and to come near. I was scared stiff. Instead of moving
toward her — what I actually thought I was doing! — I moved away,
and my mother was upset, and she came and started pushing me

to go near, to go near. That's when I said words I never wanted to say; they just came out of me: 'I don't want to be so close to death; we're close enough now, here, the whole family, all of us, everyone in the favela, every single one, no one excepted, even the kids who are tough and can hit you and punch you, they could die overnight, and they do, lots of them, all the time.'

"I said even more. I was talking and talking — like one of the drunk men, like the priest, when he wants to show us who's the master of Portuguese, and who's the dumb, dirty dog, the dog afraid to bark when this man opens his mouth. My grandmother must have heard me, because she lifted her arms up (and I thought she was going to die, then and there, for sure!) and she got them working together: a big clap, and then another, and another, like in a soccer game for the star player!

"What did I do? She called me over, and by then I was glad to come. I was so curious that I moved near her: When she applauded I didn't know why, and I wanted to know — and besides, I realized that this old lady was a stranger, and here was my only chance (in my whole life!) to know her. She'd begged herself when she was young, I knew that — from men. She'd been hit by them, and she had scars to show for her nights with them, and scars from the cigarettes they'd stuck on her body. My mother told us all that when we were young, when we were old enough to understand. I have the memories! My mother wanted us to know why her mother was so quiet. Quiet! She could be silent without interruption for days and days and nights and nights. When we were younger, my sister and I thought she was dead — a corpse sitting there. One day I saw tears coming down her cheeks, and I heard her blow her nose. Then I knew she wasn't dead. She was remembering!

"My grandmother told me that she was going and she was glad the time had come, and she wanted to say goodbye, and she thought I knew the street better than any of her grandchildren. She said I should tell everyone what she said — that it's no good to be there on the street, begging from those people; but some of them are better than others, and some are worse, and even inside the lobby of the fanciest hotel, it's the same, and here where we live it's the same, too. She said I should always pray to the Mother of God, because She might give you luck. That's all she could say; she started coughing, and then I saw her turn gray, and I could see that her chest stopped moving, and she was still, completely still. I heard a gurgle in her stomach, but afterward, not a sound. I think she was going to say that the best luck is to meet a friendly person who doesn't want to hurt you — cheat you, hit you, steal from you, trick you, use you, set you up, make a fool of you, make you feel bad and rotten and lousy, give you trouble, make you sick, take you for one long ride, grind you down and turn you into shit, and make you think it's so bad there's no reason to try to get through the day, or the night afterward, or the next day. That's what she wanted to tell me; and even if she didn't say it all, she said enough for me to fill in the words for her, and I told my sister, and she started to cry. My sister knows her way around, and she knows lots of men, and she never cries, but she did then. My sister thinks she may meet a man who will be good to her and stay with her. And she may, with luck, meet that man! But she may not! My grandmother was hoping we'd have some luck with the people we meet. You can't think of all Rio as bad luck. My friends and I, we have good-luck days in Rio."

In the presence of such unyielding hopefulness one is ready to mobilize a psychiatric vocabulary: The "denial" of an exceedingly scared and gloomy child who (let's face it) has few if any prospects. Nor is it wise to overlook this boy's handicaps, the extreme vulnerability and marginality discussed in an earlier chapter. Nor ought one to blur the desperation of poverty with the reasonable optimism of an affluent family that all will go well. Still, even if we conclude that Manuel is whistling in the dark much of the time, and headed in the long run for a grim life, we must not ignore his reluctance to absorb others in his own turmoil — make a "them" the instrument of his self-assertion.

I have heard children, when describing the Other, be less outrageously explicit than Dorrit, yet far more interested in the psychological maneuver than Manuel ever has been. When I worked in the South, studying children going through the social, racial, and educational crisis of school desegregation, I fear I heard enough moral attribution from children and parents and teachers to fill long shelves of tightly packed tapes. Yet many of us who observe or treat children may overlook the ethical dilemmas that confront even children in primary school as they resort to attribution, projection, introjection. The superego, like the ego, has a good deal of energy at its disposal, and so too does that important ego ideal discussed earlier in this book.[5] Especially in a tense historical moment, young people put a lot of effort into "placing" themselves vis à vis all possible antagonists, as my wife and I were told in Atlanta by the thirteen-year-old (younger) sister of a *white* youth whose high school was soon to be desegregated by no fewer than two black students: "It'll be the whole school against them. They'll want to leave, I'm sure. It's foolish of them to go along with the civil rights people and be their slaves and come to our schools. They'll regret it. They must be nervous as can be. If they stay a few weeks, they could just collapse, my daddy says, and then they'll blame us, the white folks, but we tried to warn them. There's a lot of people who don't want to see what's right before them, so they go for pie in the sky, and then they fall flat on their faces; that's how daddy reckons it's going to be with all this integration.

"But meanwhile we'll all have to suffer, and it's too bad. If people didn't use others, like with the nigra kids coming to our schools, then we could all be friends. There's no trouble between us, between the races, until people start pushing other people, and then there's trouble, because you have to leave people to be themselves, and not try to turn them into what you want them to be. This is our school, right here where we live, and it's not supposed to be turned into the property of all the pressure groups in Georgia and the whole country, my daddy says; and it may take us time and a fight, but we won't just pick up and walk away before those people, no sir."

All those pronouns — we and us and they and them: This child testifies how many distinctions between people can become worked into one's way of both thinking and talking. This white girl, like boys and girls by the millions all over the world, has already acquired a complex manner of dividing up the world psychologically and morally. Other children in the Atlanta of the early 1960s could be heard making similarly arbitrary judgments — with racial polarities yielding to those of class, of neighborhood, of ethnic background, of region. We all know how clear-cut the segregationist rhetoric of, say, 1961 or 1962, was in Louisiana and Georgia; and we all know that schoolchildren were well able to mouth such rhetoric; but one wonders how much of our own inclination to divide up the world with a similar passion for *either* as against *or* is at all evident to us. The moral geography of others — the Dorrits, the Brazilian *favelados*, the Southerners we automatically call "racists" — is easy to discern and approve or disapprove: those rich hypocrites and pretenders, those poor innocents in the third world, those victims of a "poor-white" or "redneck" cultural tradition.[6] Yet, how many of us are comfortable spotting similar inclinations in our own world, that of our children, our next-door neighbors, friends, colleagues?

"Don't linger here too long," a Louisiana member of the segregationist White Citizens Council (long since disbanded, thank God) admonished me in 1964. "You'll just be feeding off us! You'll be so happy that you can see how bad and mean we are, that you'll never want to go home and take a look at your own backyard! No one wants to see himself in the mirror, warts and all. Everyone wants to pretty himself up, and also get a boost by looking at someone else's warts. You Yankees come down here, and oh, you're in heaven: You've got all us bad people to spot and write home about! When you do go back yourselves, you can make the rounds, giving pleasure to all who hear you — talking about *us*, those awful Southern folks who hate the nigras and lynch people and are so bad, just as bad as can be. That's a good deal for people, to have someone else to blame for the world being bad!"

Given his public attitude toward black people in his home city of Baton Rouge, I was content at the time to take him gladly at his word — keep blaming him, because he was, indeed, contributing to the world's badness. Nor would I now want my writings — with their reminders of how complex and flawed we *all* are — to undercut my personal responsibility to make judgments with respect to issues, people, statements. Still, there have been sobering moments when that segregationist's admonitions have resounded loud and clear in my head. Listen to a twelve-year-old girl from the wealthy Garden District of New Orleans musing (in 1962) about some other white people in her city: "It's causing us lots of embarrassment all over. My mom and dad went skiing in Colorado, and that's all they heard — our race troubles. I wish the colored people would stop pushing this; but I wish our white folks — the ones over there near the Industrial Canal — would stop behaving like a lot of silly, silly people. It's ridiculous the way they go out in the morning and stand in front of those schools and scream at those colored kids. *We're* the ones who are suffering — the people from New Orleans who travel to other parts of the country, and have to listen to how awful this city seems when those television stories come on the news programs. It's awful — all these cracker types, swearing and waving their hands. Everyone in the country can see them.

"I think one type is as bad as the other: the people in the mobs, and those colored folks, who are being used, everyone knows, by the NAACP from New York City. Daddy says they come down here, the lawyers, and they recruit these colored families to go and volunteer for the integration. You mix them up with our poor-white element, and you've got a witch's brew. That's how my mom sees it! If it spreads uptown, all the trouble, we'll just get out of New

Orleans. We'll have to move! We have our 'retreat' in Slidell, and
we'll stay there; or with my grandmother in Gulfport for the summer. We go there to swim, and dad says we can just stay into the
autumn. But he says it's not going to end up nearly as bad as you
hear some say it will — because even animals have sense, and know
when to stop doing something that's going to hurt them, and all of
them over there, whether they're colored or white, are going to
wake up one morning and realize that their bread and butter is going
down the drain, and so they'd better stop being so dumb.

"We know the people who own the companies near that part of
the city, and if they say so, there'd be no jobs, and *then* what would
all those people do! My dad says that most people, they behave by
instinct; they don't have their minds educated, so they can be intelligent, and do what's right. He's a lawyer, and he says he sees a
lot of people being pushed into corners because they follow someone
else's lead, and they don't think for themselves. So, we've got your
NAACP types pushing the colored, and you have the Klan and all
these trashy people shouting Klan messages, and between the two
there's all this trouble, because people get scared, and they do what
they think is going to be easiest for them, and there's no *right or
wrong* being made the issue, and that's what you need, people who
are educated and they know how to behave, and they decide what's
right to do, and they do it, so that everyone doesn't feel ashamed
of their city."

I fear that such remarks lend themselves readily, indeed, to the
satirist's pen, and yet also require serious attention as an instance
of how a child's moral life has been substantially shaped by age ten
or twelve. This girl's father was a prominent attorney, and of course
he was the one who had to take his marching orders, so to speak,
from the wealthy storeowners and factory owners of an old, cosmopolitan port city. A word from them would mean the end of one
lawyer's job — and this girl, not yet in high school, knew enough
about the sociology of the law to say out loud one day that "there
are oodles and oodles of lawyers, and the trick is to be a member

of a top firm." When my wife asked how that "trick" is accomplished, the child was quite forthright and forceful: "It's getting in with the right people. My dad says he knows lots of his classmates from law school who haven't done well, because they're not mixers. You have to go and meet people, and you have to talk with them and get their support and then you'll be their friend." When my wife asked about this "them," the girl was equally crisp, authoritative, candid: "They're the ones who own the city. There are these families, I don't know how many, and the leading lawyers have to help them, with their companies and their taxes. Daddy knows the tax laws inside out, my mom says."

This "them" and that "them," and yet another "them" over here: individuals of various backgrond whose habits, desires, motives, purposes, personal attitudes, moral values, have become the subject of a child's conversation — as if she'd taken the time to get to know a lot of people, and accordingly, obtained an exact notion of what they thought and why. Her parents' apprehensions are hers; their social or economic considerations are also hers. She is not shy of words such as "right" or "wrong." Her values sometimes come across indirectly — through statements she makes about others. The blacks of New Orleans, for instance — they ought to realize where their best interests lie; and similarly the working-class white people of that city. She certainly has come to understand where power and money are located in her native town. Those less agile at *Realpolitik* will be in jeopardy — but then, her father would also be in trouble if he started staking out any moral territory that set him aside from the "top" families whose names and addresses she knows well. Morality means decorum and social sophistication and a canny estimate of the propertied class — or so a daughter of one of their privileged retainers has come to understand. But much of this comprehension is expressed indirectly through description of others: a moral ascription that enables the speaker to have the comfort of privacy, anonymity, and a sanctuary of sorts, because a "they" allows an "I" to wax free, even eloquent, without fear of indictment by others, or even, one's own self.

In that last regard, a child who goes to an Episcopal church every week, and who attends Sunday school, has to be careful, even as she talks about the carefulness she desires from others: "They showed a picture of one of the colored kids [pioneering school desegregation] going to church, and then there was an interview they did with Martin Luther King, their leader. He said Jesus was on their side. How does he know whose side Jesus is on? Our minister said that Jesus doesn't get Himself into every squabble in every city and every country. How could He find the time? He left us to ourselves, the minister said, and my dad said 'that's right,' and when we got home he said he'd never heard a better sermon.

"The other day on television a man said it was 'un-Christian,' what's happening here, with the integration trouble. My father said the man was from New York; you could tell by his accent. I've been there, and it's dirty, and they have a lot of crime. We know someone who went there and his camera was stolen from his hotel room. He never even got to use it. Here people are nice to each other. The colored and the white are friends, except for this trouble in the schools. If people are left alone, they'll be all right. You can't take Jesus and bring *Him* into all this! My father said that if Jesus wanted *anything* done, He's got the power to get it done! If He'd wanted there to be only white people, or only colored people, He'd have done that! There's lot of people who keep trying to drag Him into everything that's happening here, and it's because they don't want to stand up and say what *they* believe, so they hide behind what they say *He* believes, and they expect everyone else to go along with them. But it doesn't work out like that. He's not in anyone's pocket, our Sunday school teacher said, and the more people try to take Him over, the more they show that they're not Christians, and they're just trying to use Him when they want Him to use, and the rest of the time they don't care what He has to say.

"Either you're a believer or you're not! If you believe, that means you go to church and you read the Bible and you say your prayers. If you're trying to win over your neighbors, that doesn't have anything to do with Jesus and His life. Jesus wanted people to listen to Him, and behave in a good way. He wasn't telling people where they should live and what schools they should go to. Our minister told us we have to protect Jesus from all His enemies who call themselves His friends, and that was the best advice we could hear, last Sunday."

As one listens to such a child trying to make sense of what others are telling her to be the plain truth, if not the Gospel truth, one begins to realize, yet again, how convenient others are for us, as we struggle with our often shaky convictions. Through others we try to settle things for ourselves. William Dorrit wanted to send a gift of money to *them* at Marshalsea because he assumed in *them* what was so much a part of himself — the lust for coins and more coins. This charming, polite, talkative, observant, intelligent, pretty New Orleans girl is instantly able to spot the moral vacillations and evasions of others because she senses her own parents' willingness to follow the leader.

The child's use of Sunday school lessons is not surprising. The parables Christ used provide enough ambiguity to cover many motivational tracks.[7] Any historical person can become a foil for children. As with Dorrit, the child's show of anger is often a prelude to this psychological maneuver of moral attribution — a warning to the listener that the speaker is stirred, upset, ready to go on the attack. It is as if the child has perceived a threat, and must at all costs ward it off. A threat to what? Sometimes the young person is quite willing to answer such a question and then proceed to construct a line of moral argument meant to shield him or her from all possible imputations or slurs. The show of agitation tells of moral unrest, and warns that an attempted solution to a psychological impasse is about to come.

* * *

When President Kennedy died, in November 1963, I heard southern children respond to that extraordinary moment in our history, even while those same children were making history themselves.[8] An assassination dovetailed morally for many of those children with the racial conflict they were trying to understand. I wanted the children to concentrate on the matter at hand, as I saw it — an account of what was happening to them in those classrooms. I failed to see that the moral life is an imaginative (symbolic) one not only for novelists and critics but the rest of us as well.

Listen to how Ruby, now eight, tried to make sense of the senseless, and in so doing, fashion some view of how the world works, how the world ought to work: "I don't see why anyone would want to kill him. He was just sitting in the car and he wasn't hurting anyone. There are people who won't let other people be! That's what my mother said when she saw the news on television. She said there's no end to this — people hurting other people. I know they'll swear at you and curse you, but it's hard to believe someone will just go and kill you, and he doesn't even know you, not really!

"The other day I saw a kid, and he was shouting at another kid — the kid shouting was white, and it was a Negro kid he was shouting at, right in our schoolyard. So, I waited for the teacher to come and stop them. I was near her, the teacher on patrol, and I kept thinking: Now she'll do something. But she didn't. She just kept talking to the other teacher, and I heard her say that *those kids* are always getting into trouble, and it's best to let them fight it out. But I could tell that the two kids aren't the troublemakers the teacher said [they were]. The Negro kid was scared, and the white kid was being pushed into hollering by two other white kids. They told him what to say, and he went and said it. They were daring him, I heard! He didn't even seem to want to obey them, but they were two and he was by himself, and they were bigger. So he kept talking about us bad niggers, and the kid, the Negro kid, he kept saying it's not so, and he should shut up, the white kid should. Then the Negro kid said the white kids were showing everyone in the yard what they were like, but he wasn't going to blame the whole white people, all white folks, for what they were doing, him and his two buddies. So, the two others went over and pushed the Negro boy, and he fell down and he started crying.

"That teacher, she'd been watching, and she'd been saying that the Negro boy was always getting into trouble — 'ever since the court order.' Then she saw the kids pushing, and she said to her friend: 'Look at them.' But she still didn't do anything to stop the fight. Then I was ready to cry, and I was going to go and speak to her, but the bell rang, and she did go over and she called them all 'troublemakers,' and I saw the look on the [Negro] boy, and I couldn't stop thinking of that teacher all day. When they called us together and talked about the President being dead, I kept seeing the kids fighting and that teacher, and like the principal said, you mustn't have hate, and if you do, then you're being like that man who killed the President. There's a lot of people who hate other people, and especially if you're Negro, you know about the hate. It's too bad they never stopped that guy in time, the man who killed the President; and our teacher here should just go up and stop the fighting in the yard, during the recess, because when you hear people saying bad, bad things about other people, then you know there's more trouble around the corner, because lots of people, the more they say, the worse they get, and then suddenly, they'll shoot, like that man did when the President drove by."

Apart from her shrewd and unfortunately well-practiced powers of social observation, Ruby had touched upon an extremely important matter, much discussed by psychiatric clinicians: Does a venting of anger, does the spoken exercise of moral attribution, help diminish the personal worries or anxieties that prompt such behavior? Or does the person only become upset, confused, enraged, self-righteously vocal, and more likely to move from words and projected moral sentiments to deeds? Rather obviously the matter is individual —with some getting satisfaction from (and others only being excited all the more by) the words that have been spoken, the attributions made. I do think children are less likely to gain emotional peace and quiet from this sort of moral maneuver than their parents (or teachers) do — because, after all, children are still struggling with the question of control over their impulses.

Ruby saw that those two schoolyard boys were not only being indulged by what they were saying, but were also excited to action, because at their age (and especially in a schoolyard recess) action is the norm. Ruby also noticed that the Negro boy was able to sense the attributive thrust of the allegations being hurled at him, and thereby in a position to disarm his antagonists verbally, hence their rising frustration and anger: the red glow in the cheeks that responds to the arrival of an apt truth. As for the teacher, *her* attributions were all too dismaying for this child who heard them unfold — an adult using children to confess her own indifference, her own resentments and inadequacies. Ruby certainly made a significant leap, psychologically speaking, from that schoolyard scene in November 1963 to the Dallas street scene of the same month, the same year; but she had a right to wonder exactly who and what it was that Lee Harvey Oswald actually saw as he took aim and pulled the trigger of his rifle — Lord knows what repository of hopes and fears and hates, aspirations and disappointments, all foisted on a distant figure, passing swiftly through the streets of a Texas city.

Haters, or those caught in a social network of prejudice and hate (such as the segregationist structure of the old South) are perhaps the easiest to understand, if one is trying to study how children or adults indulge in moral attribution to the Other. It is sad, and sometimes startling, to hear schoolchildren make strong statements about people different from themselves — statements saturated with imputation, accusation, denunciation. That adults — parents and others — are the original authors of such remarks, have handed them down as a birthright, doesn't really help the listener as he hears the familiar stereotypes being trotted out by a boy or girl of ten or twelve who, at other moments, seems so amiably innocent.

* * *

Skin color, ethnic background, "foreignness," social status — these are common sources of unfriendly characterizations. One of the most touching and instructive experiences I have had in more than two decades of interviewing parents and children took place in a wealthy Garden District home in New Orleans in October 1964, just after completion of the Mississippi Summer Project, whereby a number of black people were persuaded to make an effort to register as voters. The home belonged to a businessman and his wife. She had been born poor, in a small town in the northern part of Louisiana. Her life's story, by her own description, had elements of obvious drama: "I was one of eight kids. My father was a drunk, that was his real occupation, though he went through the motions of being a janitor in the regional high school. The teachers and the school kids, too, I think, protected him. Everyone thought he was such a good-looking man, and he'd fought in World War II and that made him a military hero, and no one can do wrong who's worn the United States army uniform and gone into battle. Well, he went from bottle to bottle, my mother would tell us. But she never got half the sympathy he did. She was just a poor country woman, trying to do her best to keep a brood of kids fed and clothed, and trying to keep her husband half sober. Everyone fussed and fretted over poor Jim, my daddy!

"When my father wasn't taking his whiskey in, he was 'spitting out dirt on people,' that's how my mother described it. Thank God for her! She was the one who encouraged me to try to be a beauty queen! If I hadn't gone down that road I'd probably still be up there, near Shreveport, poor as can be, but white, God almighty, white! And every colored person — man, woman, child — would be my painkiller, my morale booster, my outlet for the 'miseries,' as my mother called them. Our kind of people had to accept the 'miseries' as a fact of this life: little money, bills always pushing on you — and the worst of it, not having the excuse of being colored! You know, I think my daddy *envied* the colored folks: they could look at their skin and figure out why they were dirt poor; but not him!

"I've told you the rest [how she met her well-to-do husband], and for me it's been a wonderful life here in New Orleans. I always knew my husband had married me because I was pretty, a beauty queen; but I think I surprised him (I know I surprised myself!) by teaching myself through all the reading I've done, and through the courses I've taken at Tulane. My mother's heart and soul are inside me: She saw so very much, the poor, dear woman — that was her terrible agony, being a woman who had a lot of native intelligence, and who had to suffer all those years, living with my daddy. I remember when I was seven or eight, figuring out that my mother hated my father, that she really wished he'd die, but that she couldn't say so out loud to anyone, and maybe not even to herself. She knew she was doomed! And she knew most of us kids were doomed, too. She told me when I was a teenager that if I could escape, I should — any way I knew how! She said to me once: 'If they'll stare at you and hunger after you, fine — so long as you're the one who's running the show! Take the clapping and the awards, and leave here and go find a better life somewhere else!' At the time I was hurt; I thought she was sending me away!

"My mother worked all the time to keep us from hating the colored, and from hating all the other people my daddy hated, the Catholics and the Jews. He taught us hate in the cradle, I'll tell you. I remember his speeches. He'd come home drunk, and start in: blah, blah, blah! I was cured of hate by my own hate — for him, a drunk and a real loudmouth! I remember when I started school, I'd been taught who to hate before I'd learned how to read or write or do my numbers. When my father was sober, my mother used to tell us kids, he hated himself; when he was drunk he hated everyone else, even people not so different from himself. In between screaming about the niggers and kikes and Papists, he'd throw in some garbage-talk against 'filthy New Orleans' and the 'whores' there, and the 'filthy-rich' three families who owned our county, he claimed. We'd look over at our mother, and she'd wink. At least I saw her wink. My brother, one year older than I was, would repeat what my father said, word for word. He's the one I mentioned to you [that he belonged to the Klan], and I'll tell you right now, he didn't get converted by the literature those bigots hand out now; he was saying terrible things before he even started school. I remember when my brother turned five and he swore at a colored lady walking down the street, and we were with our mother shopping, and she told him to shut up. Later he told my father, and my father went wild, shouting at the niggers, and our mother, and then he gave my brother five dollars, one for each year of his life, and told him to 'keep the faith.' Later, I asked my mother what faith. I was yellow with envy that he'd gotten all that money! She said a hundred dollars wouldn't make it right to be mean about people — and I'll tell you, I've never forgotten that moment, and I never will."

This woman was especially sensitive not only to race but class — how a person's social standing can influence the way his or her children think about others, whose circumstances are different. Her own children had cousins who were full of scorn for "rich New Orleans people," for "nigger lovers" and "snobs" and "phony race-mixers" and "big-shot types." Those cousins were not beyond using a few spicy swear words, too. Nor were her own children unable, unwilling to turn on others in a fit of denunciation, outrage, and not least, moral smugness. At nine her daughter had told her that she didn't like her cousins, whom she'd recently visited, and didn't like some children she saw on the St. Charles Avenue streetcar, who reminded her of her cousins. The mother realized the child had, in fact, listened all too closely to occasional breakfast or supper conversations between her parents, not to mention remarks made by her school chums.

As I got to know the daughter, a well-brought-up, intelligent, and introspective girl, I began to realize how hard it was for her to resist honorably the various allegations and snide references she found her apparently confident and secure friends making. In the fourth grade of an uptown private school, she concluded this about the world she knew: "There's more than one New Orleans, I'm sure.

A teacher told us that you have to realize there are people who live in the same city, but it's not the same for them as it is for others, even if they only live a mile alway. And I'm sure she's right. My friends laughed after class; they said that teacher is real poor. They said she lives in the [Irish] Channel section, and she's a cracker who made good, and got herself an education at some school, and she's got a chip on her shoulder about the poor, and it spills over, so she worries about everyone, the colored, even. The teacher told us a week ago about some Chinese people in Mississippi, and they're supposed to feel left out of it! Why would anyone who's Chinese want to live in one of those small towns? My mother grew up that way — in a town where there wasn't more than a store and a gas station and a post office, and the same person ran all three! — and she said the best thing was getting out, and she hates, she really hates going back, even to spend a single night away up there. So, maybe the Chinese deserve the trouble they're in — because they must have *wanted* to go live in one of those Delta towns!

"A lot of your poor, and the colored and the Chinese, I think they're still living in the past. The Indians, too. I mean, you have to forget about the troubles of yesterday, and try to get ahead, and be positive. My dad says if you don't have a positive outlook, you'll end up getting nowhere; you'll be one of those pins in a bowling alley, and someone who's positive will just throw a ball and it'll come right down on you and all the other pins like you, and that's it, you're down and out! It's not right to be a bigot; you should treat everyone with respect. But some people will push and some are lazy, and some are sort of dumb, and if you can't see that, you need glasses! My father was born rich, I guess, but he never sat on his trust fund, waiting for his monthly check. He told the man at the bank that he didn't want any of his money; that he wanted to start out on his own, and see what he could do — and he succeeded. And my mother was born as poor as you can be. They both had a positive outlook, daddy says — that's what they have in common.

"Lots of kids say I'm too easy-going about people, but I don't agree I am. I just don't want to say some of the bad things I hear from my friends. My mother says you can criticize people without swearing at them! If you ask me, people should just leave each other alone. The colored should go to their own schools, and the white folks should have their own schools, like before. The people who are poor don't feel good going to school with kids who aren't poor. There's jealousy, you know. Some kids have waited outside our school, and gotten into fights with us. They're 'rednecks'; my mother says she knows the type, and she hates to use the word, but it's true; there are these poor white people, and they're not very smart, and they're slow, like the colored are, a lot of them, and that's why the two are at each other's throats, daddy says. But when my friends say they're *all* dumb, the colored and the 'crackers' are dumb, I just don't say anything. You can't argue. It's a half-truth, daddy says. Some of the teachers are on the side of the colored, you can tell, and some are on the white side. The best thing is for people to stay out of each other's way. I don't like riding the school bus much, because everyone gets jumbled up, and you can smell the bad breath and the body odors, and they'll step on your shoes, just to get more space to stand in, or a seat!

"Even in our school, there are some people who are nicer than others. There are always going to be the ones who do better in school, and the ones who don't. There are some kids who don't really belong here. They can't keep up. I think the best answer is for people who think the same way to stick together, and then no one will be left out, because there's always someone who's like you. A lot of our trouble is because people aren't happy staying where they are, and having their own friends; instead, they try to move in on others, and then you have trouble. There are some Jewish kids in my class, and they're different. They talk different. They don't bother us, but I don't know what to say to them. When our maid brings her kids to our house, it's the same thing: you try to be polite, but that's as far as it can go! The Jews are always raising their hands in class. If we had colored in our school, they'd probably *never* raise their hands!"

She had, months earlier, described her closest friend as being a "real whiz" at school — alert, outgoing, quite able as a student, and yes, ready and willing to volunteer with the quickly raised hand. Yet this girl, despite her sensitivity and thoughtfulness, was not likely to give individual favorable recognition to a Jewish child, who might raise a hand often in class, or a Catholic working-class white child, also a hand-raiser, and struggling with social unease. One afternoon, after a difficult day of two tests, in English and math, she was especially outspoken about the teacher her friends had branded a "redneck." (Ironically, it was this teacher who was known to favor "integration" of that private school — the acceptance of a few black students, if necessary with scholarship aid.) I hadn't before heard such strenuous criticism directed at any teacher by this child: "She's more worried about the colored, who aren't even here (and they'll never get here, everyone I know says, all my friends!), than she is about us. She's supposed to be teaching us, not them. She's supposed to be on our side, not theirs. If they are so good, why don't they prove it, by doing good work in school! The papers say the colored do real bad in school, but everyone's beginning to feel sorry for them. It's a reverse prejudice, one of my friends said. She's right, I'm beginning to believe. We got a lecture from that teacher on 'prejudice,' and how bad it is. But she's prejudiced! She gives us her sour look, and tells us how nice those poor kids are. Why doesn't she go teach them?

"I saw a colored boy steal, right in a supermarket. He was stuffing candy in his pocket. I knew he'd never pay for it. If he was here at school, he'd be cheating, probably, and some of our teachers would be saying he's a nice kid, and it's awful, how his relatives, 'way back, were slaves. My grandma, she's still poor; but my mum worked hard. My other grandma, she's rich, but you'd never know it. She doesn't spoil us. She gives us ten dollars on our birthdays, and we put it in the bank. With a lot of people, when you get money, you go and spend it, that very day. They'll buy lots of candy. They'll get sick, afterward, eating all they've bought. Then they'll complain that they don't have any money, not a cent to their name, and someone should give them an allowance, or they'll go and complain, or steal what they can get, without being caught. It's unfair, the way some people get away with things, and others don't, and then everyone is supposed to feel sorry for the ones who are having it easy."

There was in her that day a controlled fury. The weather was unstable after a late-afternoon drenching, accompanied by bursts of thunder and stabs of lightning — and she took note of the weather by reminding me that God had His bad moods, and so did everyone. I avoided looking too intently at her, perhaps because I had resented experiencing such scrutiny myself at times in my life. She next told me that her dog had "fits" upon occasion — mild bouts of epilepsy. He was a black cocker, and the attacks came suddenly, out of no-where, it seemed, but left rather quickly. The veterinarian rec-ommended *not* starting medication. As for school, there were days, she remarked, when she wished she could take that dog with her to classes: A dog is less demanding, provocative, enraging than certain students, certain teachers. Even her closest friends, she went on to say, disappointed her at times. Others may dread loneliness; for her, at least on that muggy day, there was every reason to enjoy being alone.

Still, she wasn't alone. She kept mentioning particular friends — this one and that one, this group and that group. Only gradually did I learn that she had not done too well in the English test, she was fairly certain, and she had done quite poorly (she knew for sure) on the math quiz. Now, she was faced with a social studies paper to write — for that teacher who had "a crush on the colored." The girl had spent so much time studying for her tests, she had little time left to prepare herself for her paper, never mind the actual writing of it. The result: blast after blast directed at the teacher. The teacher had failed to teach the class well. She had failed to give clear-cut reading assignments. She had been distracted by her manifest interest in those colored children and those "poor whites." No wonder that in a grand effort at restitution, at distraction, at glorious escape, this child took to her rather impressive easel, box of paints, and stack of brushes (Figure 3), in order to paint what she hoped would be a magnificent garden, packed with flowers of all kinds; she added a bench or two amid them, unoccupied, some tall trees in the background, and behind a large fence some huddled, poorly formed figures — a *Lumpenproletariat*. A *them*, a group dark and ill-formed and very much apart. "Who are they?" I asked. "Oh, some people." "What are they doing?" I asked. "Nothing." I dropped the matter — only to be told later, as I was hearing about the kinds of flowers in her mother's (real-life!) garden, and in the one she had painted, that "those people are the busybodies who come to the Garden District to peek at our homes." Having been told earlier that the infamous social studies teacher had a "bad habit" of opening up desks, to see if anyone was (illegally) stashing candy or gum, I decided to pursue this matter no further.

Ironically it is the poor and the persecuted who are often saddled with an additional burden — the claim that they, themselves hard put, uneasy, anxious, and vulnerable, are inclined to fasten on one or another excuse to make things easier. Without any doubt, the Klan has no monopoly on prejudice and hate, on "projective distortions," as psychiatrists put it. Nor should the legendary apprehensiveness of the "working class," or the "middle-middle class" as some like to call millions of their fellow citizens, be claimed as the sole source of prejudice, hate, "distortions." Snobbishness among the well-to-do, among the very rich, among the well educated, is a reminder that no amount of money, no accumulation of diplomas, and no top social position, seem able to offer immunity to the darker side of moral attribution — our need even as children to get rid of doubts, confusions, worries, and apprehensions through recourse to others, on whom we load censure too likely to be meant for ourselves.

Children of all backgrounds experience the "bad day," the moment when their own shadow looms large and menacing. Whatever threatens — a specific person, an event, a personal response hard to connect with a particular day's incidents — prompts an effort at restitution. As the girl put it one day when she felt low, "You've got to fight back." She did. She got angry. Her anger poured out; and the recipients were others — people she knew not at all: blacks, poor white people, Jews, one or two "Italian Catholics." So doing, she felt less low — but not altogether better. She actually felt ashamed of herself. She remembered that her mother had taught her to shun racist rhetoric. She began to qualify her words, add another kind of rhetoric, a mixture of American and Christian pieties, such as the declaration that "God made us all, of course," and the additional one that "every person is part of this city, and we should be polite to each other, and if we can't, we should go someplace else, where it's not so crowded!"

That sequence, from angry blame to a gesture of toleration, even generosity, is a fairly common psychological progression. Even quite angry children sometimes tire of the rage they are trying to fob off — become mellow, suddenly, or at least relatively restrained. As with William Dorrit a moment of fright and alarm, with attendant rage at a "them," can yield to a more tolerant attitude — as if someone had caught his balance, put things in proportion, and concluded that he is not as precariously situated as he may have initially felt. Then come the efforts at mollification, even an occasional cry of anguished atonement, or begging forgiveness for sins.

In a strange way, we are haunted by those we abuse, by those whose humanity becomes an excuse for jittery name-calling. And sometimes obsessions dissolve under our own moral self-scrutiny, or an occasional moment of psychological insight. "I cannot believe what I heard my child say," the mother of that New Orleans child herself said a year or so later, as she contemplated her daughter's outburst at a couple of black children who integrated her school. Such an observation marked the onset of a kind of self-consciousness; a girl's recognition, at the behest of her mother, that silence has its virtues set the stage for a reversal of attribution. At thirteen, in that same Garden District home, she spoke in this way: "You have to give people their rights. There's a lot of bad in everyone, but you can't just look for the bad. You have to think of the good, too. If you say mean things, you're not being very good to yourself, so you can't criticize others. My mother says to keep my eye on what I've got to do, and not get sidetracked by other people! My dad says, if you're jogging, and you start noticing all the other people jogging, and someone doing this wrong or that wrong or they don't have the right shoes or their way of running isn't good, then you'll never get to your destination, so you should forget others, and keep yourself on the right track."

There is, of course, a danger there — self-centeredness. But at least this young lady was learning to curb her use of a quite common psychological maneuver, and the result was a distinct wariness about her own inclinations or impulses. She began to cherish on occasions the silence her mother urged; and in time she began to find congeniality in another kind of moral attribution: "There's a nice colored girl who's just come to our school. She's real friendly. She tries to be like everybody else. I admire her: It takes real strength to come into a different world than the one you know already. The colored race has done a lot for us white folks. My mother says she doesn't know where we'd all be if it wasn't for all the colored people who help us out. I really do think God has a special place in His heart for them. He must see all they do for us, and He was a very sympathetic person when He was here, and our Sunday School teacher says He was real partial to all the persecuted people, and the colored have been persecuted for a long, long time.

"I saw a colored lady walking with her son; he was five or six, maybe. She was telling him to be good, and to say please and thank you. I followed them for a block or so; I just *had* to! I listened in; I wanted to hear more! She was being so good, the way she explained to the boy why he must be polite, and why we need to be kind to each other. I thought to myself: The colored really *are* God's people! They may not be as smart as a lot of us white folks, and they may be a little childish, like my mother says. But that's probably because God has chosen them, and they're not supposed to be like us. He liked children, we read in Sunday school, and He chose some people to stay with Him, and be more like kids. Maybe that explains why there's a difference between lots of colored people and us: they're here for a different reason than we are. I've heard our minister say it, and my mother and I believe it! I wanted to go up and hug that mother and her son, but they'd have thought I was nuts, plain nuts! But I smiled at them, and they smiled back."

We see more than a touch of sickly sentiment, condescension, and plain foolishness in these rationalizations for the status quo — but also there's a decided shift in the child's way of regarding an entire group of significant (and numerous) people in her daily life. Moral attribution need not be only negative — the child ridding himself or herself of various inclinations. Boys and girls may also look at the Other as a model for learning what to uphold, to consider good and decent in behavior. Sometimes blaming others can be a means of claiming alliance with what one believes. Not only our well-educated and obviously sensitive children find this a congenial mental maneuver.

It can be saddening to hear children who have learned to hate choose to seek out fellow haters. In the rural part of Cobb County, Georgia, one boy, whose father was no stranger to the white robes of the Ku Klux Klan, kept telling my wife that he couldn't understand "how Yankees got their ideas." When she asked him what ideas he had in mind, he answered "the ones about race-mixing." When she tried to ask him how he got *his* "ideas," he replied, "It's not only from my daddy!" My wife had, indeed, asked him about his father's views, even as we had both gone through several long, troubling

interviews with the man. But the boy wasn't simply being difficult
or eager to show himself independent of parental influence: "I get
my ideas from my friends. They're real important. When we go to
school we talk; and when we play games we talk; and we do a lot
of talking when we're fishing, or riding our bikes down the long
road and then up the hill yonder, and that's how you know what
your friend is thinking. My best friends are all real good guys! They'd
die for you! One of them almost did — for me!

"One day, Andy and I were fishing, and it was hot, very hot, and
sticky, so sticky our tee shirts were soaking wet, and so we decided
to go swimming. We'd never been in the river, because it's pretty
dirty, and we both like to go in pools, because they're clean. We're
both good swimmers, and we were splashing around and then we
decided to swim across the river, and I was enjoying myself, and
then I hit something, a tree, I think, that was underwater. All I
knew was this thump on my head, and I was dizzy, and I must have
been going under. Andy must have seen that I was in trouble: he
came and got me and rescued me. I don't remember any of that,
though. There's a blank between the time I got hit, while swimming,
and the time I woke up. I was on the bank of the river, lying there,
and Andy was talking to me. I remember seeing his face, and hearing
him say, 'Are you okay?' He kept asking, and I said yes, yes, and
then he sort of pulled me up by both of my arms, and I vomited a
lot of filthy, filthy river water, and then I sat there and slowly I got
better.

"Andy went and stopped somebody, and they drove me home,
and the doctor came, and he said I'd be fine. If Andy hadn't been
strong and if he didn't know his Red Cross rescue routine a lot better
than I do — then that would have been 'it' for me! The best part
was afterward — the way he came to my house and brought me a
chocolate bar and some of his *Sports Illustrated* magazines. He's a
real fine friend. I think he'd risk his life for anyone — not just for
me. He's working his way up as a Boy Scout; he's got a lot of merit
badges. He's the greatest person around. My mother called him 'a

true Christian,' and she's right. With Andy, you know that he's going to do what's right, not just what's convenient. Last year he ran in front of a car, to stop it from killing a dog. The dog is still alive, and whenever we drive by the house of its master, and see it, someone in my family mentions Andy. My grandma said Jesus touched him, and she's right."

A grateful boy enlarges his already favorable view of a friend to connect him with Jesus, with the highest possible moral tradition. Andy was not just a hardworking, ambitious lad who wanted very much to get ahead in this world, be an engineer at a nearby company, where airplane parts were made (he later succeeded in this aim), and to be a first-rate athlete and a popular person. Andy was, rather, a savior of sorts — not only for the boy and the dog, but also for a community of children who held a similar view of him. My wife and I knew Andy, and certainly agreed that he commanded loyalty, admiration. We'd also heard him mouth the ugliest of Ku Klux Klan pieties.

It is in a particular world that moral attribution takes place. William Dorrit might have been a little more relaxed had he met his old jailhouse friend on a deserted island. The awful price we would pay for *that* kind of "freedom" is isolation, loneliness. Not only do our parents watch us closely (at *our* behest, not only theirs), but our neighborhood friends do, and so too do our schoolmates and our coworkers — the people who, with us, populate a neighboring segment of this earth. Even as we learn to dread or dislike others, thereby feeling better about ourselves, we also learn to admire others rather uncritically, or to be hopeful about others, thereby feeling safer about ourselves. I use the words "feeling safer" because I have often heard children use moral attribution as a means of reassurance. Ruby and Tessie and other children reassured themselves when they marched past mobs on their way to school. Ruby's words: "They say all the bad things, but they'll change their minds one day, I'm sure, because they'll get tired, and they'll remember that it's not right, God says, to talk like that, to swear and all, and

I'm not sure, but I think some of them are saying the bad words, but they might be worrying if God is listening, and what He'll do." It was my wife's impression, my impression, as we talked with some of those hecklers, that Ruby was, alas, mistaken — that she was assigning to them a moral conflict we had never heard any of them express in our various conversations.

Likewise, in Brazil I have heard impoverished children express desperate optimism about a "them" that is utterly not in keeping with a given social or psychological reality. When a girl of eleven in a favela tells me that she is sure "they" in Copacabana are planning to bring food to an especially indigent, forsaken group of families (her own included), then one has only to read over some of her earlier, brutally skeptical remarks ("they never look at us, they only look at themselves") to realize that she is, alas, clutching at straws even as, perhaps, some of her more sweeping negative judgments may also reflect her own sense of self-disgust. After all, this girl, like many other *favelados,* has just started selling her body to the rich men of Copacabana: "They never want to talk. They prefer the dark. I don't think I could recognize them on the street in the daylight. They are crazy, most of them. I don't understand them. They want me to get as crazy as they are! I forget each night; the next day I sleep and forget. I forget them all! I only remember my mother and my two little sisters, and the food I'll bring home to them! Copacabana is where rich, crazy men live; their wives may live there, too — but their wives don't know the truth about their husbands. All Copacabana is a sewer! I have to breathe the air when I'm there, but I feel my chest getting heavy. When I get back home, I breathe in and out fast, and I feel myself getting clean."

An outsider notices the familiar unsanitary favela stench outside this girl's home. She is, needless to say, speaking allegorically, as we all do at moments in our lives — letting a visitor know about a hell that she enters, leaves, enters, leaves. When one hears her say, in a time of terrible fear (her mother quite sick, her younger sister dying), that "there is a lot of trouble in Rio now, but it will get better," one appreciates the reason a private agony has impinged upon an otherwise quite accurate sense of a country's social and economic difficulties. (Food riots had taken place in 1982, and many strikes, as Brazil's mixture of inflation and recession steadily worsened.) When one hears that "the rich, they are smart, and they will realize that the country is in trouble, and so they will save us," one wonders whether a child, in urgent need of help, isn't talking more confidently than her own shrewd head would ordinarily permit. If only, one thinks, "the rich of Rio" were as "smart" as this girl anticipates and declares! Meanwhile, there is her everyday life to live — its degradation softened a bit by a child's fervent hope that somehow, some day, the world (*her* world) will change for the better. In an earlier chapter, "Young Idealism," I tried to indicate how such a commitment to the future unfolds.

One need not travel thousands of miles from home to encounter grave paradoxes — take the familiar sentimental figure: the prostitute with the heart of gold. Rich children and poor children, American children and Brazilian children, all find their own convenient "them." Not only children from well-to-do southern families caught in a changing racial climate find themselves perplexed by racial antagonisms, yet stand ready to use them for a moment's psychological advantage. We will see in Chapter VII, "Children and the Nuclear Bomb," how sincerely compassionate, sensitive boys and girls are disposed at moments to construct their own kind of (occasionally self-serving) moral hierarchy. When a fourteen-year-old boy from a Boston suburb tells my wife and me that he is quite concerned about "all those people out there who are trigger-happy, and who'd let us get into a nuclear disaster," we are inclined to ask the young man exactly which individuals he knows who fit such a description, and how many similar people he's met. The answer: "I haven't talked with a lot of people from other parts of the city [let alone the country!], but I've read that there are people who don't seem to realize how dangerous nuclear weapons can be. My father is a doctor, and he said lots of people don't want to know about the dangers, so they stick their heads in the sand, like the ostrich does. They numb themselves to the danger they should be facing, when they should be scared as hell!"

Perhaps it is too much to ask of any of us that we pause and reflect upon the enormous complexity and diversity of any given "them," especially a "them" with whom one finds oneself at political and moral odds; to reflect, also, on the dangers of self-satisfastion if not smugness: a "they" that is "numb," as against an "us" that knows the score. The point is not to embrace the paralysis of a sort of analytic contemplation that has no activist agenda. We need to take a stand against the Klan, surely. We need to recognize what the proliferation of nuclear weaponry can mean to us all. But the Klan, or other groups that attract haters, do not just appear by genetic mutation, or because some moral monster has a contagious idea or two. Social and economic change wreak their havoc. The dangers of nuclear bombs are not necessarily unknown to many who don't speak their opinions on the matter, loud and clear. Here, too, class can count — the money of some people encouraging a forthrightness others don't feel able to muster. If William Dorrit could feel exposed, susceptible to attack, so too can millions of others. It is at these moments of heightened vulnerability that the mind gratefully seizes the chance to dismiss others, or obtain the protection of others. Anxious and uncertain on our own, or about our own situation, we discover and blame a hostile "them"; or we discover and joyfully embrace a friendly "them."

This tendency to flee ourselves, either to take moral cover in the company of others or to place ourselves at a firm distance *from* others, is no small aspect of a child's growing moral life. It deserves to be understood not as the exclusive disposition of kooks, of social malcontents or political eccentrics, but rather as a human disposition available to all of us, and quite evident by the time we are walking, talking, on our way to school. It is no small irony when some of us pose the "problem" of moral attribution as one for this or that "them" only — so that yet another "we" can delight in its own success at choosing suitable company.

VII

CHILDREN AND THE NUCLEAR BOMB

URING the early months of 1963, in obvious response to the recent Cuban Missile Crisis, two psychologists, Sibylle Escalona and Milton Schwebel, offered questionnaires to well over three thousand children.[1] The children were as young as ten and as old as eighteen, or seniors in high school. The point of the survey was to begin learning how the nuclear bomb, a presence on this planet since 1945, might affect the way in which children think about this life — its prospects, its possible pitfalls. Boys and girls were asked, quite directly, whether they believed there would be a nuclear war in their lifetime. They were also asked whether such a possibility preoccupied them, moved them to worry or continuing concern. The two psychologists (both of whose work was published in 1965) reported a distinct fearfulness in many of their respondents — a worry that a nuclear bomb, somehow and somewhere and sometime, would explode, with the world's future accordingly in substantial jeopardy.

These preliminary studies were not pursued further by the same investigators, or others, for some fifteen years — at least not in any systematic manner reported in the psychological or psychiatric literature. But by 1978 the American Psychiatric Association had become sufficiently concerned with the issue of nuclear war as a potential source of psychological symptoms to begin a study of "the psychosocial aspects of nuclear developments." Two child psychiatrists on the Association's "task force" tried to learn how America's children were faring. For three years (1977 to 1980) the two doctors, William Beardslee and John Mack, with their research associates, approached children as young as fifth graders, as old as high school seniors, in three cities: Boston, Baltimore, and Los Angeles. Again questionnaires were used (eleven hundred were handed out), and again they tried by asking pointed questions ("Do you think that you could survive a nuclear attack?") to obtain some sense of how this country's children have come to regard nuclear bombs. Presumably the two doctors had in mind the questions many of us would want to have answered: Do children pay much attention, in their contemplation of the future, to the nuclear arms race, and if so, how much attention, and with what possible consequences for their present and future lives?

Beardslee and Mack phrased one major finding in this way: "Approximately 40 percent of the total group reported that they were aware of nuclear developments before they were twelve." Another finding: "Approximately 50 percent of the 1979 sample of 389 high school students reported that nuclear advances had affected their thoughts about marriage and their plans for the future. A majority reported that nuclear advances affected their daily thinking and feeling." The doctors also reported that at least some students, in open-ended comments invited as additions to the questionnaire, were willing to be candid in their declared alarm: "There were vivid expressions of terror and powerlessness, grim images of nuclear destruction, doubt about whether they will ever have a chance to grow up and an accompanying attitude of 'live for now.' Some expressed anger toward the adult generation that seemed to have so jeopardized their future."[2]

In the next four years additional questionnaire studies were undertaken in various regions of our country. In New England (Newton, Massachusetts), a high school student[3] managed to get 550 of his schoolmates to respond to a version of the questionnaire used by Dr. Beardslee and Dr. Mack. About one-third of those young men and women were fairly certain that they would see a nuclear war take place. More than one-half weren't sure whether such a disaster would occur. A majority of the students, however, did declare themselves affected to some degree by the nuclear threat — in their sense of how the future might turn out. In the Midwest (Akron, Ohio) some seven hundred students (aged eleven to nineteen) responded to the questionnaire of a physician (he practices family medicine), and here again a significant number of students alluded to their fear of a nuclear disaster.[4] We are told, in testimony submitted to the Select Committee on Children, Youth and Families of the United States House of Representatives, on September 20, 1983 by Dr. Mack, that "a high percentage" of the Akron students (compared with those tested in his own 1979 research) "associated the word nuclear with destructive imagery as opposed to peacetime uses."

Of course, the Akron study was done two years after Dr. Mack's own research work had been completed, and one has to consider the consequences of change in our nation's social climate — an increasingly widespread and serious discussion of the threat posed by nuclear weapons: coverage in newspapers and magazines, movie references, television reports or documentaries. In Greensboro, North Carolina, a questionnaire with no fewer than fifty-one items was also administered in 1982. Some 372 high school students and 566 adults were asked to participate, and about two-thirds of those individuals said they were worried about a forthcoming nuclear war.[5] Just under two-thirds placed that war as quite possibly taking place in their own lifetime. In an interesting religious aside, perhaps of regional significance, 63 percent of those who took the test announced in their written comments that the Bible prophesied the arrival, one day, of a nuclear war.

In Los Angeles and San Jose, California, a psychologist and a pediatrician[6] approached 913 junior high school and senior high school youths with yet another questionnaire and found that almost 60 percent of them were worried to a noteworthy degree about a nuclear war, though the students as a whole were more worried about other matters: death of a parent, bad grades, injury in consequence of a violent criminal's actions. Meanwhile, a group called Educators for Social Responsibility took upon itself, in October 1982, to distribute their version of a questionnaire all over the country, in conjunction with a so-called Day of Dialogue, an obvious effort to get more and more people talking about the dangers of the nuclear bomb.[7] Mack's congressional testimony mentioned above reports that "many thousands" of those questionnaires were offered to high school students, and that "two thousand randomly selected responses were examined" — those from students in Massachusetts, Wisconsin, Oregon, and California. About 80 percent of these youths believed that the next twenty years would bring a nuclear war, and 90 percent were convinced that in such an eventuality life on our planet would not survive.

A psychologist working in Massachusetts and Connecticut also devised a questionnaire[8] (given in 1982 and 1983 to 100 private school, parochial school, and public school students) and also reported substantial concern among those tested — though other issues (the threat of joblessness, for example) were mentioned repeatedly. Finally, in a major study meant primarily to comprehend attitudes toward the nation's military forces and the draft, rather than nuclear weapons, Dr. Jerald Bachman submitted a questionnaire to many thousands of students in more than a hundred schools in forty-eight of our fifty states.[9] A rising concern about the possibility of nuclear war became evident in this research, done between 1976 and 1982. In 1976, 7.2 percent of the male seniors who took the test claimed to worry about a nuclear war fairly often; by 1982 that percentage had risen to 31.2. This is the only questionnaire survey, by the way, that claims to be rigorous and representative in selecting an accurate cross-section of our nation's high school youth.

So far only one effort has been made to supplement so-called survey research with an "interview study." Dr. Beardslee and Dr.

Mack presented their results in a paper titled "Adolescents and the Threat of Nuclear War: The Evolution of a Perspective."[10] The authors state their wish to learn "the perceptions and responses of these teenagers [thirty-one in all] to the threat of nuclear war," and their hope that they will be able "to determine in greater depth than is possible through surveys how these young people were dealing with the threat." The students were not chosen randomly. Teachers and parents referred them, or helped Lisa Goodman, a recent college graduate, to meet them. She conducted the interviews, which were single encounters, of three-quarters of an hour to an hour and a half long. One-third of the students had taken a high school course in which the subject of nuclear war figured prominently. The interviewees were asked a series of questions, and their answers were taped. In fairness, this singular highly structured encounter with two and one-half dozen students from the Boston metropolitan area has to be descibed as, really, an oral questionnaire — a specific and pointed inquiry made over a quite limited time.

The results (obtained in 1982) were thus described by the authors of the psychiatric article: "Reading the transcripts of these interviews makes more immediate and real the fears young people express about the threat of nuclear war. Although some students reported trying not to dwell on it, while others claim they worry about it constantly, all of the thirty-one adolescents asserted that the existence of nuclear weapons impinges on their lives on a daily basis. They report being reminded of the arms race when they read the papers or watch television, and that there is a constant worry in the back of their minds. These teenagers say they are afraid that nuclear annihilation will come, if not right away, then in a relatively short time. Some have planned to move away from the cities because of the threat; a few have decided not to have children, and they say that the threat of nuclear war has forced them to live more in the present. Young people report various ways of trying to shut out their thoughts about this matter. Some claim that the nuclear threat is responsible for their excessive use of drugs. A few cope with the arms race by refusing to lapse into helplessness and have chosen to take the course of political action."

The same psychiatric paper that offers those words is exemplary in its candid appraisal of all the research published before late April 1983, when the *Yale Journal of Biology and Medicine* received the scientific communication of Dr. Beardslee and Dr. Mack. An especially important statement is in a "critique" the two physicians make of their own work: "The questionnaire format did not allow definite answers to many of the questions to which one would want to have answers, such as the relative importance of this issue for young people in comparison with other social and technological problems, or the variation in thinking among young people from different regions of the country." This is an important cautionary reminder. At another page in their paper, Dr. Beardslee and Dr. Mack acknowledge of one study that "it was quite clear to the respondents what the researchers were interested in learning," and so "the subjects may have complied to please the investigators."

In almost all the studies there was ample room for such an outcome. The students, that is, were given the clue that the researchers had on *their* minds the issue of the nuclear bomb as a potential threat, and wanted to ask others what they thought or felt. In his presentation to the House of Representatives (mentioned earlier), Dr. Mack, with characteristic forthrightness, refers to the distinct possibility of a "researcher bias" in the various studies — as well as other so-called methodological limitations, which have to do with, again, the choice of children selected for participation in the survey research. In some of the studies it seems likely that the children chosen for the questioning have already found answers for themselves: they are aghast at the threat of nuclear bombs, here and in the Soviet Union, and are quite prepared to say so, on paper or by word.

There are additional problems with the research so far reported, and with some of the responses to it. Several investigators, not to mention such leading advocates of nuclear disarmament as Dr. Helen Caldicott and Dr. Robert J. Lifton,[11] a Yale psychiatrist, have referred to the use of "denial" or to "psychic numbing" as explanations for some people's apparent lack of anxiety about the nuclear threat. The implication is that such people are not facing up to reality — have, instead, resorted to what are often called "primitive defense mechanisms." In the California study, the authors assert that the students who are most concerned about the threat of nuclear bombs are "also aware more than their peers of other potential dangers in the environment." The authors state that "they appear to represent some of the most mature and better adjusted teens with high leadership potential." At the very minimum, such conclusions require careful substantiation. The psychological mechanism of "denial" is, of course, a commonly used one, however "primitive" some of us psychiatrists judge it to be. No one can bear paying attention, at all times, to this world's various dangers. Death faces us all, yet we often enough push aside that kind of awareness, and so doing, surely, do not put in jeopardy our claim to "maturity."

Those who conducted the California study commented that death (*apart* from the possibility of a nuclear war) is the major preoccupation of the adolescents given questionnaires. We who work with children know that they commonly struggle with fears and worries about death. How long will their parents live? How long will *they* live? Clinicians know enough to connect stated fears of an external danger with the continuing apprehension characteristic of childhood or adolescence. It is especially worrisome when, on the basis of a single questionnaire study, judgments of "maturity" and "adjustment" are so boldly offered. As Anna Freud observed, attending a conference at Yale in 1977, "it is hard for us to know what to think about any particular moment of a child's life — unless we have the time to know the child over the months and years." She also made this comment: "The better we know a child, the less inclined we are to see 'normality' and 'pathology' as distinct opposites. Children move in and out of various moods and it is the long range view that we must seek if we are to understand them."

Questionnaires given to a *representative* population tell about the relationship of a particular kind of consciousness to other "variables": the region where the various respondents live, for instance, their religious beliefs, their social background, their education. If we are to try to understand the significance of one element of consciousness, then we need to do what Miss Freud suggests: put in our fair share of time with some children, at least — enough boys and girls (who come from different enough backgrounds) to give us a sense of whether such an issue as the nuclear bomb affects them, and, if so, how often, and under what circumstances. It is context that matters — the significance of *this* matter compared with *that* one in the child's life. What in one child's life prompts worry about a nuclear war? What makes for indifference in another child? To obtain this kind of information requires rather long involvement with children — "direct observation," sustained over the years.

Even such an approach does have some limitations. A handful of children, known with some intimacy, should not be advertised as the "empirically validated" spokespersons of a giant research project, with all its claims to "objective" findings. Clinical field studies do more than risk the subjective; they embrace it. But they do contribute those details, those anecdotes, those revealing incidents, those puzzling, confusing moments which can offer their own instruction to us — the muffled ring of the small truth which brings us closer to some of this life's ironies and ambiguities. In the conference at Yale mentioned earlier, Anna Freud reminded her fellow clinicians that her father derived enormous depth of knowledge and ideas from "a handful of patients, whom he saw and saw and saw." She went further: "A single child, allowed to be our teacher for long enough, can tell us about many universal problems or predicaments — like a short story or a novel, opening up the world to us."

I remember vividly the first time I tried introducing the subject of the nuclear bomb to a child I knew fairly well. The year was 1979. I was visiting Albuquerque, where I had lived for several years in the early 1970s, and where (I now had begun to think) the nuclear bomb might well prove to be a fit subject for examination. After all, New Mexico is where the bomb was first developed and used, and where extensive nuclear research still takes place. A substantial number of families have some everyday acquaintance with the bomb — as an aspect of their continuing lives, rather than as an abstract topic. New Mexico may also be where nuclear bombs are neighbors: The West's mountain areas are known repositories for this weapon of weapons.

An Anglo boy of twelve was one of the children I knew well. I had met him initially when he was six and in the first grade. I had been eager to hear how he spoke of others, different from himself — a research effort to learn about matters described in Chapter VI of this book. His father was related to another child I had met and come to know years earlier. The father was, I thought, a sensitive and reflective high school teacher of English and of American history. He would, I felt, have some observations of his own on the subject of the nuclear bomb. Perhaps he had shared some of them with his son. As the boy told me what he thought was "good" about the Pueblo Indians he had met to the north of Albuquerque, what wasn't "too good," and what was "pretty bad, sometimes," I asked if I might ask him about something altogether different. Yes, he would be glad to oblige. I then made mention of the nuclear bomb; I briefly outlined an argument that for many years had engaged at least some people: to use or not to use, and if to use, when and with what justifying reasons. My presentation was informal and unrehearsed; at the end of it, I said this: "So that's about all. There's an ongoing discussion about nuclear bombs, whether we should ever use them. Some people say no, never. Others say no, mostly. Others say yes, under certain cirumstances. Others say, you bet — and they don't seem too fussy about the circumstances. Do you find this subject of nuclear bombs coming to mind at any time, or do you hear your friends talking about it? Do you have any thoughts at all on the subject which you would like to share with me?"

A pause. I decided that my comments had been stilted. I resolved that in future conversations (if there were to be any) I would be more relaxed, more inviting in my way of bringing up this subject. Meanwhile, the boy was saying nothing. I decided to go on: "As you know, I'm interested in what children think about various problems our country has to face — and this subject of nuclear weapons is one of those problems, and if you had any thoughts on the subject, I would be grateful to hear them."

The boy seemed lacking in interest, perhaps perplexed. He said nothing. He had been talking fairly freely thus far, and so I was made uncomfortable: I had managed to interrupt an interesting exchange of views, and now both of us were stranded. I found myself rephrasing my purportedly suggestive comments and inquiry, always a sign of one or another difficulty — and still to no effect. The boy shrugged his shoulders and said, finally, this: "Well, sir, I don't give the nuclear bomb much thought, no sir." He had not before addressed me as a "sir," and I decided to stop an exercise that was beginning to seem academic for both of us.

I tried again in Albuquerque the next day (it was late in the summer of 1979) with a thirteen-year-old girl whose father and mother are both lawyers. She was no more forthcoming on the subject: "I haven't been thinking of nuclear bombs." I tried, in vain, to get her to go on from there, so to speak. Children are great ones, after all, for self-effacing demurrers, for avowals or disavowals that turn out to be not the last word but a preliminary, testing remark, meant to see what the adult world really has in mind. But in this instance the child could say only what she distinctly meant — an absence of reflection on the subject.

The next day I went to a Pueblo reservation I know well, where I had worked for two years earlier in the 1970s.[12] I had a conversation there with several children whose older brothers and sisters I had met many times "back then." The phrase was one eleven-year-old girl's, who kept telling me that "back then" she had been only two or three, but she did remember her parents talking of "the Anglo doctor," and anyway, the family had a copy of the book I had written — one that their son, among other children, had so substantively helped me write. I remembered, in fact, some memorable statements made by that brother — outspoken condemnations of the ever domineering, combatively competitive Anglo world, including observations about the sonic boom we occasionally heard above: "The Anglos and their big noises," he would say over and over again. Now, years later, he lived in Denver, seeking training in electronics. His young sister was eager to talk about him, and indeed, about almost anything and anyone, I had noticed: a child eager, even perhaps too eager, to earn the grateful nod of her older visiting listener.

As the girl told me that she knew how skeptical her parents were of Anglos, their stated purposes and principles, given the history of their involvement with the Pueblos, I asked her about our present American dilemma of what to do about the manufacture and potential use of nuclear bombs — a problem, I told her, for all of us. I found myself, with that aside, annoyed — at myself: too didactic, moralistic, preachy, and also, rather more suggestive than I want to be in such a situation. I wondered why I was talking in this way. I decided that I was becoming impatient at getting no response from children. Had not three other children, all Indians, earlier in the day given no indication of the slightest interest in the matter of nuclear bombs?

This girl, actually, did eventually show interest. I kept bringing up the subject, and now she told me that she sometimes heard atom bombs being discussed on television, and that when she did, she was likely to stop and think along these lines: "There could be a war one of these days, and everyone would die. Then there'd be no more life left, and there'd just be a big desert here. Maybe some of our [Pueblo] people would escape, though: they'd go and hide in the caves. We know caves that the Anglos don't know. We know all the streets and the stores and the buildings. But we know the secret places up here, and we could just go and hide and wait, and then we could come out and we would be able to keep going —

we'd grow our food, and we'd mind our own business, and not get into any big fights."

I had heard such a scenario from Pueblo children years ago, though not with the atom bomb figuring in it. Again and again these boys and girls had told me of the mixture of fear and awe they felt for the powerful Anglos who run everything, and, too, of the bitterness that Indians also feel, as they think of what the future has to offer. Nor were other emotions lacking — continuing apprehension that even the land left in Pueblo hands would ultimately be seized; envy, as well, of the massive wealth and power of a people regarded, still, as intruders. Often military weapons of the United States appeared in the drawings of Pueblo children — a jet streaking across the sky, a military base placed in a desert landscape. The children, almost invariably, constructed a story quite like the one above: The Anglos are mighty, all right; the Indians can do little but hope and pray and retain some persistent sense of themselves as survivors; a moment of apocalyptic truth will somehow, somewhere, appear, and the result will be a fallen Anglo giant, whereas a saving remnant of Pueblos will survive, will start anew, and (who knows?) will yet have a chance to show what Indians can manage to achieve — peace, lasting quiet on the land, in the air, and a gentle, nourishing, harmonious social world.

I talked in 1979 and again in 1980 with other Pueblo children, some children of the children (adolescent youths) my wife had known and taught nearly a decade before. I found no specific, overriding anxiety or fear attached to the nuclear bomb as an American weapon. For these children, rather savvy in their distrust of what for them is another nation, the nuclear bomb is not much different from other aspects of Anglo dominance — always a reality, and always quite visible and audible.

Not that the Anglo outsider ought to ignore other emotional and ideological elements at work in these boys and girls. They are American citizens. Some of them have relatives who have successfully worked their way into the American urban middle-class life of, say,

Albuquerque. They enjoy the same movies and television programs as other children in New Mexico. They have watched Anglo tractors at work, bulldozers, construction workers putting up resorts, condominiums, dams, bridges, or laying down sprawling interstate highways. They see cars and motorcycles racing across the semiarid land, and dirt bikes defying any obstacle, it seems. Moreover, they have heard that those nuclear reactors, those nuclear plants, have the capacity to generate enormous amounts of energy. Such force may inspire not only worry and alarm, but excitement, admiration, curiosity, and even confidence.

A fourteen-year-old Indian youth (mostly Pueblo, but with some Spanish ancestry on his mother's side) spoke eloquently to me (in 1981) about the astonishing power of America, and his gratitude for it: "I know what it would be like if we lost to some dictator-country. The Indians would be slaves. The Anglos made mistakes here, but if you look to the south, you see that we're much better off than we would be if we lived in Mexico, or any other country in South America. I saw on television how the Russians treat people who aren't 'Russian,' the minorities. In Russia, if you raise your voice against the government, you're through. They'll jail you; they'll kill you. Here, we all love to spit at each other. We call the Anglos a bunch of coyotes, but who wants to leave this country? No one. We have to keep our guard up. It's like a boxing match. You can't give up your advantages, and let the other guy move in and take over. The nuclear bomb is one of our advantages. When we run out of oil, we'll be glad we have nuclear energy. If the Russians had nuclear bombs, and we didn't, they'd be telling us when to breathe, and when to hold our breaths!"

In the towns north of Santa Fe among children of Spanish ancestry, sometimes called Hispano-Americans, some of that youth's militant loyalty to this nation mingles with lingering distrust of the Anglos, whose old truculent ways are remembered well. Teachers have told my wife and me (as recently as 1984) that they cannot detect a special concern on the part of schoolchildren that our nuclear bombs will be used. Have those teachers heard any informal, even casual references to nuclear bombs? No. Might we talk with children separately and together in small groups? Of course — and so we did, repeatedly, in Truchas and Madrid and Taos, and later Espanola: conversations over two years, forty-three individual interviews and seventeen meetings with six boys and girls.

Some children weren't quite sure what nuclear bombs were, how they worked, let alone what havoc they might do. Nor were we, I fear, able to give them precise, simplified technological information. The longer we talked with the children, the clearer it became to us that nuclear bombs were not at all on their minds as an issue, a threat, a matter of concern or even mild interest. "I don't think these children give this topic any thought," a teacher told us, and in general we had to agree. One outspoken and perceptive boy of thirteen, quick to see *our* "thought," told us he had seen a program about the nuclear bombs dropped on Japan, and heard his father say that thousands and thousands of American lives were saved by the use of those two bombs, and "so if that was what happened, then it was good." Had he any notion of what might happen in a future war, were nuclear bombs to be employed? "Yes," he said, quickly: "Some cities would be wiped out, both here and in Russia, but our army would still have to fight theirs. I don't think we'd get any bombs dropped here."

I asked what places he thought might get hit. He hesitated, said he didn't know. I pressed the matter: Were there any cities in America he thought to be likely targets? He said nothing for about half a minute, then said "probably Washington." It was the capital, he reasoned, and herefore an inviting target. Did he have any idea what kind of damage would take place, and how many lives might be lost? He replied tersely: "There'd be a lot of buildings wiped out, and lots of people would die." I noticed that he was speaking in a quiet, matter-of-fact voice, and that he seemed not at all apprehensive. I asked him if he knew anyone who was worried about the possibility of a nuclear war, or who wanted to talk about the subject. He gave me an immediate "no" for an answer. Then he decided to tell me something: "My brother is in the army, and he's not worried. If he's not worried, why should I be?"

I felt a reprimand in his manner. He seemed grave as he looked at me, and a bit quizzical: Are *you* worried? I decided to be more assertive. I asked where his brother was stationed. In Europe. Where in Europe? In Germany. How did he know what his brother's attitude was about nuclear bombs — had he written letters home, been back on furlough? The boy said no, his brother hadn't been writing much, only brief notes, and hadn't returned to New Mexico recently, but his brother is "tough," and would never say we ought to weaken ourselves in any fashion: "This country is keeping a lot of other countries free, not just ourselves, and if we start giving up, then there won't be free countries any more. The Russians aren't giving up their bombs. They say we should weaken ourselves, but they don't let anyone push them to do anything they don't want to do." He now had to leave, because he was a patrol monitor in the school's halls and cafeteria at lunchtime.

In 1980 my wife and I started talking, yet again, with rural southern children we've known over the years — now about the nuclear bomb. In the past four years we have tried to have fairly detailed exchanges with these young people — an effort to find out how often they think about the bomb, and with what emotions. Many boys or girls complain of no real knowledge of how a nuclear bomb works; they also declare that neither they nor anyone they know are in potential jeopardy. On the other hand, I won't for a long time forget the remark made to me (1983) by a black child of ten in Greenville, Mississippi: "If the Ku Klux Klan ever got that bomb, it would be real bad for us."

It is possible, actually, to smile a little too quickly at such a comment: the condescending visitor who realizes how tough it still is for Mississippi Delta black families, and how isolated many of them are from this nation's mainstream. Yet, the boy had said what he said in response to prodding from his teacher, wanting to help me out. She had asked the class if anyone knew "about the nuclear bomb," and "what it can do, when it is dropped." No one raised a hand. She then turned to the boy just quoted, her ablest, most talkative child, and asked him directly what *he* knew about nuclear bombs. He replied, "Nothing, ma'am." The teacher then expounded upon the awful destructive power of one bomb. She added that there are hundreds "on our side," hundreds on "the Russian side." The boy's face then lit up, and he asked where the ones on our side are. The teacher wasn't sure. I said I wasn't, either — but rather suspected that significant stores of them are to be found out West, in the Rocky Mountain area. The boy wanted me to name a state. I said Colorado, Wyoming — again out of speculative ignorance. A few seconds of silence; then he made his observation about the Klan as a potentially dangerous possessor of nuclear weapons. His teacher said "true," but dismissed the comment. On her face one could see her judgment — an inappropriate connection between a national, indeed international issue and a quite local one!

Later, however, I learned of the boy's circumstances. He knew that an uncle elsewhere in the Delta had once been assaulted and injured by some Klan members. All he had done was to correct a white driver who handed him the wrong change at the gas station where he worked. That night stones had come crashing through his windows, and he had heard guns shooting sporadically in the dark for a few minutes thereafter. The uncle and his family had taken refuge with the boy's family, and the boy had heard many a frightened, angry conversation. His remark about the nuclear bomb getting into the hands of dangerous Klansmen, therefore, made a good deal of sense: a mind connecting whatever it hears to the dominant matter at hand. A fifth-grader with his own world to know and master, he had not given any thought to the danger of a nuclear war. He knew, however, that a nuclear bomb was "a big one." So with the Klan: "They're big white men, and they wear their big robes."

Some white children in the nearby Delta told me that they also knew how "big" the nuclear bomb is: "It's the biggest of them all." I wanted to clarify this impression. Is the bomb big, or its effect big? The children thought "both." One girl of twelve observed that the bomb has to be big, because it causes a lot of damage, and there has to be a lot of bomb to cause a lot of damage. No one disputed her; and I began to remember Piaget's observation — that at certain ages children have limited capacity to understand the laws of nature, of physics and chemistry. Several children thought nuclear bombs were bombs that had more "dynamite" than other bombs. One child said there was no dynamite in a nuclear bomb — only "electricity." When these sixth- and seventh-grade children asked me what I knew to be inside nuclear bombs, I was unable to reveal a great store of information — and that ended the discussion of "content." As for use, a girl of twelve said this: "It's bad to drop bombs on anyone; it doesn't make any difference whether the bomb is regular or nuclear."

In Atlanta, however, I met some children who were quite aware of the unique and overwhelming threat a nuclear war would pose to all humanity. I had first visited children in a white working-class neighborhood (1981), then a black working-class neighborhood (1982), and once again met children not at all concerned about this vexing issue.[13] In fact, I had to work hard to convey to these boys and girls that there *is* an issue. They felt that bombs are bombs, and big bombs are big bombs, and bigger bombs are — well, bigger bombs. A white boy, thirteen, the son of an Atlanta truck driver, told me this: "You get weapons in different sizes and shapes. There's so much power you need in one kind of battle, and then another kind of power in another kind of battle. But in some wars, you need all the power you can get, and as fast as possible. This is when they'd use the nuclear bomb. If we had an enemy that was going to wipe us out, like the Russians, we'd have to go right after them, and that would be all right. If we didn't defend ourselves, they'd win. They'd be figuring how much power they had to throw at us, and we'd be ready (I hope!) to throw the same amount of power back at them, and we'd have that final extra margin, I believe, to win!"

Did he worry about what might happen to our cities, to the cities of our enemy — to the ordinary people who might suffer a great deal in such a war? The question, I knew, was rhetorical, to say the least — a measure of my own frustration and even alarm: Nuclear war as merely a matter of quantitative power to be gauged by the two antagonists. The boy was not upset with me: "Sure, a lot of people would die. But if we didn't stand up for ourselves, we'd all die, or become slaves of the Russians. They even lock up and kill lots of their own people. They're a bad country, and we have to be able to beat them, and they have to know we can do it!"

This is an unsurprising analysis — heard not only from children but adults: War is hellish, yes, but if it comes, a nation can only stand fast and fight. Many years ago I had heard children talk thus, and in no way did my effort to focus on the specific nature of nuclear war seem to change their military assumptions. The moral issues were analyzed, all right, though not as a new and special instance (nuclear war) but in traditional terms. In New Mexico, Indian children, as I have said, had long had opinions about Anglo ethics, and were quite willing to cite the nuclear bomb as the latest example of American machismo, braggadocio, and God knows what else. In Mississippi for some black children, the Klan was still a living reality. For these children, "it's a hop, skip, and a jump," one black teacher told us, "from anything scary here to the Klan!" In Atlanta, among boys and girls whose parents were blue-collar workers, my wife and I thought we were hearing old-fashioned Dixie patriotism being given an airing.

In a neighborhood near Emory University, however, we met children (ten in all) who had quite a different view of this question. A medical colleague and old friend had introduced me to a number of parents whose distinct moral misgivings about the nuclear-weapons policy of this country (and the Soviet Union) were apparent, and whose sons and daughters, I was told, shared their parents' disquiet. These were all well-to-do people: doctors, lawyers, college professors, architects. The children were mostly attending private schools. They had heard, again and again, from their parents what nuclear bombs might do to this world, if ever used even in small numbers. Ellen, at twelve, was quite willing to tell me this — in response to a question about her present worries: "You shouldn't worry about anything except the nuclear bomb; it's the biggest danger to everyone. If one bomb got dropped on Atlanta, there wouldn't be any Atlanta left. We'd all be killed. It's that bad. I saw a film, and it showed the bomb going off, and it's like the world is coming to an end. If we don't stop the arms race, we'll all die! That's why we need the freeze! We have to get the freeze as soon as possible!"

I sat with Ellen and her older brother, Bill, who was then fourteen, and with some of their chums, and heard for two hours similar statements of urgency, of dread. Did they think it "likely" a nuclear war would take place? Yes, they all said — unless we of this country change our direction. How might we do so? The freeze! How might we persuade our own leaders and the leaders of the Soviet Union to accept the idea of a freeze? The children vied with each other when answering — as children so often do when they feel strongly on a subject and have worked out definite replies. The sum of their recommendations was a series of familiar steps: write letters; assemble in public to make one's views known; speak to one's friends and acquaintances; use the vote if you're old enough; keep following the news, so as to be apprised of who in which country is saying and doing what. I can only make a précis of several days of earnestly stated remarks, some delivered quite anxiously and emotionally. Ellen's best friend, Sue, also twelve, addressed herself to the indifference of others: "I'm worried because a lot of people are sticking their heads in the sand. My daddy says they're like ostriches: they don't want to see the trouble, so they bury themselves! The more who do it, the easier it'll be for the generals to go and push the button and use the atomic bombs, and then it'll be the end of the world.

"I agree, some people would survive, but millions would die, and that would mean we're no longer in the world we're now in. My father is a doctor, and he says there'd be no way for all the hospitals left, after the bombs were dropped, to keep up with all the people who would be sick. He says millions of people would die, right away, and millions more would be very sick, and even if a doctor *could* see them, he wouldn't be able to do much to help them, because they'd be dying, basically — dying.

"Why is it that more people all over the world don't push their governments to get rid of the bombs they have? They'd better do it fast, or there could be an accident, and that would be terrible. I heard a big explosion the other day, and I thought: It would sound like that, a nuclear bomb going off, only much, much worse. It would be like — as if God was coming down to judge us, and call us all bad for what we've done, for making these bombs."

That day she painted a picture of nuclear devastation — a bomb dropped on metropolitan Atlanta. She worked on the picture (Figure 4) with great care, and obvious anguish. She twice had to stop and explain her sadness — that such a scene might well represent our collective fate. When I told her, in an effort to be just a bit reassuring, that it was "quite possible" we wouldn't all be "witnesses to such a tragedy," she took exception, even became a bit reproachful: "I think you should remember that we're headed for a big showdown, and then the bombs will be used, and then we'll see black clouds over our cities, all of them, and so will the Russians, and it'll be the worst thing anyone has ever seen, and we'll all be gone, and my mother says if we're *not* gone, then we'll be in the worst trouble you can imagine, and we'll sure be wishing we were gone!"

She sat there, frozen almost. Her eyes moved from me to the window, which disclosed a bright pastoral scene: the sun gracing with its early spring light a great expanse of grass, and beyond some tall and wide maple trees — sturdy as can be, one began to think, and a presence there, surely, for decades. There was, for me, an anxious silence, which I didn't know how to interrupt. I tried not to be caught staring at this lovely child — tall for her age, with light brown hair and hazel eyes and freckles galore and a pug nose. Yet, I wondered what was in her mind, and I found myself worried about her, not so much in a clinical sense, but as a father myself, who was now wondering whether the girl had the heart on this delightful morning to resume her painting — render more corpses and collapsed buildings and rubble. I also felt somewhat intimidated, maybe even judged by this child — reprimanded for my reassurance, hence hesitant to say one word more.

After a minute or so I ceased looking out the window. My head was full of these thoughts, and I was explicitly troubled: no words, no action from Sue. Was anything "wrong" — with her, with me, with this effort I was making? What to say and do now? A gulp, then the readying of the vocal chords for a word or two — any word, any phrase, so long as this heavy hush would end. Before I could get the sounds out of my mouth, however, Sue's eyes moved away from the window, and she took up again her artist's task. I felt distinct relief in my mind and body both. The next thing I did, quite unwittingly, was stretch my feet, which had been tensely drawn together. I was ready to wait, as I had been doing for years with children as they drew. I had a book to read. Sometimes I have drawn pictures myself alongside a child — though not this one, Lord knows, with her wariness.

My relaxation was immediately spotted by Sue; her eyes lifted from the painting, went directly to my legs, fixed upon my shoes: "In a nuclear war, there'd be no safe food and water, and we'd be walking around without shoes and our clothes would be torn and dirty; I'm sure it would be terrible, and that's why we'd be unhappy, because we'd not want to be the ones who were still alive!"

Then and there I myself felt "unhappy." I felt as worried in my own way, I was beginning to think, as this child felt in her way. I felt that my stretched, relaxed limbs had offered her a message, had stated a truth that she required no all-knowing doctor to declare out loud, so quick and knowing was she. That's just the problem, she'd warned me, responding to my relative complaisance, my easy optimism, my blind satisfaction with a contemporary status quo! *You* can relax; but some people choose to face down this utterly real difficulty. Don't tell *us* about the difference between "fantasy" and "the reality principle" of psychoanalysis!

I pulled my legs back before I knew that I had done so. She thereupon went back to her paints. I decided to distract myself, because I was clearly a distraction to her. I also felt the need of some distraction for my own sake — a means of disengagement from a situation that seemed to prompt accelerating personal discomfort and perplexity, if not out-and-out confusion. I got up, and saying that I was thirsty, asked Sue if I might get her some water while getting some for myself. She shook her head — and, to my considerable relief, smiled as she said, "thank you." When I returned, however, I heard this: "I'm glad you mentioned water; I'd forgotten that everyone who survived would soon be dying from drinking contaminated water, or there might not be any water to drink, because the water pipes would be destroyed."

Inadvertently I showed a thin smile on my face; then, having realized what I had let happen, I wiped away the smile. I found myself trying to look consciously grim. How does one *look* grim? Sue was content to return to her art work, and so I took hold of my book bag, and extracted from it a stack of notes I had taken. I started going through them — reading, actually, what children of Sue's age, or a little younger, a little older, had been telling me these past few years in discussions about nuclear weaponry. Soon I was lost in that mass of paper, more than I realized. After about ten minutes of such reading, I heard Sue's voice addressing me: "Are those your notes?" "Yes." "I'm through with this." "Oh, good." "Well, it's not very good; it's awful." "I meant that I was glad you're finished." A pause. Then, her reply: "I hope we all don't get 'finished' in a nuclear war." "I do, too."

She stood there, while I looked and looked at her painting. She had used an enormous piece of paper, courtesy of a very well-equipped art studio in a private school. She had used her brushes and paints effectively — broad strokes, fine ones, and a lively mix of colors. There was a painterly aspect to her approach — the shapes of people and things suggested by shades and colors rather than by outline or contour. There was a strange openness, I thought, in this hellishly constrained world, so marked by death and destruction. I couldn't help noticing all the blood — a peculiar relief, I thought: the red a boost to the eye, in contrast to the grave black, the downward tug of the gray. Suddenly I spotted a touch of yellow — slanted lines, though, rather than the round body of the sun. I was grateful for the use of yellow, a pleasing contrast to the fiery red. Here was a girl who loved to use color! But as that thought crossed my mind, I began to feel self-conscious: how could I react so *appreciatively* to the dreadful scene? I felt glad I had kept my mouth shut as I scanned the painting.

We talked again when I was through looking. I began: "Oh, Sue, I certainly hope we're all spared this!" She replied without the slightest hesitation: "I hope so, too!" I felt better, somehow — a touching moment of agreement! I had begun to feel, earlier, some awkwardness; for, rather than admit to myself that I had been condescending to her, I dwelt in my mind upon her irritating self-righteousness. But even now she seemed uncannily "on" to me. She cast a glance at my face, which was not yet smiling but wanting to do so, and began her solemn message: "It's too bad all this might happen! I worry about my little sister; she's only two, and she doesn't know how horrible the nuclear threat is. There are times when I wish *I* was two! But my daddy is right: You can't be an ostrich! I have a cousin and she's three years older, and she and I were practicing hitting tennis balls, and then we stopped and rested, and she said she loved tennis, and I told her so did I. But if there's a nuclear war, that will be the end of tennis, and no more Häagen-Dazs strawberry." I went into a rhapsody on brands and flavors of ice cream. Even as I did so, I heard myself with some surprise! Sue looked intently at me. She had initially broken into a laugh as I answered her ice-cream reference with one of my own. But as I turned long-winded on the subject her face tightened, and when I saw that happen, I persisted with chatter, rather than shut up. I wanted her to smile again. I wanted to keep talking about ice cream so that we would *not* talk about nuclear bombs and nuclear wars and a nuclear catastrophe. She had used, once, the word "annihilation," and I remember being struck that she should know the meaning of the word so well — not the dictionary definition, but the distinct historical possibility that such a fate would be hers and mine and that of millions of others. I remember, also, being concerned, even unhappy. Across my mind this thought raced: Oh, let this child grow a bit, and let her not be so preoccupied with death — especially because there is nothing she can do, beyond worry and worry and worry.

Condescension in me had bloomed more intensely than I had realized; annoyance, too. These were the attitudes fueling my ice-cream commentary. She listened patiently. When I stopped for air, and to see what effect my mini-lecture had, she resumed with this: "My cousin said she was glad I reminded her. She said the trouble with a lot of us is that we forget. She said she'd try not to forget. We finished our tennis, and then we had our ice cream, but we agreed we would try to tell one friend that week to get her parents to speak out, to say they wanted nuclear weapons abolished all over the world. In our school there is a teacher who helps; he gives you information, an article, and you can give copies to your friends!"

No more talk of ice cream! Sue now had to go to class. I was left with my memories of our encounter, with her massive, ambitious, impressive painting — and with a strong urge to go get an ice-cream cone. That would have meant a drive of several miles. I did seek out the Coke machine, however. I went back to the room with my drink and sat there and looked again at the child's vision of nuclear annihilation: bleeding bodies, dismembered bodies, bodies piled upon bodies; wreckage of homes and office buildings, some collapsed, some with a few steel skeletons still standing — arms reaching out to the sky. And that sky: black as can be, a covering of death over the entire bleak, forsaken earthscape — with the usually powerful, penetrating sun utterly blocked. A few trunks of trees still stood, their roots drenched in pools of blood.

In a quarter of a century of work with children, some of them quite disturbed, hence hospitalized on psychiatric wards, I had never seen such an unremittingly raw, lifeless painting. If I had seen the painting before meeting the artist, I would have quickly had all sorts of gloomy, if not morbid diagnostic notions — severe depression, psychosis, or at the very least, a child paralyzed out of fear. In this instance, however, I knew Sue well enough to be reasonably sure she was not someone "in need of treatment," though I was beginning to realize that her fears were prompting at least one psychiatrist to stop and think — to see.

I sat there wondering what I had been made to see. Here was an almost Blakean vision — a child's representation of an apocalypse: life utterly extinguished, hope completely denied, death granted unqualified hegemony. Moreover, the artist knew precisely what was happening in the world around her that justified her artistic pessimism. Her pessimism was artistic and moral, not personal. Though she was a lively, cheerful girl, I was sorely tempted, sitting there, sipping a Coke, to consider her in some way *troubled*. Eventually I even went to the trouble of asking three teachers about Sue — knowing in advance that I would hear nothing to feed my clinical mind. But I had to settle some difficult account with myself: Sue as a child who got under my skin, whose painting made me feel like an ice-cream freak; made me respond like a doctor who ought to hurry and make a diagnosis; made me feel at times like an annoyed parent, tired of being pushed by a hectoring child.

Sue, I began to realize, had taken her parents' misgivings and dismay as her very own. The parents were no agitated zealots. They were a well-to-do, well-educated Atlanta couple: the father is an internist, the mother a former nurse, now a full-time mother of four children, with Sue the oldest. Both parents were Georgia-born, reared, educated; both are loyal, active Methodists; neither is of any particular political persuasion — nominal Democrats like many millions of other Southerners. They were not inspiring mad obsessions in a child.

As the southern expression goes, there is no reason to "make a federal case" out of Sue's bold challenge to my sense of what matters. She was no more or less than a feisty, direct-speaking, honest girl who knew how to call the shots as she saw them. She had a finely developed moral sensibility and an inclination to avoid evasions — hence her calm, forthright willingness to confront what quite possibly is in the cards for all of us. I believe I was angrier with her than I dared acknowledge to myself. At another moment I believe I wanted to consider her as at least on the way to being crazy. Her accomplished manner of painting, her powerful use of color, as well as that deadly black paint, had me scared. When I had given up calling her sick, or provocative, or a jejune moralist, or a smug dogmatist, I could finally let her be herself: a determined realist with an ethical worry or two.

In the metropolitan Boston area, I was able to pursue the same inquiry more thoroughly. I still wondered whether "really" (that is, well below the surface of things) Sue hadn't tapped some vein of psychopathology as she evoked so feverishly the bloody consequences of nuclear confrontation. What might a larger span of time with children like Sue, and other children utterly disinterested, or quite indifferent to the nuclear threat, tell about their respective psychological (even psychiatric) natures? Accordingly, I returned to families and friends I had known in my work in the late 1960s and 1970s — this time in various communities within and outside of Boston: working-class black and white families from Roxbury, Brighton and Allston, Lynn, Watertown, Waltham; and rather well-to-do families of Lincoln and Wellesley.[14] I talked with younger brothers and sisters of young men and women I had once come to know, and with their help got to know new families. I went back to talk with teachers, a number of whom I had kept meeting on occasion over the years. They were especially helpful, as were the parents I met, in reminding me of what matters to children in the long haul, as against what holds their attention momentarily. Sue, I learned, really did persist in her apprehensions; they had been an important preoccupation over the weeks, the months, the years. But I wondered about some other children I met, including Sue's classmates, who told me of their decided anxiety that nuclear war would demolish Atlanta, as well as Boston, but whose dread seemed (I judged) far more controlled than Sue's.

I worry about that last distinction, yet have been encouraged in it by the remarks of some teachers with whom I have repeatedly discussed this vexing issue. One of them (whose eighth-grade, suburban English class affords her ample opportunity to hear children speak their minds, not to mention read their thoughts as worked into compositions) kept insisting, a bit cynically, that all "interviews" done by people like me (never mind questionnaires!) ought be regarded with extreme caution: "I'll be blunt: I'm not so sure these children aren't conning you. Some of them are very bright; they've learned to tell people what they think those people want to hear; or they've just learned to talk a good line! I don't deny there is a true concern in some of these children about what might happen if America and Russia went to war, or if someone on either side pushed that god-awful button that sent the missiles on their way. But you have to pour salt on some of the words, the expressions of panic these kids can sometimes come up with. You have to ask why is the kid saying this. You have to notice who is being told what story. You have to keep your eye on the kid, so you know what he's like before and after he says what he says (or he writes what he writes).

"I saw one boy go in and talk with you. He'd been horsing around; then he knew he was going to be talking about a serious matter, so he straightened up and put on a serious face. I saw him after he left you, and in a second he was back to being the thirteen-year-old wise guy he is, most of the time. Unfortunately (for him!) he talks too much and has a booming voice and he's completely unaware of anyone but himself, and so he gets overheard all the time, sometimes making remarks that offend those who overhear him! In this case, I heard him at lunch laughing and telling his best friend that he convinced you 'the world is coming to an end'! The friend asked him how he did it. He said he told you about all the people who would die, and how everything would be ruined: there would be no electricity and gas and the water would be poisoned and it would be 'all bodies and rubble'; he said he told you several times, 'all pure bodies and rubble.' Then the friend asked him how he knew he had persuaded you. He said he knew, because he had met people like you, friends of his parents, and 'if you cry, they cry' were his words!

"I wanted to go and choke him! I get angry at kids every day, though I don't think I let on *how* angry! Sometimes an outburst from me is their only hope: to be told that their early adolescent, self-centered rudeness will simply not be tolerated! But I was eavesdropping, and I suppose I deserved the frustration I felt! Anyway, I hear these children say the most awful things, and I know in my heart that I *mustn't*, I just *mustn't* take them at their every word! Sometimes they're ashamed of their good-natured, considerate, and polite side; it's as if they have to show each other — and us teachers, of course! — how tough and callous and even crude they are. It's a terrible age! But it's also a wonderful age — because so much is happening. Every day, practically, you see amazing spurts of growth. I don't even recognize some of these kids from week to week! Well — an exaggeration, because there's a lot that doesn't change, in them and in everyone!

"I'm wandering off the subject! All I'm trying to say, really, is this: I'm sure that boy *was* sincere, just as I'm sure he was also putting you on a bit, *and* also putting on his friend as well. Most of all, he was telling himself (by hearing himself) that it's *appalling* what those nuclear bombs signify in our lives — that we're on the brink, every minute, of planetary extinction. Now if you stop and think about it — what is a thirteen-year-old boy to do with that? This boy's father is a lawyer, a law school professor, and his mother is a professor, too, and they sign all the petitions. I shouldn't talk like that! They're very compassionate people, and they've been active a long time in the nuclear freeze movement. But just picture all this from their only son's point of view! His older sister has echoed everything her parents say and do. I know. I taught her. The boy has the *three* of them to contend with. Frankly, I think he's bored by all this talk of a 'nuclear holocaust.' For him, it's almost everyday shop talk! But I also think he's scared, just as you and I are!

"What do *we* do? We forget. We say a nuclear war will never happen. We turn to matters we *can* control, or matters that will divert our attention from this worst of all possible events. When that boy tries to trick you, he's trying to say that the whole thing is a game. And for *him*, as a member of *his* family, it is, in a way: something that unites some members of the family, and divides others. The boy wishes his parents would every once in a while put aside their nuclear freeze passion and pay a little attention to him! I have overheard him saying that his parents are more worried about a nuclear holocaust than they are about his health! He has had asthma in the past, and he takes medicine, and they haven't yet taken him for a half-year checkup, and he wants to play lacrosse, and he's afraid, I think, because the last time he went out for a really tough sport, his asthma got much worse.

"I don't know why I'm telling *you* all this! I suppose I've become as jaded as these kids. Some of them are as sincere as Helen Caldicott: they're only twelve or thirteen, and you can hear them at lunch, worrying about Pershing missiles being deployed, and telling one another the terrible, terrible facts they've heard their parents recite at the dinner table. But many of them are quite intent on turning their backs on their parents — and even have trouble sitting down for half an hour with their parents, to eat together at the dinner table. These are the children who will use anything their parents say against them, and if you and I happen to be around, against us, too! Remember, this is not something — the nuclear bomb, the nuclear freeze — that these children can *experience*. One girl, a black girl who is bused out here [under METCO, a voluntary program to bring some of Boston's ghetto children to suburban schools] put her finger right on the nub of all this; she said to me she thought 'all this talk about nuclear this and nuclear that is head talk.'

"What did she mean? When I asked her that, she said I knew the answer! I told her I didn't. I wanted to hear *her* answer. Well, she said: 'When I talk about "racism," I know what I've gone through. It's not an idea, "racism." It's not one of your "theme subjects." It's me being called "dirty nigger" by a honky on the bus. These kids, they've never been through that. They talk a big line about "racism" and "nuclear disarmament," but it's like going to a class or something!' I couldn't get her words out of my mind for the rest of the day! She keeps her eyes on these kids; she knows them, in ways, better than anyone else. Wait: I should qualify that — she knows them better *in certain respects* than anyone else. In some ways she doesn't know them at all."

Much more was said over many days by this high-spirited and hardworking teacher. At her suggestion, I did, indeed, get into many talks with the black youth quoted here, and heard extended versions of what the teacher heard. This young woman of thirteen became both passionate and agitated in her delivery — and hard to ignore in the tough substance of her reflections: "I've been here two years. It's not my world; it's theirs. Today I might wish it was mine, but tomorrow I might tell every one of them they can damn well have everything they've got! You hear them talking about the new cars they'll get when they can drive, and what new country they'll go see this summer, and how they really get bored, so they're glad *this* weekend they're going down to their summer home on the Cape, or up in New Hampshire someplace — and then they tell you that 'this nuclear thing is a real bummer,' that's what a kid told me, and she's *so* proud because her father went to protest at some nuclear plant someplace. Do you know what she had the nerve to come and tell me? She finished showing off her new necklace to her friends, and then she spots me, and she asks me if I know about 'the big meeting tonight to get people organized for a nuclear freeze,' something like that. I was going to say: Honey, I leave here to take my bus back to that 'awful place, Boston' (I hear them say that, and they mean the rich part, Beacon Hill, not Roxbury where I live!), so I just can't join your 'party.' That's what they told me they're having, a 'party' after the meeting! And they tell me the 'nuclear issue' is for them what 'racism' is for me! I told that to my mother, and I'm not going to tell you what *she* said!

"You know what? They get a kick out of this! If it wasn't for the nuclear bomb, they'd be in trouble; they'd have to find some other reason to show everyone that they're the top dogs, and they're the leaders, and we should listen to them. I heard one of the kids say: 'My dad says you have to get involved in the *big* issues.' She was so excited: they were going to meet someone famous who's against the 'nuclear holocaust,' just like them. I get so mad sometimes I'm ready to drop a nuclear bomb on all of them!"

She was, she reminded me, "only talking"! She saw their finer moments, their less pretentious, less self-important sides. They could be (both to her and to each other) sweet and solicitous and generous. She knew, and in candid moments could say, that the heart of the trouble between her and "them" came down to (what else?) class as much as race. And so it has seemed to me after several years of trying to understand why some children become so awakened morally to this issue and others seem so thoroughly unconcerned with its possibly life-and-death meaning to all of us. In other words, I find that the children I have met who have taken this issue to heart, whose moral life has become, as with Sue, quickened by discussions of what so threatens this very planet (the chance that an "exchange" of nuclear missiles will one ghastly day take place) are children, again and again, from well-off families whose parents are themselves involved in the so-called nuclear freeze movement. Class, then, is a primary determinant of how children sort themselves out on this issue — but also the presence or absence of parental encouragement. Some affluent parents, after all, give nuclear bombs no thought at all.

Ought not *everyone* (in his or her right mind, one wants to say as a matter of common sense) be opposed to the use of nuclear bombs, and want to see their manufacture stopped everywhere, their use absolutely prohibited, their very presence on the earth eliminated? Yet, many people have deep and abiding fears about the Soviet Union. Whether such fears are reasonable or not, they are widely entertained, the polls tell us, and I have in my home-to-home visiting experience heard them expressed quite often. Moreover, the "working-class" people I have known, and their children, too, in Massachusetts as in New Mexico or Georgia, and black and white alike, have, by and large, not made the nuclear freeze theirs as an emotional issue, nor does one hear their children taking it into themselves, "crying with it out of the heart," as I used to hear Dr. Martin Luther King say. Often, in fact, I have heard class animosities all too grimly and vigorously expressed by working-class children on this issue — for example, the angry scorn conveyed by the black youth quoted above.

As for Sue, who made such a strong impression on me, I have returned often to Atlanta and followed her progress into adolescence. She has been doing "right well," as it is often put in the South. She still worries earnestly about the thousands of nuclear bombs scattered over this earth. But she has been heard to talk about other matters, also important to her: "I forget about nuclear bombs for days, and then I wonder if I'm losing my conscience. I hope not! Every Sunday I pray to God to help us end this nuclear madness. I hope He hears me!" In Boston, I ended up meeting several children, boys and girls, rather like her — though none quite so compelling in his or her moral directness and earnestness.

I think the black child's critique, and the schoolteacher's, tell us something important about anyone's moral life — and tell us something important, as well, about what must precede moral involvement, namely what I suppose might be described as the criteria a person has for *moral notice*. Each of us seems to have the time, the inclination, the disposition to regard only selected matters or issues as morally compelling. As one listens to our young, white poor, they can often be heard raging at the terrible disparities of wealth, comfort, power in this nation. For black people, or Spanish-speaking people, or Indians, it is a similar asymmetry — some of us with so much going for ourselves, others with so little. Among "working-class" people (not poor, but surely not rich and influential, and, they know, thoroughly vulnerable even to slight economic downturns) it is often a matter of keeping one's head above water: meeting this day's hurdles, a demanding enough task. As one thirteen-year-old Boston boy put it: "My father can barely remember to obey the speed limits while he tries to get to work and punch the clock on time. He says he's got no room for any other worries inside his head than the big ones already there!" I doubt that such a moral lesson will fail to have a continuing hold on this child. But for some of us there is another life — one that offers the time, the ease, the personal and economic security, the social assurance that permits the mind to wander and wonder, to take up issues and causes, to take stands unconnected to a wage struggle, say, or to a racial conflict. Children born in such circumstances can find broad leeway for moral reflection of the kind Sue pursued. Needless to say, as Sue herself observed, the advantages of life don't guarantee an outcome such as hers. There are lots of influential people, as mentioned, whose children could not care less about the nuclear threat, or for that matter, anyone's welfare other than their own.

Children know and favor the concrete. An abstract moral issue is hard for them to comprehend as thoroughly real and pressing. Thus it was that Sue did her best to make some concreteness for herself, for me — that unforgettable painting. She, too, I suspect, worried that a mere exhortation followed by the contrasting expanse of a particular life may offer meager moral nourishment indeed. In Sue's words, at fifteen: "I hope a lot of people become better people by the time we get the nuclear freeze; we've got to be — because if we're not, there will be another close call, like this one."

Immediately, she went on to hope that *she* would become "better." I wondered out loud in what respect she thought she ought to improve. She smiled but was silent for ten seconds or so. "I should leave my friends alone sometimes. They tell me I drive them 'crazy' with my sermons! They stop listening to me after a while." She had been so advised repeatedly by one of those friends, was at first disbelieving, but finally saw her point, and did not forget it. She began to worry about self-righteousness — a work of the devil, surely, as she had often been told abstractly in church, but now had occasion to consider in concrete connection to her very self.

This youth was struggling to reach others by breaking down a large barrier between them and herself. Who among us, however older and more educated than she, can clearly see the moral assumption of others — or even those we ourselves have come to hold dear? Even as this child had gradually learned how hard it is to understand friends, and to be understood by them in turn, the rest of us find out, in time, about the barriers separating this planet's human beings: nationality, race, class — the three most important. The more time I spend talking with children, the more I am brought face to face with the question of class, its enormous influence upon boys and girls as well as grownups. For a while I could not quite see what a child's attitude toward the nuclear bomb had to do with his or her parents' social and economic background. The nuclear bomb threatens all of us, and surely all of us have an interest in staying alive, in preventing the extinction of the species to which we belong, and all other life, as well. But few of us seem able to regard this matter of human survival, however universal, in the clear light of its unparalleled significance. Class persuasively tells us what really counts in this life.

Poor children, for example, have told me for years that they do indeed worry about extinction: hunger and malnutrition are their lot, and their drawings reveal again and again recognition of terrible, persisting vulnerability. When such children *do* mention nuclear bombs, they seem transformed into symbols of other, more immediate threats — the apocalypse of a broken ghetto world, the holocaust of a dazed, despairing migrant farm community, the sense of utter futility some Indians feel as they look back at the past, contemplate the present, speculate about the future. I simply do not hear children of poor families mention the threat of nuclear war as a major worry for them. True, they watch television, and without question that produces a heightening of awareness: There are thousands of these almost infinitely lethal weapons, and in a war, everyone in America would be in mortal jeopardy. But the black youth bused to a suburban school knew well the world she left five days a week. As I have talked with her younger brother and two sisters, with a cousin of hers, with other children who live near her in Boston's black neighborhood of Roxbury, I have not heard nuclear bombs mentioned; only dope and coke and smack and needles and syringes and booze, bottles and bottles of booze, and a future of no work at all, and bold, hungry rats and brassy cockroaches who seem to know no fear and stairs that cave in and fires — the arson that earns slum landlords lots of insurance money. It is *this* nightmare, this complete devastation these children know and want to depict with crayons or paints, and not rarely mention in conversation.

As for children whose parents are so-called blue-collar workers or white-collar workers, they, too, take their cues from a given world, learn its preoccupations, worries, apprehensions — wherein, "you have to work overtime just to keep up," to quote from remarks made by a girl whose mother is a nurse, and father is a factory worker in Lynn, Massachusetts. The father offered an example of what he meant: "You ask what my big worries are, day after day. I'll tell you. It's whether I have enough cash to fill up my gas tank, after all the bills are paid. I have this terrible nightmare sometimes — that I've run out of gas, and there's no more money to get more, and the last week of the month there *isn't* any money, so I drive slow to save gas!"

That statement has continual echoes, one begins to realize, in family after family. I have sat with that factory worker's daughter, who is now thirteen, and with her brother, who is eleven, and heard them in these recent years notice a news item one day about the nuclear bomb, or a "docudrama" on another day, such as *The Day After* — but always at my prodding. Left to themselves (and how else does a child psychiatrist find out what a boy or girl *on his or her own* deems worthy of mention, discussion, conjecture?), there is scant concern with nuclear bombs, the possibility of nuclear war. Rather, one hears about first communions, toys purchased on the cheap, toys too expensive to be purchased, toys one day to be purchased, if enough can be saved; and one hears about Scouts and bikes and the cars parents have bought or hope to buy, but are always paying off; and one hears about trips to the beach for the day, and ice skates, which can be costly, oh so costly; and about bills — hospital bills and mortgage payments, and high, high interest rates, and loans, and loans to pay off loans, and credit cards that can't be used for a while, or credit cards newly "operative" because "the balance has been reduced." The Lynn girl just mentioned told me this family news, and more, too, in response to my inquiry, one week, about how things had gone recently for her and her brother and their parents: "This has been a good week all around. We can use the credit card, and my father got a better second job. We'll have more money coming in, so we'll be nearer to even. We'll never break even, though — my mother says: only when we go to heaven, if we're good most of the time. There's a man across the street, he works like a dog at his job, and then it all disappears in hospital bills and doctor bills. His wife is sick. It's like the end of the world. There's always a bill collector at their door!"

In some homes of the well-to-do one hears different notions of how it will go when "the end of the world" arrives. I refer, of course, once more, to children whose parents are themselves deeply concerned about the nuclear issue. Rather paradoxically, the Sues of this world worry hard and long about nuclear accidents or wars, yet have everything to live for — and seem to me comparatively hopeful most of the time about their prospects in life, nothwithstanding their responses to questionnaires. (Sue took one in 1982 and quite truthfully proclaimed her horror of a nuclear war. That very evening she had a great time at an elegant party given by her cousin.) In a similar vein, a youth of fourteen, a freshman at a private suburban school north of Boston, tells me worriedly what he heard his parents tell — Dr. Helen Caldicott's conviction that if President Reagan were to be reelected "accidental nuclear war becomes a mathematical certainty." When I question the lad about the accuracy of the quote, he brings out a copy of the *Harvard Crimson*[15] brought home by his older brother, who works earnestly, conscientiously, and at some sacrifice to his schoolwork in the Cambridge Nuclear Freeze Movement. The boy has repeated exactly what he has heard his parents declare, and himself has read. Yet, like Sue, he plans ahead — for ski trips to Colorado and summer vacations on the coast of Maine and scuba-diving lessons and sailboat races. He lets a visitor to his home know that he expects to go to college, and he knows that for him "the place will be Dartmouth," and the only impediment to such a future he sees is his grades: "If I do work, I'll be there. My best friend's brother is a sophomore there, and we've visited him. It's a good place if you like skiing the way I do!"

This polite, kindhearted youth doesn't get upset about money the way lots of working-class youths do. He *expects* to be in college the way ghetto youths *expect* to stand idle in the street. Though he has in mind for himself all sorts of wonderful plans, this youth declares himself to be "sick" over the possibility of a nuclear war, and "really pessimistic" about what the next few years may bring. He would enter Dartmouth, if all went well, at the very end of what would have been a second term for President Reagan, if all had gone well for *him*.

Even as class separates children with respect to their thoughts (if any) about the nuclear bomb, class separates their parents — something our politicians surely know. Some of us have the leisure to worry about some issues that others ignore, because they are overwhelmed by different issues. In *The Road to Wigan Pier*,[16] Orwell reminds his relatively small number of educated, well-intentioned readers that they may well be fatally separated from millions of ordinary working people, whose lives demand their own priorities and set limits on all other concerns. In that book, a precursor in some ways to *Animal Farm* and *1984*, Orwell prophetically warns of the consequences — a drastic misunderstanding between a privileged and decent (if occasionally smug) intelligentsia, on the one hand, and on the other a working class that is precariously situated, as well as inclined to intense patriotism (with, meanwhile, millions of the poor battered into indifference or worse). Such a misunderstanding, of course, presents not only dangers but, to some, clear-cut opportunities — as in the old saying, "divide and conquer," this time with the fate of children all over the world quite possibly at stake.

NOTES

INTRODUCTION

1. Miss Freud's book *Normality and Pathology in Childhood* (New York: International University Press, 1965) has helped all of us in child psychiatry to pause and wait, lest a moment's diagnostic and categorical zeal be wonderfully or sadly mocked by time — a symptom, gone, or a spell of progress undercut by trouble that seems to have come from nowhere. She was a great one for what she called "watchful waiting" with respect to children. When she was told that America's President Woodrow Wilson had used that phrase as a means of conveying his policy during World War I — to be carefully, observantly neutral — she smiled and remarked winningly: "Children have their small wars, and often we have to suspend our judgment about their significance until we know enough; and it takes time, a long time, to know enough." Her emphasis on time, on longitudinal assessment, is especially noteworthy and exemplary at this time of fast survey research, of questionnaire studies analyzed by computers, of hasty hour-long interviews all too obviously geared to a specific "topic" through directed inquiry. She was willing to let children lead her where *they* wanted to go, and the press of a research project, of data and results, be damned. Always she asked us to spend *time*, with boys and girls, if we would gain some overall sense of what had been occurring to them, and why, during a span of their lives. I have tried to acknowledge my admiring obligations to Anna Freud in "The Achievement of Anna Freud," *Massachusetts Review*, VII (Spring, 1966), and in "Children's Crusade," *New Yorker* (September 23, 1972).

2. Her phrase "direct observation" was meant as a suggestion and rebuke both. She urged her colleagues to give children the most extended of scrutiny — *and* to be cautious about the way in which they use theory. "We must back up our conclusions with concrete details," she said — a novelist's vision as well as a scientist's.

3. We have learned in our medical offices to listen for these "voices," but most children, please God, don't go to see child psychiatrists. Moreover, how do children who aren't patients get on, as thinkers and worriers and dreamers (literal or symbolic) in their ordinary lives? Here the researcher's "location" can mean a lot — out in that so-called field, sitting in a kitchen, a living room, standing

on a schoolyard or neighborhood playground: repeated and unashamedly casual chat (at times, seemingly wandering or pointless). Yet, over the years the "moments" reveal themselves — when a powerful personal eloquence, a pointed psychological acuity has been, almost in an offhand manner, conveyed to the listener.

4. The philosopher Gareth Matthews has done enormous justice to this matter — what children can comprehend, morally, on the spur of the moment — in his brilliant and knowing *Philosophy and the Young Child* (Cambridge: Harvard University Press, 1980), and in *Dialogues with Children* (Cambridge: Harvard University Press, 1980). I can only repeat here, in essence, what I wrote (in an introduction to the latter book) about his work — the gratitude a person feels when he meets a thoughtful friend walking down a road that does have its pitfalls, but deserves to be traveled.

5. It was in Cape Town, South Africa, ironically, that I began to have some second thoughts about my American work — as happens, often enough, when one goes abroad, only while there to return home in one's head by virtue of a moment of contrast. At the University of Cape Town I was questioned intently about the United States by South African students, and when I was back in my own country I tried to think about what answers their questions required. It was then, too, more than a decade ago, that I began my work in Brazil. See "Children and Political Authority," the T. B. Davie Memorial Lecture, published by the University of Cape Town, August, 1974, and also in the *New York Review of Books*, February 20, 1975, March 6, 1975, and March 20, 1975; and "Children of a Brazilian Favela," *Harvard Educational Review* (February, 1981). The South African work, needless to say, is written up at some length in the companion to this volume, *The Political Life of Children*.

6. As I have stated in separate essays on "Method" in the *Children of Crisis* series, and begun to say once more in an earlier footnote to this chapter, my work entails a lengthy effort to get to know a relative handful of children. I have kept up with about half of the children I've come to know during these past twenty-five years — watched them grow up, marry, become parents. A visit or two a year has given me some knowledge of how these fellow citizens, once so vulnerable as children, and rather often, poor children at that, have managed to do in this life. When I decided to look at the moral lives of children I approached a number of these families and asked their help. Rather quickly I was put in touch with friends, neighbors, younger brothers and sisters, cousins — and the result was a new group of children to meet and get to know: five in the Belle Glade area of Florida, where I did my earlier work with migrant farm workers, five in Albuquerque, where I'd lived and worked with Indian- and Spanish-speaking and Anglo children, two in Atlanta and three in New Orleans, where I'd worked with well-to-do white families as well as black families struggling with school desegregation, and ten in the greater Boston area, where I have put in years among a range of families — some quite well off and rich, some working-class, some rather humble, to say the least. Moreover, I met (in 1980) an entirely new group of young people who had a lot to say, and they are described in the chapter "On Character" — a research project involving interviews with high school students in Massachusetts, Georgia, and Illinois. Some of these young people, their younger brothers and sisters, their friends, helped me enormously on the subjects of "character," of "moral purpose," and too, helped the explo-

rations I have pursued on the attitudes of children toward the nuclear bomb. I have worked rather closely with many of these younger children, visiting some of them (in Massachusetts) twice a week for three and four years. The individual interviews (no child was seen fewer than twenty times) are recorded, transcribed, edited, analyzed by subjects discussed, and compared with interviews of other children on the same subjects. The problem, believe me, is not the difficulty children have in talking about important matters, or again, the significance, the lucidity, the persuasiveness of their comments, but rather the complex, thickly textured character of all those young minds at work, their sensibilities responding to one or another issue put to them, or, not rarely, raised by them: the difficulty in distilling so many thoughts, suggestions, passionate preferences, strongly stated objections, doubts, worries, hopes, dreams, so many stories, really, into the chapters of a book. I suppose our work can be called a kind of documentary child psychiatry harnessed to efforts at thematic analysis — and, as anyone who makes regular home visits knows, the constraints of a book's covers seem very narrow when so much is said, when compelling personal narratives are necessarily sacrificed.

7. See the article mentioned in footnote 5. I am especially indebted to Ms. Adriana Monteverde Elia for her important help with translating and making favela (and nursery schools) visits in Rio de Janeiro.

8. A meeting with her at Yale University in 1979.

9. Tillich's popular *Courage to Be* (New Haven: Yale University Press, 1952) and his *Systematic Theology,* in two volumes (Chicago: University of Chicago Press, 1951) give obvious evidence of his strong psychiatric interests.

10. From *Paterson,* Book I. I have tried to indicate my deep debt to Dr. Williams in *William Carlos Williams: The Knack of Survival in America* (New Brunswick: Rutgers University Press, 1979 and 1983), and in *The Doctor Stories of William Carlos Williams* (New York: New Directions, 1984).

I. PSYCHOANALYSIS AND MORAL DEVELOPMENT

1. See his *Young Man Luther* (New York: Norton, 1958), and *Gandhi's Truth* (New York: Norton, 1969). I have tried to indicate the extent of his influence on psychoanalysis and the social sciences in *Erik H. Erikson: The Growth of His Work* (Boston: Atlantic-Little, Brown, 1970).

2. This discrepancy between professed ideas or ideals and everyday conduct, between character and intellect, has haunted all sorts of intellectuals over the centuries, and not a few ordinary people, who have witnessed that discrepancy in the flesh, so to speak — authoritative and learned voices that have become strangely silent in the clutch. Dietrich Bonhoeffer could not forget (as he sat in a Nazi concentration camp and awaited his death) how many of Germany's educated cadres, even its (Aryan) intelligentsia, even its philosophers and clergy, yielded to the blandishments of Hitler's demonic tyranny. See his *Letters and Papers from Prison* (New York: Macmillan, 1967). The chapters "On Character" and "Young Idealism" discuss this matter at some length — and it preoccupies Walker Percy throughout his five novels and his many philosophical essays. I have tried to give an account of Percy's moral examination of our contemporary life in *Walker Percy: An American Search* (Boston: Atlantic–Little, Brown, 1978).

3. The reader will, no doubt, sense in this first chapter evidence of struggle in the

author: strong respect for the work of Jean Piaget, Lawrence Kohlberg, Carol Gilligan, and yet perplexity that sometimes slides into pique as I compare their ideas about "moral development" with the thoroughly complicated matter of moral (and yes, spiritual) *behavior* in children, and will notice irony, at the very least. How do children prove themselves capable of such brave, exemplary acts — and would the wisest, most morally sensitive and subtle philosopher or clergyman or social scientist or physician ever be able to muster up similar responses under the same fearful, if not murderous circumstances? I edited out the somewhat truculent tone that appears here, now and then, in favor of a flat and aloof mention of a paradox — that the best experimental information, carefully worked into a suggestive theoretical statement, does not necessarily (and indeed, was not meant to) preclude magnificent moral "moments" in children, whose behavior can still be regarded as, say, fearfully or compliantly motivated. But my wife urged me to leave the manuscript as it was. Perhaps the "problem" is my own "counter-transference" — a fiercely irrational protectiveness causing me to insist that Ruby, and others like her, be granted judgment by their deeds, no matter her age or her unconscious or quite conscious motives. (After all, adults, too, can be "moral" as much out of anxiety and apprehension as out of the workings of ethically advanced contemplation.)

Perhaps, too, my "problem" is cognitive as well as emotional, an unnecessary edginess based on a miscomprehension of what Piaget and Kohlberg and Gilligan mean to tell us. And they tell us a lot — how children (and in the case of Gilligan, how boys and girls with important differences) think about moral matters, and how that thinking changes over the years. For me, Piaget's *Moral Judgment of the Child* (New York: Free Press, 1965) has been, all along, a touchstone — constantly *there*, as I have watched and heard children struggle with ideas, with possible choices or courses of action. Similarly with Lawrence Kohlberg's *Philosophy of Moral Development* (New York: Harper & Row, 1981) and Carol Gilligan's important and powerfully instructive *In a Different Voice* (Cambridge: Harvard University Press, 1982). I can only get a bit mystical here, summon the notion of action as "transcendence," and, admittedly, risk murkiness or evasion. I have discussed these matters, in the past, with Professor Kohlberg and his students, and have been correctly reminded by Professor Gilligan that I may be worrying this matter too hard — at a University of Michigan conference on April 9, 1980, when I presented a paper, "Children as Moral Observers," later published in *The Tanner Lectures on Human Values* (New York: Cambridge University Press, 1981). The point of a body of psychological research, she pointed out, has to do with an analysis of moral thought, of moral judgment and moral values; and moral behavior, indeed human behavior, is by no means necessarily a direct consequence, in anyone, of ideas.

Still, Kohlberg especially has tried to straddle these two words; he has tried not only to explore "thinking" but to have an influence upon behavior — as in his efforts to teach high school students and influence prisoners. Words such as "intervention" and "practice" appear in his writings, even in their titles. And why not? We all want to see our ideas make a difference in this world. If the risk is the "sin of pride" (or a "narcissism" out of control) then the hope can be honorable and necessary — that knowledge in some fashion, at least some of the time, will inform our daily lives as we in our halting and stumbling or all-too-sure manner struggle to live them. My wife feels this is a dilemma that won't be solved, ever, to anyone's complete satisfaction — hence the research and more research, the ideas generated, and yet our not-so-hidden awareness (as Flannery O'Connor said it in a public lecture my wife heard) that "Pascal's old division between mind and heart was no mere pre-modern superstition, but an important piece of psychological information that probably scares many of us a great deal." A good discussion of this matter by a thoughtful psychologist, Augusto Blasi, may be found in "Moral Cognition and Moral Action: A Theoretical Perspective," *Developmental Review,* III (1983), pp. 178–210.

4. The quote is from Lawrence Kohlberg's essay "A Cognitive-Developmental Approach to Moral Education," published in *Humanist* (November–December, 1972).

5. Little that happens in this life is not to some degree explored in *Middlemarch* — a novel of special psychological acuity (and with high tolerance of ambiguity and paradox). I have tried to offer an extended appreciation of that novel in *Irony in the Mind's Life: Essays on Novels by James Agee, Elizabeth Bowen and George Eliot* (Charlottesville: University of Virginia Press, 1974, and New York: New Directions, 1978).

6. See "On Narcissism," in Volume XIV of *The Complete Psychological Works of Sigmund Freud* (London: Hogarth, 1957). An extremely helpful essay on the ego ideal is to be found in Volume XVIII of *The Psychoanalytic Study of the Child:* "The Ego Ideal and the Ideal Self," by Joseph Sandler, Alex Holder, and Dale Meers (New York: International University Press, 1963).

7. In Chapter I of the first book of *Dark Night of the Soul,* by St. John of the Cross (New York: Image, 1959) Gerald Brenan's *St. John of the Cross* (London: Cambridge, 1973) offers a fine examination of this psychologically knowing saint — who, somehow, managed to transmute harsh suffering into gentle charity.

8. In Volume I of *Children of Crisis: A Study of Courage and Fear* (Boston: Atlantic–Little, Brown, 1967).

9. Dated June, 1966.

10. See "Understanding White Racists," originally in the *New York Review of Books,* December 30, 1971, and in *The Mind's Fate* (Boston: Atlantic–Little, Brown, 1975). C. Vann Woodward's *Tom Watson: Agrarian Rebel* (New York: Oxford, 1963) provides indispensable assistance to anyone who wants to comprehend how a social system, a historical era come to bear on a gifted individual's political and moral life. The transformation of an ardent populist into an unremitting racist is rendered with comprehending subtlety and ironic sadness.

11. I have found *The Interpreter's Bible* quite helpful here: Volume I (New York: Abingdon, 1952).

12. In Volume XVII of *The Complete Psychological Works of Sigmund Freud* (London: Hogarth, 1955).

13. So we are told in the "Editor's Note" that precedes *Moses and Monotheism* in Volume XXIII of Sigmund Freud's *The Complete Psychological Works of Sigmund Freud* (London: Hogarth, 1964).

14. *Middlemarch* by George Eliot (New York: Signet, 1964), p. 809.

II. MOVIES AND MORAL ENERGY

1. See discussion of "method" in Volume 1 of *Children of Crisis* (Boston: Atlantic–Little, Brown, 1967).

2. In *Flannery O'Connor's South* (Baton Rouge: Louisiana State University Press, 1980) I try to do a particular kind of "reading" of Miss O'Connor's stories and letters, and tell of my wife's friendship with her.
3. I have been helped considerably in the task of summarizing these movies not only by a review of my own tapes and notes, but a reading of sections of two volumes of *Magill's Surveys — Cinema* (Englewood Cliffs, N.J.: Salem Press, 1980 and 1981).
4. Andrew Young's documentary films, as well as this dramatic enactment of the South that immediately preceded the civil rights movement, have especially touched a number of young people who have worked in the rural parts of that region to change it — yet love some of its people, as they are, for their continuing dignity, their quiet everyday heroism.
5. *The Moralist* is a powerful effort by a psychoanalyst, Allen Wheelis, to acknowledge the ethical side of his life, his work, and has meant a lot to my students and me over the past decade (New York: Basic Books, 1973); and similarly with Erik H. Erikson's *Insight and Responsibility* (New York: Norton, 1964). The acknowledgment, without apology or disdain, on the part of these two essayists of the clarifying value of moral subjectivity in the psychoanalyst's daily struggle to understand his or her professional situation, not to mention a patient's life, has given courage to many of their students and readers.
6. *Movies* by Manny Farber (New York: Hillston, 1971).
7. *Agee on Film* by James Agee (New York: McDowell Obolensky, 1958).

III. MORAL PURPOSE AND VULNERABILITY

1. In Chapter 12 of George Orwell's *The Road to Wigan Pier* (New York: Harcourt Brace Jovanovich, 1958).
2. Op. cit., Chapter 2.
3. I have taught Orwell's documentary books for many years (*Down and Out in Paris and London, Wigan Pier,* and *Homage to Catalonia*) and some of his essays ("Hop-Picking," for instance), and the students keep noticing this tendency in him, an intellectual's distrust of his own kind.
4. Eugene Brody's psychiatric work in Rio de Janeiro, Brazil, is pioneering and much to be recommended: *The Lost Ones* (New York: International University Press, 1973).
5. See Volume II of *Children of Crisis: Migrants, Sharecroppers, Mountaineers* (Boston: Atlantic–Little, Brown, 1972).
6. There is a growing literature on "deprived" children — often described as "at risk." See John Bowlby's *Attachment and Loss* (London: Hogarth, 1969), Jerome Kagan's "Resiliency and Continuity in Psychological Development" in A. M. Clarke and A. D. B. Clarke, *Early Experience: Myth and Evidence* (New York: Free Press, 1976), and Michael Rutter's extremely edifying psychiatric work in *Maternal Deprivation Reassessed* (Harmondsworth, Middlesex: Penguin, 1972).
7. Christopher Lasch's *Culture of Narcissism* (New York: Norton, 1978) is a spirited discussion of our contemporary, affluent culture. In Volume V of *Children of Crisis* (Boston: Atlantic–Little, Brown, 1978) I try to indicate the vicissitudes of "entitlement" among many "privileged ones."

IV. ON CHARACTER

1. A good summary of Allport's sensitive moral and psychological writing is found in *Personality: A Psychological Interpretation* (Holt: New York, 1937).
2. See R. J. Havighurst and H. Taba, *Adolescent Character and Personality* (Wiley: New York, 1949). Also, more recently, R. Havighurst and R. Peck, *The Psychology of Character Development* (Wiley: New York, 1960).
3. See *Disorders of Character*, by Joseph Michaels (Thomas: Springfield, Ill. 1955), for a suggestive discussion, with a first-rate bibliography.
4. Wilhelm Reich, *Character Analysis*, 3rd ed. (New York: Farrar, Straus & Giroux, 1972), p. 169.
5. In his well-known oration, "The American Scholar," delivered before Harvard's Phi Beta Kappa Society on August 31, 1837.
6. See my *Children of Crisis: A Study of Courage and Fear*, Volume I (Boston: Atlantic–Little, Brown, 1967).
7. See the section, "Schools" in Volume 3 of *Children of Crisis: The South Goes North* (Boston: Atlantic–Little, Brown, 1967).
8. Sören Kierkegaard, *The Present Age*, translated by Alexander Dru (New York: Harper & Row, 1962), p. 43.

V. YOUNG IDEALISM

1. Dated October 17, 1972.
2. Her letter, mentioned above, was a response to this description.
3. New York: International University Press, 1936.
4. Psychoanalytic "revisionists" such as Karen Horney addressed this subject; see her *The Neurotic Personality of Our Time* (New York: Norton, 1937). Wilhelm Reich did, too, in the early and important days of his research — in, for instance, *Character Analysis* (New York: Farrar, Straus & Giroux, 1972). Of course, implicitly or explicitly all psychoanalytic theorists who have tried to connect the life of the mind with social, cultural, or political institutions (Erikson, Laing, Wheelis, Fromm, Bettelheim) wrestle with this matter of relativism.
5. In *Ego and the Mechanisms of Defense*, op. cit.
6. I tried to discuss the moral transformation (self-described and witnessed and discussed by others) in "What Can We Learn from the Life of Malcolm X?" *Teachers College Record* (May, 1966).
7. Interview with me, January, 1971. See my book *A Spectacle unto the World: Dorothy Day and the Catholic Worker Movement* (New York: Viking, 1973).
8. See an article I wrote in the midst of working with the civil rights movement in the South in the early 1960s: "Social Struggle and Weariness," in *Psychiatry* (November 1964), and Volume I of *Children of Crisis*, op. cit.
9. I wrote an article in response to that memorable meeting: "Danilo Dolci: The Politics of Grace," *New Republic* (August 19, 1967).
10. In a conversation held on August 28, 1964.

VI. SOCIAL CLASS AND THE MORAL OTHER

1. The quotation is from pp. 691–695 of the Penguin Edition of *Little Dorrit*. I use *Little Dorrit* in a seminar I teach, "Dickens and The Law" at Harvard Law

School; we work with it and other novels of Dickens's late period: *Bleak House* and *Great Expectations*, for example. I describe the thrust of our studies in "Charles Dickens and the Law," *Virginia Quarterly Review* (Autumn, 1983).

2. No one does better justice to *Little Dorrit* than the Leavises in *Dickens the Novelist* (London: Chatto & Windus, 1973). Excellent essays on Dickens that I use in the seminar are George Orwell's "Charles Dickens," in *An Age Like This* (New York: Harcourt Brace Jovanovich, 1968), and Edmund Wilson's essay on Dickens in *The Wound and the Bow* (Boston: Houghton Mifflin, 1941). Both these critics emphasize Dickens's interest in examining the social world of nineteenth-century capitalism, as do the Leavises in their book, especially in their chapter on *Hard Times*.

3. Stated in "Morality and the Novel," in *Phoenix: The Posthumous Papers of D. H. Lawrence*, Edward McDonald, ed. (New York: Viking Press, 1968).

4. See article mentioned above, "Charles Dickens and the Law."

5. See the Freud essay "On Narcissism," mentioned earlier, and the article "The Ego Ideal and the Ideal Self," also mentioned earlier.

6. There is a fairly well-known psychological and sociological literature on prejudice, and class-connected envies or rivalries. *Social Change and Prejudice*, by Bruno Bettelheim and Morris Janowitz, is particularly helpful (New York: Free Press, 1964). Freud himself was interested in this matter — as in *Moses and Monotheism*, op. cit., and a little gem, "A Comment on Anti-Semitism," in Volume XXIII of the *Complete Psychological Works* (London: Hogarth, 1964). A distinguished list of psychoanalysts and social psychologists — Erich Fromm, Theodor Adorno and his associates, Gordon Allport, Abram Kardiner — have looked long and hard at the phenomenon of religious and racial hate. See the bibliography to Volume I of *Children of Crisis*, op. cit. An especially suggestive book by a moral philosopher, Max Scheler, is *Ressentiment* (New York: Free Press, 1961). This is an effort by a penetratingly wise essayist to understand why we need others so much — to hate as well as love. Nietzsche was the first modern psychologist-philosopher to look at *ressentiment* and its connection to the moral life (in *Genealogy of Morals*) and he (and Scheler) leave the rest of us little to do but continue to illustrate concretely the ideas they set forth, as I have tried to do here. See also the article mentioned earlier, "Understanding White Racists."

7. A delightful and instructive book on this subject is Sallie McFague's *Speaking in Parables* (Philadelphia: Fortress, 1975).

8. See *Children and the Death of a President*, op. cit.

VII. CHILDREN AND THE NUCLEAR BOMB

1. Escalona, S. "Children and the Threat of Nuclear War," in *Behavioral Science and Human Survival*, ed. by M. Schwebel (Palo Alto: Science and Behavioral Books, 1965).

2. The literature on the way in which American children regard nuclear bombs, and the possibility of nuclear war, is relatively small, as mentioned in this chapter. The best summary statement has been made by my colleague and friend Dr. John Mack in his testimony to the Select Committee on Children, Youth and Families of the United States House of Representatives, on September 20, 1983, titled: "The Psychological Impact of the Nuclear Arms Competition on Children and Adolescents." This excellent, comprehensive paper is a careful, balanced

critique of the various research efforts, and provides a necessarily brief bibliography. Many of the studies described had not been published at the time of the presentation to the Congressional committee, and some may never be published — but are, rather, informal attempts by doctors or social scientists to talk with young people and report on what was said, heard. One suspects that this body of literature will grow in size and in methodological sophistication.

Another paper of Dr. Mack's (and of his colleague Dr. William R. Beardslee) also offers a comprehensive review of the literature — and is itself in that literature, and so is readily accessible to the interested reader: "Adolescents and the Threat of Nuclear War: The Evolution of a Perspective," as mentioned, by Dr. Beardslee and Dr. Mack, in the *Yale Journal of Biology and Medicine*, 56 (1983), pp. 79–91. I also suggest a reading of "The Threat of Nuclear War and the Nuclear Arms Race: Adolescent Experiences and Perceptions," by Lisa A. Goodman, John E. Mack, William R. Beardslee, and Roberta M. Snow, *Political Psychology*, 4, No. 3 (1983). These authors describe the one study, so far, in which *any* interviewing was done — a single meeting with thirty-one youths.

Robert Lifton's work with Hiroshima survivors is, of course, an enormously significant contribution to this century's psychiatric *and* moral literature — a powerful and brilliantly analyzed study of the one (and we all hope and pray *only*) occasion for the use of nuclear bombs. His work was not done with children, and of course the Japanese whom he interviewed were not struggling with fantasies or fears so much as terrible memories — aspects of a reality the twentieth-century world has come to know with a shudder. See Lifton's *Death in Life* (New York: Vintage, 1967). In the tradition of Lifton's work, I recommend an especially moving essay by a gifted anthropologist, Lisa Peattie: "Normalizing the Unthinkable," in *Bulletin of the Atomic Scientists* (March, 1984). Professor Peattie is grappling with our own grappling — as all of us try to live our lives yet know somewhere within ourselves that virtual extinction of our species is now all too possible. Whether we ought to call children (or adults) who think much about this dread possibility "sick" or victims of pathological denial ("denial," "psychic numbing") is, needless to say, no easy matter to decide, often entails considerations best described as sociological and existential as moral. Again and again one hears even elementary schoolchildren wondering, and sometimes explicitly, wondering who, living what kind of life, makes judgment (ethical or psychiatric or both) about whom, as I try to say in this chapter. We certainly could do with more studies of this difficult kind of social and psychological inquiry meant to tell us what matters to whom and why, including (in the write-up) an Augustinian self-scrutiny on the part about the values, the purposes, the social and economic circumstances of who do the studies.

3. Unpublished manuscript reported by Beardslee and Mack, of
4. Ibid.
5. Ibid.
6. Ibid.
7. Ibid.
8. Ibid.
9. "American High School Seniors View the Military: 1976– man, *Armed Forces and Society*, in press.
10. See mention of this paper in footnote 2.

11. See Footnote 2.

12. See *Eskimos, Chicanos, Indians,* Volume IV of *Children of Crisis* (Boston: Atlantic–Little, Brown, 1978) for description of work done in New Mexico and Arizona.

13. During the follow-up of families previously seen in connection with work for *The Middle Americans* (Boston: Atlantic–Little, Brown, 1971) and also the study described in the chapter "On Character."

14. In addition to the follow-up interviews (now in the North) mentioned in footnote 13, my wife, Jane Hallowell Coles, and I began a separate study in 1974, jointly pursued for five years, and described in Volumes I and II of *Women of Crisis* (New York: Delacorte, 1978 and 1980). We visited a substantial number of families in connection with that project — ranging in background from poor to working-class to well-off, and they were extremely helpful to us when we wanted to explore the issue of nuclear bombs and nuclear war with them, parents and children alike.

15. *Harvard Crimson,* March 20, 1984: "Caldicott Charges Nuclear War Is 'Inevitable' under Reagan."

16. I have been teaching George Orwell's *Road to Wigan Pier* (New York: Harcourt Brace Jovanovich, 1958) for many years, and have discussed this provocative book, a mixture of documentary reportage, social reflection, political analysis, and moral exhortation, in "Orwell's Literary Sensibility," a chapter of *Orwell* (Athens: University of Georgia Press, 1985).

INDEX